THE ORIGINAL BLACK PANTHER

THE ORIGINAL BLACK PANTHER

PRINCE RIVERS AND THE LOST CITY OF HAMBURG

STEPHEN BERRY

The University of Georgia Press
Athens

A Sarah Mills Hodge Fund Publication
This publication is made possible in part through a grant from the Hodge Foundation in memory of its founder, Sarah Mills Hodge, who devoted her life to the relief and education of African Americans in Savannah, Georgia.

Athens, Georgia 30602
www.ugapress.org

Designed by Melissa Buchanan
Set in Miller and Champion

The paper in this book meets the guidelines for permanence and durability of the Committee on Production Guidelines for Book Longevity of the Council on Library Resources.

Printed in the United States of America
26 27 28 29 30 C 5 4 3 2 1

EU Authorized Representative
Easy Access System Europe—Mustamäe tee 50, 10621 Tallinn, Estonia, gpsr.requests@easproject.com

Library of Congress Cataloging-in-Publication Data
Names: Berry, Stephen William author
Title: The original Black Panther : Prince Rivers and the lost city of Hamburg / Stephen Berry.
Other titles: Prince Rivers and the lost city of Hamburg
Description: Athens : The University of Georgia Press, 2026. | Includes bibliographical references and index.
Identifiers: LCCN 2026012575 | ISBN 9780820377506 hardback | ISBN 9780820377513 epub | ISBN 9780820377520 pdf
Subjects: LCSH: Rivers, Prince | African Americans—South Carolina—Beaufort County | Enslaved persons—South Carolina—Beaufort County | United States. Colored Troops | African American legislators—South Carolina—Hamburg | African American mayors—South Carolina—Hamburg | United States—History—19th century | Aiken County (S.C.)—History—19th century | LCGFT: Biographies
Classification: LCC E185.97.R58 B47 2026
LC record available at https://lccn.loc.gov/2026012575

For Booster and Beans

CONTENTS

ILLUSTRATIONS

PREFACE

> The lion cannot protect himself from traps, and the fox cannot defend himself from wolves. One must therefore be a fox to recognize traps, and a lion to frighten wolves.
>
> Niccolò Machiavelli, *The Prince* (1513)

The enslaved leave their traces on the historical record in glances and glimpses. We find them enumerated in a shipping manifest, listed on a bill of sale, cataloged in a probate proceeding as part of a property dispute. Mostly we find them in a long list of names as given by their enslavers: Venus, Jupiter, Cicero, Titus.[1]

There are exceptions. When Sojourner Truth was told that racists planned to burn down the building where she was scheduled to speak, she responded: "Then I will speak upon the ashes." When Frederick Douglass was invited to speak at an American Independence Day celebration, he asked famously: "What to the Slave is the Fourth of July. I answer: a day that reveals to him, more than all other days in the year, the gross injustice and cruelty to which he is the constant victim."[2]

Such indignation is easy to quote, easy to feel, easy to recover. Harder to find whole are the enslaved of the South who remained in the South, men and women who were never published by the abolition press, never interviewed by the Works Progress Administration, never given the opportunity to write out their life story. Beyond Frederick Douglass, Nat Turner, Harriet Tubman, and Sojourner Truth, how many hundreds of Black leaders lived and died in relative obscurity, forever altering the flow of history, without ever writing a letter?

Everything Prince Rivers ever wrote—all that we can be sure he said—could be transcribed onto a single page. And yet, like a storm over a darkened landscape, his record roars to life in scenes so searing they stir the blood or break the heart. And then all goes dark, sometimes for years at a time. What Rivers bequeathed to historians is not an archive of records but an "archive of action"—a set of particular choices made in particular circumstances for particular reasons, which we are left to interpret.[3]

In interpreting those actions, I occasionally ask questions and answer them speculatively, weighing all evidence and alternatives, always hoping a next generation of scholars will follow up with better questions, answers, and information. What I never do is claim more than the evidence allows. The only assumption I make is the one every biographer makes: My subject knew what he was doing. So far as I can tell, Rivers never made a precipitous decision in his life. Even his most spontaneous act—his flight to freedom on horseback—seems to have been carefully considered. A legendary carriage driver and boatman, Rivers could have fled from enslavement a thousand times. Instead, he waited thirty years for an opportunity to flee toward real freedom. The second it was offered? He was gone with the wind.

In closing this preface and absenting the scene, I leave only this of my own perspective: Rivers never sought our pity. He sought a country worthy of his name. Amid calls for a "Third Reconstruction," we would do well to remember a forgotten leader of the first, the original Black Panther, the man who, more than any other, helped create the United States Colored Troops, the man who built a "lost city" for his people and spoke for the "choked voice of a race, at last unloosed" when he exhorted his men to arms: "This is our time!"[4]

THE ORIGINAL BLACK PANTHER

THE COACHMAN

There is no secret so close as that between a rider and his horse.

R. S. SURTEES, *Mr. Sponge's Sporting Tour* (1853)

He knew the roads by heart. He knew his horse even better. How many times had they ridden this way together? Ten? One hundred? One thousand? The popular historian Will Durant famously said, "We are what we repeatedly do. Excellence, then, is not an act but a habit."[1] If so, the enslaved were prodigies in their own narrow fields. All that excellence rarely won them more than better rations or fewer beatings. Very occasionally, it won them their freedom.

Prince Rivers was, first and last, a splendid horseman. "When he made his first appearance upon his coach-box," noted the *Charleston Mercury*, "you were at a loss which to admire most—the polish of his horses, the polish of his manners, the polish of his skin, or the resplendent polish of his shirt collars." Such observations, and many like them, were meant as dog whistles to racist readers that Rivers "put on airs." Such backhanded compliments, however, can also be read as genuine.[2]

Every source we have, Black or white, sympathetic or otherwise, cites Rivers's perfect poise and manners. "His manners are not surpassed on this globe," noted one of his future officers. "I feel my awkwardness when I meet him. This because an officer ought to be as polite as a soldier." In every historical record, Rivers comes across exactly this way—capable, honorable, and a little "squared away." The origins of these attributes of mind—how he came to understand self-discipline as the measure of a man—are lost to time. All we can know is what is plain on the page: Rivers was one of those men who, putting his mind to something, became not just good at it but graceful. Whatever Rivers became as a soldier and a statesman, he learned as a horseman. As one white witness noted,

Rivers was uniquely poised on a horse and was universally understood as the "crack coachman of Beaufort."[3]

In the antebellum South, riding a horse was something white people did, especially white men. The entire regime that kept Rivers enslaved depended on whites' capacity to leverage animal intelligence and attributes. Slave patrols (and later the Klan, and even later prison guards) routinely used horses for mobility and intimidation. An escaped slave on foot could never cover as much open ground as a white man in a saddle, and in the field overseers depended on horses to clear the space around them. Horses are huge, their movements startling and random. From the seat of a horse, white men could survey a broad landscape and rain down blows or withering fire. (And when fugitives took to the swamps or the thickets, white men could always unleash the dogs.) As William Tecumseh Sherman later noted, all this equine training became a military asset for the Confederacy. "The young Bloods of the South," he said, "as long as they have good horses, plenty of Forage, and an open country, they are happy. . . . They are splendid riders, shots, and utterly reckless. . . . They are the best Cavalry in the world." (By comparison, Yankee horsemen, according to an English observer, could "scarcely sit their horses even when trotting.")[4]

In Rivers's world, Blacks walked; whites rode. This was just one of a thousand indicia of power in the antebellum South, with effects both subtle and profound. In writing his *Autobiography*, Frederick Douglass attributed his mother's very absence to her lack of mobility. Since she worked on a neighboring plantation twelve miles away, her daily commute was the thing that most kept them apart. "I never saw my mother, to know her as such, more than four or five times in my life," Douglass noted, because "she was a field hand" and had to travel back to him "the whole distance on foot, after the performance of her day's work." Meanwhile his "master [had] three splendid coaches, three or four gigs, besides dearborns and barouches of the most fashionable style." "In nothing," Douglass said, was his enslaver "more particular than in the management of his horses."[5]

Rivers's understanding of horses was as much a marker of status among the Black community as among the white. "There is no race in the world with whom a little *state* gives so much power as the African," noted one white witness traveling to Rivers's hometown in 1862. "They have always seen a white man on a horse, and have to think it so far a badge of power & caste, that they will hardly lift their hats to a white man on foot." In ways that would become especially legible during the Civil War, Rivers's ability to command horses predicted and implied his ability to command men.[6]

For thirty-seven years, Rivers quietly perfected his skills until excellence became a habit. By middle age, he was at the height of his powers—beautiful, graceful, and physically imposing. Given his sense of direction, knowledge of geography, and touch with a horse, he must have contemplated escape a thousand times. Solomon Northup called enslavement "one long dream of liberty." His fellow slaves said the same. "My feelings were all centred in the one idea of liberty," said Williams Wells Brown, "of which I thought by day and dreamed by night." Another fugitive, Lewis Clarke, "thought and dreamed of liberty" incessantly before making an "effort to gain it." "No tongue can tell the doubt," Clarke said, "the perplexities, the anxiety which a slave feels, when making up his mind upon this subject. If he makes an effort and is not successful, he must be laughed at by his fellows; he will be beaten unmercifully by the master, and then watched and used the harder for it all his life."[7]

In the stillness of an early November night, 1861, Rivers decided not to dream of liberty but to seize it. Rather than hooking his horse to the carriage, he threw a saddle on its back and alighted. The journey would be arduous. He would need all his skills. But tonight, for the first time in his life, he wouldn't carry someone else to their destiny. He would race toward his own. And with every horse length—with every collective breath of horse and man—Rivers's past receded and his future heaved into view.

"the fayrest haven of the worlde"

Prince Rivers was born and raised in Beaufort, South Carolina, an Atlantic Seaboard town located halfway between Charleston (to the northeast) and Savannah (to the southwest). Early surveyors assumed Beaufort would become just as significant as these other ports, and perhaps more so. In 1562, the French explorer Jean Ribault called the area around Beaufort "one of the greatest and fayrest havens [where] without danger all the ships in the worlde myght be harbored."[8]

Gradually, one empire after another discovered that Beaufort was a saltwater cul-de-sac. Yes, the port was good, which made getting coastal goods in and out easy enough. Connecting Beaufort to the American interior proved a thornier problem. More than Savannah or Charleston, Beaufort was sliding into the sea. "The whole Country is nothing else but severall Islands," noted the first English surveyor of the region in 1666, "made by the various intervenings of Rivers and Creeks."[9]

Strictly speaking, these "intervenings" were not rivers or creeks but "arms of the ocean," and the sandy, soggy soil made it difficult to build good roads (and later railroads). Not until the twentieth century would bridges and causeways link Beaufort to the wider world of the American interior.[10]

What the sandy soil and sound port did permit, however, was the production of cash crops for markets abroad, especially indigo and long-staple cotton. (Rice, another crop critical to America's early success, grew farther inland, where the estuaries became less brackish and paddies could be flooded with fresh water.)[11]

Chartered in 1711, Beaufort was the second-oldest city in South Carolina (just behind Charleston). On the strength of its export economy, the financial significance of the town quickly ballooned, though its relative isolation created a society dominated by a handful of large coastal planters. At the height of the market, the indigo grown around Beaufort accounted for a third of all colonial exports. During the Revolution, when the bottom dropped out of indigo, local planters made a smooth transition to long-staple cotton. By the time Rivers was born, Beaufort and its environs had been dominated by the same crops, same routines, and same white families for a century.[12]

Mythologically, Beaufort wasn't just the Old South but the Oldest South, a jewel of the "enchanted isles"—a place like *Gone with the Wind*'s Tara. The moss and mist hung heavy in the trees. Time glided serenely on from generation to generation. All of the money was old and all of the society respectable. In 1957 a historian published (with a straight face) an article in an academic journal entitled "The 'Periclean Age' of Beaufort." "Just as a galaxy of eminent men adorned the Age of Pericles," the author noted sagely, "so a notable group of gifted men was the brightest ornament of antebellum Beaufort. A scion of a prominent family of this 'Newport of the South,' in recalling her golden years, went so far as to call her planter aristocracy that 'noble form of society which rose like an exhalation from the sea . . . bloomed as bright as the flowers of Eden, and shone as beautiful as a rainbow in the sky.' This grandiloquent tribute is, of course, exaggerated."[13]

Exaggerated, indeed. By their own admission the scions of Beaufort belonged more to the Dionysian Age than the Periclean. The "brightest ornament" of the town, poet William J. Grayson, described his own neighbors as a "jovial and somewhat rough race, liberal, social, warm-hearted, hospitable, addicted to deep drinking, hard swearing, and practical joking, and not a little given to loose language and indelicate allusions." The cornerstone of Beaufort's social scene was the monthly meeting of the "Agricultural Society," a rotating feast in which one man was required to bring all the food and "no man was permitted to go home sober."[14]

Beaufort's white men were equally obsessed with sport, another sure sign that they had too much time on their hands. In his justly famous *Carolina Sports*, local planter William Elliott described the regional culture as an endless bacchanal of hunting, fishing, and goofing off. Complaining to his wife about the agricultural "in-com-pe-ten-cy" of his neighbors, Elliott was interrupted by a group of "Young Gentlemen" who, for days, had been "popping away at the ducks," scaring them from one yard to another until the whole neighborhood seemed to be at war. (His fit of pique past, Elliott grabbed his gun and joined the fun.)[15]

Like any bacchanal, such surfeited pleasures reveal an underlying existential exercise in managing boredom. Composing an ode to his hometown, Elliott wrote something closer to a lament. "Oh, Beaufort!" he declared, "thou mother of beautiful women and illustrious men, who devotest thy daughters to Heaven, in this world and the next; but dismissest thy sons in an opposite direction. . . . Thou financial wonder! whose taxes increase as thy means diminish, and whose inhabitants grow rich by borrowing from each other. Oh, Beaufort! lovely always, but like a freckled beauty, loveliest at a distance."[16]

Trapped in a saltwater cul-de-sac, Beaufort's money wasn't just old but decomposing. "In proportion to their Fortunes," noted one white witness, the denizens of Beaufort "are the plainest people I ever meet with." The walking avatar of that plainness—and the harbinger of the financial collapse none of them saw coming—was the most hapless of the local planters, Thomas Chaplin. Inheriting wealth, Chaplin spent his time suing his extended family for whatever they had left. Fully hammered at each meeting of the "Agricultural Society," he dreaded the month when the hosting duty came around to him. Speaking of the blame Chaplin heaped upon his slaves for his own financial reverses, Chaplin's late biographer aptly said of him: "*He* could not relax, thinking of all *they* had to do."[17]

So, what were *they* doing, these overworked "servants" of the idle rich?

Like a photograph printed without black ink, the mythologized picture of Beaufort is washed-out and gauzy. If Beaufort was a comparatively timeless and stable place overseen by distracted and dithering enslavers, what did this mean to the enslaved? To understand Prince Rivers, our entire portrait of Beaufort, our entire frame of reference, needs to be reversed.

"This land is our family"

Prince Rivers was born on land that breathed with the sea. Even as local whites drained the swamps and cursed the soggy soil, the enslaved community nestled into terrain that protected and defined them. When the tide rolled in, the estuaries swelled and the salt marshes became passable by boat, creating paths for furtive travelers that conveniently closed behind them. When the tides rolled out, the estuaries shrank, exposing a dominion of edible crabs and other shellfish. For the enslaved, their sea-sopped, tidal landscape pulsed with protection and mystery and natural arteries to family and food. "This land is our family," Rivers's forebears said, "and the waterways are our bloodline."[18]

The original Africans dragged to South Carolina's coast had been captured less for their labor than for their agricultural knowledge. Indigo and rice had been their success story. Fleeing the work, weather, yellow fever, and malaria, the whites were only ever around to oversee planting and harvesting before setting off for their summer homes and winter retreats.

Given their overwhelming numbers and critical contributions, local Black communities always lived with a sense that Beaufort belonged to them, and the whites were just visiting. This is not to say that their enslavement wasn't brutal. It certainly was. Especially in the rice fields, the enslaved were knee-deep in mud from before they could see, scanning the black-dark for the snakes and alligators that might make quick work of their children, working blindly beside them. For generations, however, these Africans in America were in a stronger position to negotiate the terms of their enslavement. And from the beginning they had demanded and received a certain amount of autonomy and salutary neglect. The result was the "task system," a regime in which they completed their hellish tasks as quickly as possible and then went fishing or tended their gardens. As one Lowcountry planter put it, "We don't care what they do when their tasks are over—we lose sight of them till the next day."[19]

This "time until the next day," coupled with Beaufort's relative isolation and economic stasis, produced the unique Gullah-Geechee culture, a rich inheritance with one foot in the Americas and the other in Africa. Spared the constant dislocations and displacement that plagued enslaved communities elsewhere, South Carolina's coastal Black population created creole enclaves in which African folk beliefs, crafts, music, cuisine, and language survived and thrived in the Americas.

"On St. Helena Island," noted historian Guion Griffis Johnson in 1930, "where there were some two thousand slaves to a little more than two hundred whites, the Negroes learned very slowly the ways of the whites. Their mastery of English was far less advanced than that of the Piedmont slaves. They spoke a garbled English, imperfect words and expressions they and their parents and grandparents had learned from the few whites with whom they had contact."[20]

What Johnson saw as cultural backwardness, Rivers's ancestors experienced as cultural resistance. If their speech "mystified" outsiders, so much the better. As Johnson herself noted, the Gullah-Geechee "didn't want to be 'uplifted'; they wanted to be left alone." This extended to their language—a mix of African terms, phrasings, and cadences with just enough English mixed in that they could communicate with whites or exclude them altogether. Even the name of their language—"Gullah"—was a masquerade, a probable bastardization of "Gola" or "Angolan." But the creole language they invented carried hints and carried forward multiple traditions from West Africa.

Within this Black community, "household slaves" like Rivers were understood as "swonga Negroes" with deep knowledge of "buckra" ways. Far from being resented, they served as a natural buffer between the "white house" and the slave quarter. This communal sense of solidarity was amplified by the ocean and the sense that they were never so far from their spiritual home. "The water brought us here," goes the Gullah-Geechee saying, "and the water will bring us back."[21]

"a parentage of its own kind"

Rivers was born simply Prince, enslaved to Henry Middleton Stuart Sr., owner of Oak Point Plantation on Kean's Neck on the north bank of the Coosaw River in Beaufort, South Carolina. If Rivers ever knew his mother or father, he never said anything about them. (If you can imagine not knowing these things, coming to terms with them, and then excelling in spite of them, you will have taken your first small step in imagining his remarkable rise.)

There are things we do know. Throughout his life Rivers was described as having luminously dark skin, "light" eyes, and "curly" hair (rather than the typical white pejoratives of "woolly" or "kinky"). Another witness put it more plainly: "His features are not very African." His physical features, coupled with other evidence—the fact that he was "raised in the white folks' house," according to his daughter, and that he was a trusted household servant and not a field hand—point toward a possibility that Rivers was a mixed-race child of a dark-skinned enslaved mother and an enslaver father.[22]

The late historian Isabel Vandervelde speculated that Rivers's mother might have been Linda Middleton, born enslaved around 1809 on Wadmalaw Island near Charleston. Vandervelde based this notion on a somewhat slender reed: In 1873 Middleton filled out a Freedmen's Bureau card listing a child, Prince, and a father, Prince. If Linda *was* Rivers's mother, however, she was fourteen when she gave birth to him, a fact that invites disturbing speculation. Certainly, she would have been unmarried, and her pregnancy would not have been of her choosing. Then, too, there's the listing of "Prince" as a father, almost certainly a man enslaved, which doesn't fit the typical pattern for a son born with dark skin but other features suggesting a mixed-race heritage. All we can say for certain is that Rivers "coded" Black, not "mulatto." His "light eyes" were all the more striking for the fact that he was dark-skinned.[23]

In one thing, Rivers was perfectly typical: He didn't know his own birthday. Such petty assaults on the psyche were part and parcel of the enslavers' regime. "I have no accurate knowledge of my age," Frederick Douglass complained in his *Narrative*, "never having seen any authentic record containing it. By far the larger part of the slaves know as little of their ages as horses know of theirs, and it is the wish of most masters within my knowledge to keep their slaves thus ignorant. I do not remember to have ever met a slave who could tell of his birthday. . . . The white children could [all] tell their ages. . . . A want of information concerning my own was a source of unhappiness to me even during childhood."[24]

After he became famous, Douglass gave himself a birthday, though it always sat uneasily with him. In an emotional confrontation with his former enslaver later in life, Douglass learned that he was probably born in February 1819. He coupled this with the last memory of his mother in which he clambered up to her lap to share some cake. "The 'sweet cake' my mother gave me," he recalled, "was in the shape of a heart, with a rich, dark ring glazed upon the edge of it. I was victorious, and well off for the moment; prouder, on my mother's knee, than a king upon his throne." These were the kind of memories an enslaved man made a meal of, because he had to. As a friend later said of Douglass: "After he got his freedom he celebrated St. Valentine's Day as his birthday, since he felt he had as good a right to have a birthday as other people, and he liked the traditions surrounding that date." Even so, the question of his birth date remained a subject of annoyance to Douglass. Attending a fete for himself late in life he crankily declared: "Birthdays belong to free institutions. We, at the South, never knew them. We were born at times: harvest times, watermelon times, and generally hard times. I never knew anything about the celebration of a birthday except Washington's birthday, and it seems a little strange to have mine celebrated."[25]

As he aged (and became famous in his own right), Rivers underwent something like Douglass's process of constellating memory and sentiment to create an origin story for himself. The hard facts are these: The 1870 census gives Rivers's age as forty-five; the 1880 census gives it as fifty-six; and his obituary, printed in 1887, notes that he "died . . . in the sixty-fifth year." Together these sources suggest a birth year between 1822 and 1825. Louisa Rivers, Rivers's second wife, added a handwritten note to their marriage certificate, likely referring to her husband: "December 25, 1823. April 10, 1887 total 64 yrs, 3mos, 16 days, up to death." Absent better information, we should assume Rivers's birthday was December 25, 1823.[26]

Was Rivers really born on Christmas? Or did he, like Douglass, pick a day that was psychically comforting or personally significant? It is impossible to know. Rivers attended church, but he wasn't especially religious. Probably, as with Douglass's story of the heart cake, Rivers associated Christmas with family and a feeling of freedom.

What we can know is that Rivers grew up Gullah. Multiple sources emphasize Rivers's Gullah accent, which would have made him sound roughly Jamaican or Barbadian to modern ears. This accent would prove an occasional embarrassment to him in public life, just as, much later, it proved an embarrassment to another South Carolina native, Supreme Court Justice Clarence Thomas. Asked by high school students why he didn't pose more questions in oral arguments, Thomas noted:

> I'm going to give you a more personal reason, and I think this is probably the first time I ever even told anybody about it. . . . How old are you? . . . You're 16. . . . When I was 16, I was sitting as the only Black kid in my class, and I had grown up speaking a kind of dialect. It's Geechee. Some people call it Gullah now, and people praise it now. But they used to make fun of us back then. It's not standard English. When I transferred to an all-white school at your age, I was self-conscious, like we

> all are. It's like we get pimples at 16, or we grow six inches and we're taller than everybody else, or our feet grow or something, we get self-conscious. And the problem was that I would correct myself midsentence. I was trying to speak standard English. I was thinking in standard English but speaking another language. So I learned that [and here he paused]. . . . I just started developing a habit of listening.[27]

Later in life Rivers developed a similar habit of reticence, especially among whites. But as he grew to manhood, Rivers drew more confidently on other aspects of his Gullah-Geechee heritage. Not knowing his mother or his father, he still knew who he was—heir to a rich tradition of organic resistance to local whites. More than anything, he knew the land of his birth, a parentage of its own kind.

"the best-looking enslaved person in Carolina"

Rivers grew up attuned to his environment. Barely a teenager, he became renowned throughout the Lowcountry as an "accomplished whip" and "stellar boatman," a skill widely prized amid the tortuous rivers and marshes of his youth.[28]

In an age before GPS, Rivers's knowledge of every nook and cranny of the countryside became a treasured intelligence, hard-won by experience. Mark Twain famously made a meal of his "commoner" origins as a riverboat pilot in similarly unstable terrain. Twain's ample riverboat salary told the truth, however. Before there were reliable roads, road maps, or signage, the talent for reliably getting people from point A to point B, especially over long and arduous distances, was invaluable. At a young age, Rivers drove his enslavers from their plantation in Beaufort to their vacation home in Flat Rock, North Carolina, then known as the "Little Charleston of the Mountains." (In ways that would later become ironic and even iconic, Rivers also drove the future Confederate General P. G. T. Beauregard from Beaufort to Charleston.)[29]

Another thing that set Rivers apart was his literacy. Thomas Wentworth Higginson, Rivers's future colonel, said of him: "He writes well enough to prepare for me a daily report of his duties in the camp."

"Raised in the white folks' house," according to his daughter, Rivers may have been educated by one of his enslavers, but there is no record of it, and they would have been flouting the South's antiliteracy laws to do so. Or he may have learned his letters the way Frederick Douglass did, by daily acts of will and clandestine opportunity. "Nothing seemed to make her more angry than to see me with a newspaper," Douglass said of his enslaver. "She seemed to think that here lay the danger. . . . If I was in a separate room any considerable length of time, I was sure to be suspected of having a book."[30]

In his knowledge of geography and ability to read and write, Rivers would have been unusual among the enslaved. What set him most apart, however, were certain intangible qualities of mind. As he came of age, Rivers grew tall, strong, and physically attractive, with an almost military air and bearing. Every source admits he was good-looking, with one source calling him simply "the best-looking enslaved person in Carolina." Six feet tall, broad shouldered, and barrel chested, with dark skin and strikingly light eyes, Rivers possessed an intensity that exuded command. From an early age, he sat straight, walked straight, and thought straight, saying only what was needed and letting his actions say the rest. Reading the sources, one is reminded of Rainer Maria Rilke's famous stanza in *The Panther* (not least because so many witnesses later compared Rivers to a panther):

> As he paces in cramped circles, over and over,
> the movement of his powerful soft strides
> is like a ritual dance around a center
> in which a mighty will stands paralyzed.[31]

At ease on a boat or in a saddle, Rivers always knew where he was going, even if he could never go where he pleased. As he reached maturity, his mighty will stood paralyzed. Among all the indignities of enslavement, Rivers resented most the impossibility of reaching his own potential. Frederick Douglass captured a similar feeling, watching from his plantation as little white triangles appeared and disappeared over the horizon of Chesapeake Bay. "You are loosed from your moorings," Douglass told the ships, "robed in purest white . . . [but] I am fast in my chains."[32]

"The Governor sent him home to his master"

In his late teens, Rivers married Elsie, one of Ol' Man Stuart's field hands. Whether it was a love match or an arranged marriage is unknown. Rivers was an epic Lothario, a source of endless mirth among whites, especially as his entanglements brought him and his lovers to grief. According to a newspaper, Rivers once "exercised his [literary] genius on writing passes for some sable damsels, omitting at the same time to put his own signature to the document. This performance brought him under the notice of that awful tribunal the town council of Beaufort." (The record of that "awful tribunal," like so many other records of Rivers's early life, is lost to time.)[33]

We do know that when Rivers married Elsie, he settled down, producing a dozen children before the Civil War. Such epic fertility could be possible only if they were married as teenagers, a fact supported by the typical birth interval among the enslaved. By all evidence Rivers and his wife were devoted parents, but they also suffered tragedies innumerable. Infant mortality was grossly high in the era, especially in the South, especially among the enslaved. Even so, the deaths of their babies must have struck their marriage like a relentless hammer. Ultimately, they would lose ten of their twelve children, leaving only a grown son, Jack, and a grown daughter, Pattie.[34]

In 1856, when he was thirty-two, Rivers was chosen "to present a petition to the Governor of South Carolina on behalf of slaves, for the redress of certain grievances." The specific grievances are unknown and the petition itself has never been found. Most likely Rivers was agitating for something quite modest: the right of the enslaved to hire themselves out, a question then agitating the legislature. Throughout the South, enslavers rented their slaves to other parties and pocketed the proceeds. Rivers and the petitioners wanted the right to sell their own labor and keep some portion of the profit.[35]

Rivers's petition was rejected. (According to a witness, "the Governor sent him home to his master, telling him the State could not interfere with the relations existing between master and slave.") By the 1850s, the Southern legal system had reached the end logic of racialized slavery.

As Thomas Ruffin put it succinctly from the bench: "The power of the master must be absolute, to render the submission of the slave *perfect*."[36]

The fate of Rivers's petition is less interesting than the fact that it was presented in the first place. The American enslaved population was more politically savvy and organized than we generally realize. Even in rural areas, Black people in the antebellum era built an effective labor movement, culminating in a massive work stoppage and sit-down strike we call the Civil War.[37]

In choosing Rivers to present the 1856 petition, the broader Black community implicitly recognized him as a leader of this nascent movement. As a Black coachman, Rivers was a sort of "secular pilgrim"—a man who creates a larger community by moving between smaller ones. "Those who can journey from one community to another can also interpret and describe those communities," one historian has suggested, "navigating not just streets but relationships." Traveling throughout the tidewater, Rivers was a natural interlocutor. Like a cabby on Wall Street, Rivers sat quietly in his carriage and listened, perhaps reading the cast-off newspapers left behind by the swells. After work, bedding down the horses and bedding down himself, Rivers attracted a throng of Black locals eager to hear the news from afar. Even as men like Ruffin worked to ensure that the power of the master was absolute, the submission of the enslaved was never perfect. Beyond the ken of his enslaver, Rivers created and constituted whole neighborhoods and networks after dark.[38]

According to a witness, Rivers's petition *did* elicit a reaction. Shortly afterward, "every gun, pistol or other weapon was taken from the slaves [even as] the chivalry took fine care to say nothing about it in the papers." Even after the purge of things, however, the idea of freedom remained. Hope can't be taken from human beings, no matter how draconian the regime.[39]

The story of the slave who personally petitioned a governor became the stuff of lasting legend among Black communities in the tidewater. Traveling the region with the Fifty-Fourth Massachusetts a decade later, Corporal James H. Gooding found that the story was still being circulated by Black locals. According to tradition, there had been a "conspiracy hatching among the slaves, as far back as 1856, the year [John C.]

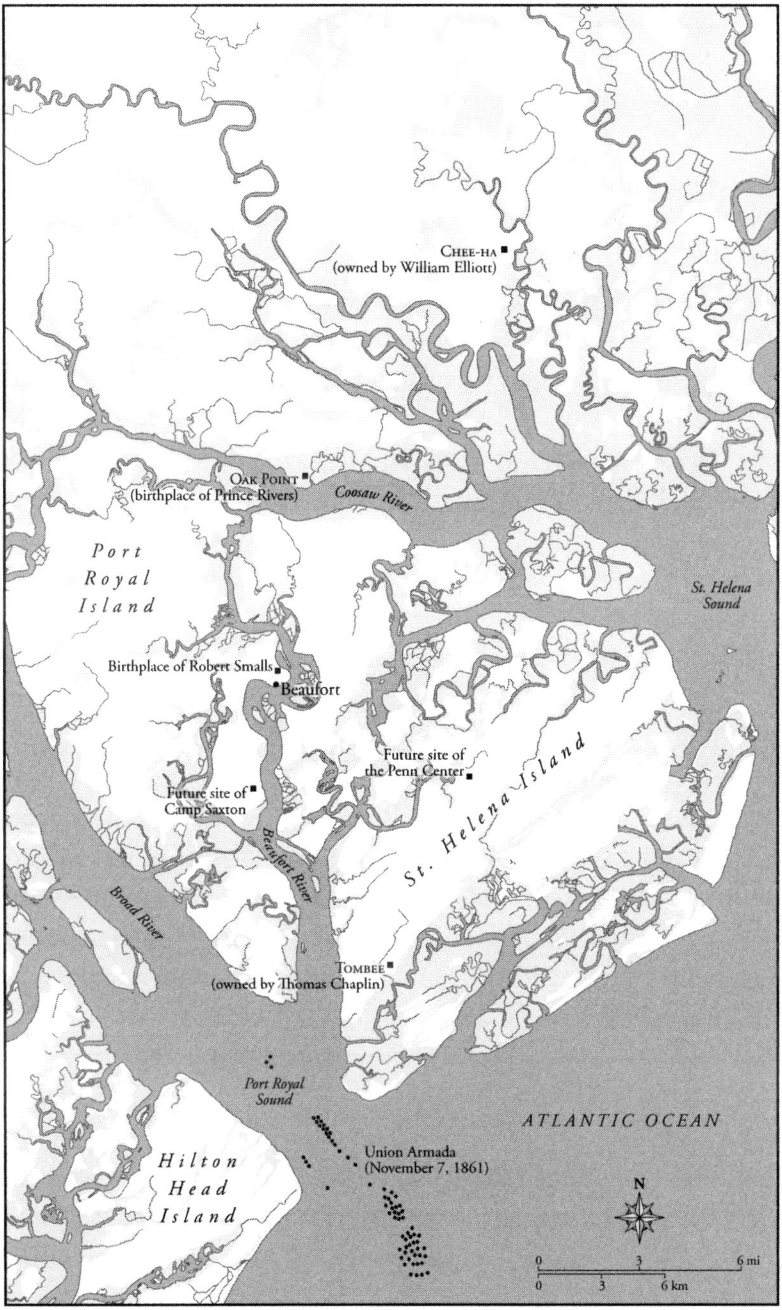

A stellar boatman and crack coachman, Rivers knew every nook and cranny of land that seemed to be slipping into the sea. Map by Mapping Specialists, Ltd.

Fremont was up for the Presidency. The negroes had heard through their masters that Fremont was a 'damned abolitionist'; they then began to lay plans to escape, or if necessary to fight." When Frémont was defeated that November, the enslaved population decided to stand down but not before they elected Prince Rivers to travel "to Charleston, in the name of an organized committee, praying the Governor of the State to recommend to the legislature to so modify some certain statutes that the negroes could live a little more like civilized people."[40]

While he would never have used the term, Rivers became by his thirties a natural politician. The enslaved did not practice politics as it is traditionally understood. They couldn't vote, couldn't participate in elections. The regime struggled to keep them ignorant, illiterate, and isolated. As one field hand understood it, when someone left the plantation, they had "left the United States." But men like Rivers circumvented these systems, creating networks of information that linked Black communities together across vast distances. "And people talk before them as if they were chairs and tables," Mary Boykin Chesnut famously said of her own "servants." "And [yet] they make no sign. Are they stolidly stupid or wiser than we, silent and strong, biding their time?"[41]

Rivers was biding his time. For two decades he sat silent and strong, hooking and unhooking the horses from his carriage until the time was right. And then, one night in early November 1861, during what became known as "The Grand Skedadle," Rivers's panicked enslaver came to him to demand that he ready the family to take flight from the invading Yankees.

With that, Rivers's long wait was over.

"The Grand Skedadle"

The war correspondent Noah Brooks dubbed the rebel evacuation of South Carolina's sea islands "The Grand Skedadle." Certainly, it was a chaotic scene. To understand the collapse of the Confederate position, one needs to understand strategic decisions made by two groups: a small cadre of men in Washington and a massive number of enslaved people on the South Carolina coast.[42]

Immediately after the fall of Fort Sumter, U.S. President Abraham

Lincoln announced a blockade of the Confederate coast. For that blockade to be effective, however, the Union Navy would need anchorage and coaling stations along the coastline to allow the fleet to repair and refuel without returning north. A week into the war, the greatest naval minds in the North were preoccupied with one question: Where could they find a strategically located port in the South that was poorly defended, underpopulated by whites, capable of harboring a massive number of boats, and relatively protected from potential assaults from the Confederate interior?[43]

The answer was the land Rivers knew best—the salty, soggy triangle formed by Port Royal and St. Helena Sound, with Beaufort at the apex. Here the Union Navy could create a beachhead to menace marine traffic coming out of Savannah and Charleston without having to directly attack either. Here also the Federals would discover something they hadn't anticipated: invaluable allies. The Gullah-Geechee, we have noted, had been enslaved the longest and enslaved the least. They were a people with deep roots, strong families, and a tradition of cultural autonomy. They say no war plan survives first contact with the enemy. The Union war plan wouldn't survive first contact with its allies.

On October 29, 1861, seventy-seven Yankee warships put to sea. Each captain carried a sealed envelope revealing the fleet's destination. Scattered by a gale after rounding Cape Hatteras, several ships were lost or run ashore, and seven men were drowned. Even so, by November 3, the largest armada ever amassed under the American flag had gathered outside the mouth of Port Royal Sound. For several days, according to a rebel witness, the "great fleet" lay motionless "in such street-like lines that our camp called it the city of Lincolnton." On November 7, Lincolnton attacked.[44]

The resulting Battle of Port Royal proved a low-casualty, high-ordnance affair, in which the Yankee gunboats quickly got the better of Confederate land batteries located on either side of the sound. One insouciant rebel tried to make light of the catastrophe, chiding the Federals for sending such "an immense armada to rout a handful of men from their sand holes," but then the men from the sand holes fell back on Beaufort wailing, "The Yankees are coming!" and sent the entire region into panic.[45]

The federal force sent against Port Royal was the largest armada yet assembled by the United States. As federal soldiers swept ashore, Rivers was tasked with ferrying his enslavers to the safety of the interior. Image from "Bombardment and Capture of Port Royal, South Carolina," November 7, 1861, *Harper's Weekly*, July–December 1861, 760–61.

The resulting "grand exodus of the secesh," Noah Brooks said, was an almost comic spectacle. Enslavers who, in the months before, had refused to send enslaved people to help the Confederate army build fortifications at the mouth of the sound seemed startled to learn that the forts had fallen. Leaving their suppers on the table, the great men of Beaufort threw their wallets in their hats and "left everything else to the invader." "Everything locomotive was pressed into service," Brooks remembered—leaky boats, rickety carts, anything that could be rowed or rolled was on either the river or the road, bearing away the fleeing whites.[46]

For the most part, the Black residents just watched them go. More even than their sudden military reversal, the whites found the conduct of their own enslaved population the most incomprehensible thing about the day. Reporting back to Confederate high command, one rebel officer tried to explain the disaster by saying that as "soon as it was understood . . . that a retreat of our forces . . . might become necessary, every hand was employed and every individual busied in gathering together the flats and boats from every quarter of the Island. This duty was rendered doubly arduous by the unwillingness displayed by some of the negroes." The officer posited that the local Black population "shrunk from executing the order" because they were paralyzed with fear by the cannonade. Smarter whites realized that the Blacks had dropped their mask. Most ran off. Others refused to comply. Reduced to begging, one enslaver implored his Black seamstress, Susannah, to accompany his family in retreat. Susannah refused. He then told her that if she stayed she would either be killed by the Yankees or sold to Cuba. Again she refused. "Why should they kill [us]?" Susannah responded. Later that night the enslaver's son stole back to Beaufort to tell her that she should burn the cotton to keep it out of Yankee hands. Again Susannah refused. "Why should we burn the cotton?" she asked. "How else will we get the money to buy clothes, shoes, and salt?" Instead of burning the cotton, Susannah and others "guarded it every night, the women keeping watch and the men ready to defend it when the watchers gave the alarm."[47]

For time immemorial, the Black population around Beaufort had felt that the land belonged to them. Now with the whites finally gone, things could proceed as they should. Some celebrations probably did get out of hand. You have to imagine this moment from the Black perspective, however. The war had barely started when suddenly there were seventy-seven Yankee gunboats thundering up the river. Of course, the mood was electric. According to Noah Brooks, Black residents

> were left behind to riot in the halls of the Beaufort Montezumas. . . . The slaves, intoxicated with their sudden freedom, ransacked the houses of their proprietors, plundering and gutting the wardrobes of masters and mistresses, jumping, in very wantonness of unrestraint, with their rough shoes on, into downy, snowy beds, dancing upon the polished pianos or marble tables, feasting upon choice dainties, decking themselves with gorgeous finery, and "closing out, regardless of cost" the stores of the town. Probably such another saturnalia was never witnessed before in this country, and such another mad set were never let loose from serfdom as the emancipated slaves of Beaufort, left to shift for themselves by their skedaddling owners.[48]

Brooks's portrait reeks of racial stereotypes. More important, it ignores the scenes of Black people keeping silent vigil over the cotton, understanding that it was the key to buying "clothes, shoes, and salt." Before the Yankees had even set foot in Beaufort, the Black population was sending a message. This land is ours, not yours. And we intend to live here.[49]

"he 'expropriated' his master's horse"

Rivers's experience of the Battle of Port Royal was complicated. Stuart's plantation was situated barely north of Beaufort, giving the whites just a little more time to evacuate. Stuart undoubtedly came to Rivers, as the most dependable member of the household, and asked him to ready the carriage. In that moment, Rivers would have seen something on the face of his enslaver he had never seen before: *fear*. Whether out of pity or otherwise, he decided to comply.

Stuart threw his most portable valuables into a case and the case into the carriage with his wife and three young daughters. Then, as he had done a thousand times, Rivers shut the door, alighted the box, and cracked the reins. All around him he saw the House of Dixie falling. The "famous sporting avenue of Beaufort, embowered with trees and flagrant flowering vines," was now eight miles of "hurrying confusion, dismay and wild disorder." We can't know what Rivers thought as he took the last carriage ride he would ever undertake as a man enslaved. All we can know is that sometime after he saw his enslavers as far as Edgefield, he unhooked the carriage and raced the horse back to the coast.[50]

Rivers's ride to freedom became legendary during his lifetime. The press found it especially amusing that he had "expropriated his master's horse." In their glibness, reporters failed to understand why their own story worked. There was something iconic about riding to freedom. If Rivers had walked back to Beaufort, the story would never have captured the public imagination. Instead, in the liberation of horse and man, in the whipping wind and galloping pace, Rivers captured the zeitgeist of African Americans' pell-mell quest for emancipation.[51]

A year later the painter Eastman Johnson captured a similar scene in *A Ride for Liberty*. Based on an event he witnessed near Manassas, Johnson depicted an enslaved family (husband, wife, and child) atop a horse, "charging for the safety of Union lines in the dull light of dawn." At the time the painting was unique for giving a Black family full agency and making them the sole focus of the canvas. Johnson's point was as clear as it was powerful: Emancipation is their journey, not ours.[52]

Johnson's family needed to ride three miles to freedom. Rivers needed to ride 136. This is what the more iconic versions of his escape miss.

Rivers's iconic flight to freedom on horseback was reminiscent of the scene witnessed by painter Eastman Johnson near Manassas, Virginia. Eastman Johnson (American, 1824–1906). *A Ride for Liberty—The Fugitive Slaves* (recto), ca. 1862. Oil on paperboard, 21 15⁄16 × 26 1⁄8 in. (55.8 × 66.4 cm). Brooklyn Museum, Gift of Gwendolyn O. L. Conkling, 40.59a-b.

Rivers's challenge was geographic. He needed to travel more than a hundred miles across politically impossible terrain where any Black man on a horse would have seemed as fantastical as a hippogriff.

As the miles whipped by between Edgefield and Port Royal—between slavery and freedom—Rivers undoubtedly drove himself and his steed to the edge of endurance. A typical carriage horse is bred for stamina, not speed. This trip would require both. The first night, Rivers knew, would be key. More than anything, he needed to stay ahead of the news fanning out in his wake. Henry Stuart was apoplectic when he discovered that Rivers had fled. We may never know why he was so angry. Was it a matter of Rivers's financial value, the fact that he was irreplaceable?

While the exact route of Rivers's ride is impossible to know, he would have avoided major towns and roads while still striving for speed. This path approximates his likeliest route down underused but still serviceable plank roads in his quest to meet the Union Army. Map by Mapping Specialists, Ltd.

Or did the wound go deeper—a sense of betrayal, a toppling of the conceit that an enslaver could be respected, even loved, by a man he enslaved? Regardless, Stuart was and would remain preoccupied by Rivers's loss. Years after Rivers's escape there was still "a placard, offering two thousand dollars for his recapture," on the road between Beaufort and Charleston. (Two thousand dollars in 1861 would be the equivalent purchasing power of $60,000 today. It is a staggering sum in the history of American slavery.)[53]

Rivers knew how Stuart would react. He had built this into his calculus. The two men had been close, just not in the way Stuart thought. Undoubtedly, Rivers left at night, seeking to cover the greatest possible distance in the shortest possible time. This would have taken him down the Edgefield to Hamburg plank road, the longest in the state, already undertraveled and poorly maintained as the state turned its attention to railroads. By dawn, Rivers would have made it twenty-five miles and could turn southeast toward the coast on roads less populated and policed. He would have known enough to slow down. Horses are tricky animals—kegs of energy on champagne legs—and if his broke down, he was doomed.

When Rivers trotted back into Beaufort is unknown. He must have been exhausted . . . and elated. For the first time in his life, he had used his encyclopedic knowledge of the terrain to go exactly where he wanted. Falling back into the fold of his family, he was overwhelmed by a single feeling: *I am free.*

THE SOLDIER

Discipline is the soul of an army.

GEORGE WASHINGTON (1757)

Call it fate or luck that Rivers's backyard was the first territory the Federals invaded during the American Civil War. Certainly, the trajectory of his life would have been different if the Union Navy had never steamed into Port Royal Sound. "Fate," "luck," and "irony" are not words historians like to use, however. We prefer explanations. The Union Navy's decision to take Beaufort and Port Royal made sense: They were in search of something unique, a deepwater port that wasn't really being used. They wanted what the land itself made possible, a coastal way station easy to get to from the ocean, difficult to get to from the Confederate interior.

What they got, in addition, was something else the land made possible: a unique set of allies starving for self-Reconstruction.

Returned to Port Royal after his horse-borne escape, Rivers was greeted by a chaotic scene. In their hasty retreat, the "great families" had left behind ten thousand enslaved Americans destined to become the heart of the Port Royal Experiment, a model for what Reconstruction might have been. Working largely on their own initiative, Rivers's and the rest of the Black families got to work raising cotton for the U.S. government, using their resulting wages to buy land abandoned by their former enslavers. This wasn't a government giveaway or a "land redistribution" program. Port Royal was a market-based solution to Reconstruction, and the mood in the Black community was profoundly hopeful. Their war was already over, and they intended to get on with the rest of their lives.[1]

Literate and magnetic, Rivers cut a commanding figure in the early days of the Port Royal Experiment, but we cannot say with certainty what he did before he became a soldier. We know what the Black community most wanted, in addition to land, was health care and education, and Rivers was among those who prevailed upon the local Union commander to arrange for both. Thus, in January 1862, a steamship arrived bearing fifty-three teachers, ministers, and doctors, the core of what became the Penn School and the model for the Freedmen's Bureau.

Had Thomas Jefferson lived longer, he would have been staggered to discover that the deepest urge of those he enslaved was not for revenge but for education. "They believed, as perhaps no other people had believed so fervently, that knowledge would make them truly free," Pauli Murray said of her grandfather's generation. Working at the Penn School, Laura Towne concurred. "Their steady eagerness to learn is just something amazing," she noted. "To be deprived of a lesson is a severe punishment. 'I got no reading to-day,' or no writing, or no sums, is cause for bitter tears. This race is going to rise."[2]

In addition to helping to establish the Penn School, federal authorities around Port Royal had been empowered to avail themselves of anyone, "whether fugitives from labor or not [as] ordinary employees, or, if special circumstances seem to require it, in any other capacity, with such organization (in squads, companies, or otherwise) as you may deem most beneficial to the service; this, however, not being a general arming of them for military service." Working within the interstices of the order, General David Hunter, commander of the Department of the South (South Carolina, Georgia, and Florida), effectively began recruiting Black troops in May 1862. Whether Rivers was literally his first recruit or simply one of the first is open to debate.[3]

Regardless, Rivers and Hunter immediately understood each other's value. Both were practical men. Paunchy and balding, Hunter was also brusque and fierce, with a wide moustache and penetrating stare. Rivers likewise seemed preternaturally "military"—squared away, centered, stoical, and self-disciplined. More important, he knew every inch and acre of the area Hunter now commanded, making his utility immeasurable. As it happens, we know exactly what Rivers was thinking when he signed up. Asked in August 1862 by James Miller McKim, a Presbyterian clergyman and antislavery advocate, why enslaved people had not risen

Impatient and brusque, Rivers's first commander, David Hunter, saw Rivers as a powerful tool for recruitment. Image courtesy of the Library of Congress.

en masse before then, Rivers was clear: There was no defeating the Slave Power without an army. Denmark Vesey had tried and been hanged. Nat Turner had tried and been hanged. John Brown had tried and been hanged. "What would have been the use?" Rivers told McKim. "We would have had no chance. . . . No gun, no sword, no knowledge, no chance—no nothing." "But suppose you had a chance," McKim then asked him. "Would you all fight then?" "Yes," Rivers replied, "I *know* we would. Only let us know for sure—*for sure*, mind you—that the white people mean right; let us know for sure that we're fighting for ourselves, and I *know* we will fight." "Well, Prince," McKim responded, "wouldn't you call this a good chance?" "Yes, sir, I do," Rivers said. "And I tell my people this may be our *last* chance. That's the reason I joined as a soldier."[4]

Focusing on white generals rather than Black communities, historians have largely failed to appreciate the role of men like Rivers in establishing what became the United States Colored Troops. Like his former commander, John C. Frémont, David Hunter is rightly classed among those generals well out in front of the Lincoln administration in their determination to use the Civil War as a pretext to strike at slavery. In command of the Department of the West, Frémont hadn't even notified Lincoln when he summarily declared martial law in Missouri and freed people enslaved by Confederate supporters on August 27, 1861. In the ensuing brouhaha, Lincoln rescinded the order and ultimately fired Frémont for insubordination. Promoted to the Department of the South, Frémont's protégé, David Hunter, sought to pick up where his mentor had left off, attacking the Confederacy by freeing, organizing, and arming Black people in his district such as Prince Rivers. As we will see, Hunter ultimately exceeded his authority and got reprimanded as well. For good reason, historians have generally credited these men for leading from the front even as it damaged their careers.[5]

What gets lost in this version of the story, however, is the pressure men like Frémont and Hunter were under from the Black communities in their departments. To be sure, both men were well to the left of Lincoln politically. They were also responding to exigencies and opportunities they saw on the ground. When Hunter arrived in his department, he was greeted by a massive Black army already self-organizing around him. Immediately upon signing on with Hunter, Rivers took over as a recruiting officer and, starting out on a "Sabbath day . . . got thirty-nine men before sundown." The point is a simple one: Hunter did not build his Black army alone; Rivers built it too.[6]

In building that army, both men knew they were fighting a two-front war, against the Confederacy on the one side and Northern prejudice on the other. Top Union commanders and a vast majority of the Northern public were deeply against the idea of Black troops. As commander of the Army of the Potomac, George McClellan, put it bluntly: "I confess to a prejudice in favor of my own race, & can't learn to like the odor of either Billy goats or n—s." William Tecumseh Sherman was equally comfortable with the N-word: "A n—r as such is a most excellent fellow," he told a friend from St. Louis, "but he is not fit to marry, to associate, or vote with me, or mine." Seth Rogers, the First South Carolina's regimental surgeon, put it best: "Remember, it requires not only *time* but *deeds* to undo the hateful lesson this Republic has been so long teaching. The public heart has a virus in it, and nothing but the flow of arterial blood can purify it."[7]

Their regiment recruited, Hunter and Rivers embarked on a "consciousness-raising" tour of the North. Rivers was more critical to the endeavor than Hunter. An eloquent, imposing former slave capable of commanding a room, Rivers embodied the case they sought to make to Northern audiences: Black Southerners were ready to fight. In New York the fight became literal when Rivers was set upon in a public street by Northern bigots. According to Higginson, Rivers was "taken by General Hunter to New York last spring, where the *chevrons* on his arm brought a mob upon him in Broadway, whom he kept off till the police interfered." Seth Rogers, the new regimental surgeon, was undoubtedly referring to the same event in a January 3, 1863, letter home: "Serg't Rivers, our Provost Sergeant, is as black as the ace of spades and a man of remarkable executive ability. He is the one from whom some Philadelphia soldiers attempted to strip the sergeants' stripes and found [it] wiser and safer to leave him alone." The fate of the Civil War may have been determined at places like Gettysburg, but its significance was made in moments like these on the streets of New York.[8]

If Rivers and his sergeant stripes created blowback on Broadway,

Hunter and his fugitive regiment created a national conflagration. On June 9, 1862, Charles A. Wickliffe, representative of Kentucky, stood indignantly on the floor of Congress to demand by what authority "General Hunter has organized a regiment of . . . fugitive slaves." Had he been "authorized by the [War] Department"? Had he "been furnished clothing [and] arms"? Returned to camp, Hunter spent a stormy night in his tent crafting his response, which was read on the floor of Congress to the deep amusement of Republican House members and the deep indignance of Democrats. Tongue firmly in cheek, Hunter noted that if it pleased the House he had not armed fugitive slaves but had organized a regiment of loyal Southern Unionists prepared to take the war to "fugitive masters" who had fled their homes, their flag, and their country. To the question of whether he had received supplies from the War Department, he said it was his "painful duty to report" that he hadn't, but he would be glad to receive them whenever convenient. In the meantime, he had taken it upon himself to ensure that his men had everything they needed. "To me," said Hunter, "it seemed that liberty to employ men in any particular capacity implied with it liberty also to supply them with the necessary tools; and acting upon this faith I have clothed, equipped, and armed the only loyal regiment yet raised in South Carolina."[9]

Hunter's rhetorical flourishes may have satisfied him personally, but they proved impolitic and counterproductive. Belittling Congress and embarrassing the administration, Hunter betrayed a heavy-handedness evident in other aspects of his regimental administration. Even Higginson would later complain that Hunter's recruiting process had been so aggressive it bordered on dragooning. On this point, Rivers may have been a willing accomplice. As Rivers saw it, the enslaved population had been forced into illiteracy and lied to for years; their brains were just as subjugated as their bodies, and what they most needed was to be deprogrammed in a Union army camp. Others believed, and not without right, that freedom must be freely chosen if it is to mean anything. As Lincoln's secretaries, John Nicolay and John Hay, later put it: "There is no disguising the fact that the members of Hunter's regiment were to a great extent forced into it, and had no heart in the matter." This exaggerates the case and borrows much from malicious rumor, but there is probably a kernel of truth here. At the very least, the regiment suffered from one insurmountable problem: Hunter and Rivers were so far out in front of the government that they could not pay their troops, a material reality that ate deeply into the morale of a body of men who had labored for decades without compensation.[10]

In August 1862, Hunter was ordered to dissolve the bulk of his regiment, leaving only Rivers's Company A. It is significant that Rivers's company was kept quietly in service. Under newly made Captain Charles Trowbridge, Company A was ordered to occupy St. Simons Island. Like Port Royal, St. Simons' whites had fled to the interior, and the island was now left to five hundred Black people and one particularly vicious band of rebel guerrillas. Arriving to take up the manhunt, Rivers and Company A found that those who had formerly been enslaved on the island had already organized and armed themselves for the same purpose. The two parties determined to make a common cause and thus began a ten-day chase that drove the rebels into the swamps and finally off the island altogether. As the guerrilla band's captain noted in a letter to a friend: "If you wish to know hell before your time, go to St. Simon's and be hunted ten days by n—s." All of this was so early in the war that Trowbridge's men had no uniforms, meager supplies, and no thought of payment. Still, "not one of his men flinched," Higginson later recounted. "They kept up their spirits . . . and they seemed to take delight in the pursuit, though the weather was very hot, and it was fearfully exhausting."[11]

These actions received exactly zero press. The vultures who wanted the war to be a white man's fight ignored the continuing service of Rivers's Company A and declared complete victory as the administration sent Hunter to the sideline (though he was effectively kicked upstairs).

Capturing the prevailing white mood, an editorial in an otherwise sympathetic newspaper celebrated the death of Hunter's dream:

> It is to be hoped . . . that after the failure and disbandment of this negro brigade we shall have no more such foolish experiments. The axe, the shovel and the hoe, pots, kettles and pans, the wheelbarrow and the teamster whip, are the proper implements for these negro contrabands in the service of our land and naval forces. Having been tried as a soldier under the most favorable circumstances and inducements, and by a competent officer, and an emancipation enthusiast, we think it is

> proved, in the result, that the negro has been properly judged by President Lincoln as unfit for the musket. Let us have a place for everything and everything in its place; but no more negro brigades.[12]

Dressed down and disbanded, the First South Carolina seemed as much like the end of a story as the beginning of one.

"the only Harvard Phi Beta Kappa . . . who has led a storming party against a federal bastion with a battering ram in his hands"

Thomas Wentworth Higginson, a captain in the Fifty-First Massachusetts, had just sat down to dinner in his regimental barracks when a letter was thrust into his hands. Higginson was in his mid-thirties, abstemious and attractive. ("He prided himself not a little on his good looks," said a female friend.) Slicing open the envelope, he unfolded a note from General Rufus Saxton, now in Hunter's old job as head of the Department of the South. The letter offered him the colonelcy of a newly reconstituted First South Carolina Colored Troops. "Had an invitation reached me to take command of a regiment of Kalmuck Tartars," Higginson later said, "it could hardly have been more [un]expected."[13]

Higginson was right to be surprised. He wasn't a perfect fit for the post. Certainly, he was antislavery. Henry David Thoreau called Higginson "the only Harvard Phi Beta Kappa, Unitarian minister, and master of seven languages who has led a storming party against a federal bastion with a battering ram in his hands." (He was referring to an 1854 incident in which Higginson had stormed a Boston courthouse trying to liberate Anthony Burns, a man forced to return to his enslaver under the new Fugitive Slave Law.)[14]

Higginson had also been a key member of the "Secret Six," the Northern backers of John Brown's raid. Higginson had lamented the "madness" that dwelled within Brown—"the insanity that sat stealthily beside his great, selfless nobility"—and yet it didn't stop Higginson from standing his ground amid the blowback from the raid. When three of his co-conspirators ran off to Canada, Higginson publicly dressed them down.

"Can your clear moral sense justify our holding our tongues in order to save ourselves," Higginson wrote, "even as that nobler man whom we did provoke to enter into danger becomes the scapegoat . . . going for us even to the gallows?"[15]

Higginson was bold. His antislavery credentials were impeccable. David Hunter had been bold. David Hunter had been rabidly antislavery. This wasn't the problem. The problem was that Hunter hadn't condensed the nation around the idea of Black troops, and he hadn't condensed those troops around an idea of themselves. What was needed was someone who was simultaneously better at politics and better with the men. This was probably why Saxton had thought of Higginson in the first place. Higginson had a massive amount of what we now call "emotional intelligence." His gift wasn't just his boldness but his empathy and his capacity for carrying empathetic arguments.[16]

There was another problem, however: Higginson had zero military experience. Granted, he had stormed that one barricade, but he seemed more like a zealous preacher, professor, or protester than a military man. For most of his life he had been preoccupied with nature writing and poetry. (He would later help shepherd Emily Dickinson's verses into print.) In short, Higginson seemed built for the pen, not the sword. What Carl Sandburg famously said of Lincoln might also be said of Higginson: He had "streaks of lavender [and] spots soft as May violets." "The birds are as real and absorbing to me as human beings," Higginson mused to a friend, and "I will trust this butterfly against all the dyspeptic theologians or atheists of the world." Military men don't trust butterflies. They trust plans.[17]

With the letter in his lap, Higginson asked himself: So, what's the plan? Hunter (and others) had tried and failed to formally organize Southern Black troops. All had been thwarted, Higginson believed, not by the troops, but "by the pro-slavery influence that had still so much weight at [Union army] head-quarters." Having worked so long to change Northern hearts and minds, Higginson knew too well what he would be up against. "The prevalent tone of public sentiment was still opposed to any such attempts," he noted, "and it did not seem possible that the time had come when it could be fairly tried."[18]

Looking at the letter, Higginson was almost sure the government wasn't serious; he was almost sure he would find himself "after all, at the head of a mere plantation guard or day-school in uniform." And yet . . . if he took the job, he might be the first man to *formally* command Black troops in battle . . . and not just Black troops—formerly *enslaved* Black troops. With the official sanction of the War Department, Higginson mused, a reconstituted First South Carolina could be something closer to a government-sanctioned slave insurrection. "I had been an abolitionist too long, and had known and loved John Brown too well," Higginson later recalled, "not to feel a thrill of joy at last on finding myself in the position where he only wished to be."[19]

In late November, the Fifty-First Massachusetts steamed out of Boston, bound for New Bern, North Carolina. Captain Higginson wasn't with them. Instead, *Colonel* Higginson was steaming into Beaufort to join the First South Carolina.

Bathed in sunrise beneath fading stars, Higginson caught a glimpse of his new camp above a morning tide, "softened into picturesqueness by the early light." He had an immediate urge to meet his men . . . and just as immediately put it out of his mind. "The first few days on duty with a new regiment," he told himself, "must be devoted almost wholly to tightening reins" and tightening supply chains. "The men concern me chiefly in bulk," he wrote in his new journal, "as so many consumers of rations, wearers of uniforms, bearers of muskets."[20]

Higginson's priorities weren't entirely wrong. Hunter's regiment had been ill supplied, ill clothed, and ill paid, all of which had eaten into morale. And morale would be key. The regiment would be "watched with microscopic scrutiny by friends and foes," Higginson knew. "A single mutiny, a single miniature Bull Run . . . and it would all [be] over with us." As curious as he was to get to know his men, Higginson remained standoffish. "Discipline must come first," he told himself.[21]

All of this explains why Higginson came to rely on Rivers. As the regiment's role model and disciplinarian, Rivers could take Higginson's or-

Rivers's second commander, Thomas Wentworth Higginson, relied on Rivers for the implicit obedience of the men. "If there should ever be a black monarchy in South Carolina," Higginson said, "[Rivers] will be its king." Image courtesy of the Massachusetts Historical Society.

ders and execute them perfectly, allowing Higginson to remain a remote figure, acting through his first sergeant. The arrangement had another historic consequence: Higginson and Rivers became friends.

Rivers and Higginson were the same age, born within three days of each other in 1823. Rivers and Higginson saw the political landscape the same way; both believed that "the destiny of the negro race might rest" on the performance of the First South Carolina. Like Higginson, Rivers loved his men, but he didn't court their love. His men didn't need a friend; they needed to be ready. "As to actual discipline," Higginson said after watching Rivers put the men through yet another drill, "it is doing no injustice to the line officers of the regiment to say that none of them receive from the men more implicit obedience than Color-Sergeant Rivers."[22]

"No anti-slavery novel has described a man of such marked ability"

Shortly after his arrival, Higginson confirmed Rivers as color sergeant, company A, First South Carolina Volunteers. One has to understand military organization to know what this means. Regiments and companies are formed in order. To belong to Company A in the first regiment formed in a state meant you were the first of the first. To be color sergeant, as a Black man in that era, meant that Rivers occupied the highest-ranking position he was allowed to occupy. Higginson trusted Rivers to carry the American flag into battle because he trusted him to understand that wherever the flag went, the men went. In the first regiment of Black soldiers ever formed by the United States, Rivers was the first of the first of the first, the tip of the Black spear.

Of all the pen portraits drafted into his diary, Higginson reserved his most flattering ink work for Rivers, and it deserves unpacking here, especially since it says so much about both men.

Higginson's first impression of Rivers focused explicitly on color: "He is jet-black, or rather, I should say, *wine-black*; his complexion, like that of others of my darkest men, having a sort of rich, clear depth, without a trace of sootiness, and to my eye very handsome." Higginson had counseled himself again and again to remain aloof and at a distance, but everywhere in his private journal he comes across as a neophyte anthropologist, captured by his subject, grappling with the mysteries of a people he is struggling to understand. Higginson could just as easily have said that Rivers was "handsome," but he didn't. Instead, he said that Rivers was "to my eye very handsome."[23]

Higginson's second observation is more telling: "His figure is superior to that of any of our white officers," he said of Rivers, "being six feet high, perfectly proportioned, and of apparently inexhaustible strength and activity. His gait is like a panther's; I never saw such a tread. No anti-slavery novel has described a man of such marked ability. He makes Toussaint perfectly intelligible; and if there should ever be a black monarchy in South Carolina, he will be its king."[24]

Again, Higginson might have said that Rivers made Toussaint perfectly intelligible *to him*. Toussaint Louverture had been born enslaved on Saint-Domingue (later Haiti) in a brutal slave regime. He had also grown up, like Rivers, an equestrian and coachman who later led his people in one of the most successful liberation movements in the history of the world. "I've been fighting for a long time," Louverture famously said, "and if I must continue, I can." Ultimately, he did continue, liberating Haiti in the only nationally successful slave revolt in human history.[25]

Think, then, about all that Higginson was admitting to his journal. In important ways, he saw himself as a participant in a slave revolt led by men like Rivers. This makes sense. This was why he had sponsored John Brown. His job was to light the fire. The tinder, the combustibles, were already on the ground in the South. Higginson's biographer, Brenda Wineapple, has speculated that, because he was "born a sickly 'half-dead' child," Higginson became obsessed with "exercise, bodybuilding . . . and forcible political action." Whether this is true, Wineapple is certainly right that Higginson was almost unique in his admiration for the physical valor of those who escaped slavery. "These men and women," Higginson said, "who have tested their courage in the lonely swamp against the alligator and the bloodhounds, who have starved on prairies, hidden in holds, clung to locomotives, ridden hundreds of miles cramped in boxes, head downward, equally near to death if discovered or deserted,—and who have then, after enduring all this, gone voluntarily back to risk it over again, for the sake of wife or child,—what are we pale faces, that we should claim a rival capacity with theirs for heroic deeds?"[26]

This was a view of the matter David Hunter had never taken—that his job was to run interference with the army brass and then get out of the way. Rivers saw it similarly: Black Southerners didn't need white leaders to lead; they needed them to be allies in a liberation movement that was already taking place. No wonder, then, that the two men got on so well. Higginson wanted to be John Brown without the "madness." Rivers wanted to be the sort of man John Brown had dreamed of meeting when he first set foot in western Virginia.[27]

Over the course of two months, gradually and by degrees, both men came to feel that their regiment was ready. Higginson also began, gradually and by degrees, to forget that he was white. "I am growing used to the experience," he said, "at first so novel of living among five hundred men, and scarce a white face to be seen, of seeing them go through all their daily processes, eating, frolicking, talking." For all his empathy, he could only dimly understand how perfectly he'd been captured by a lib-

The area where Rivers and his men first bivouacked and celebrated Emancipation Day is now part of the Reconstruction Era National Historical Park. (In this image, originally published in *Frank Leslie's Illustrated Newspaper*, a figure that may be Rivers can be seen in the right foreground, reviewing troops.) Image courtesy of the Library of Congress.

eration movement led by others. "Each day at dress-parade," Higginson said, "I stand with the customary folding of the arms before a regimental line of countenances so black that I can hardly tell whether the men stand steadily or not; black is every hand with moves in ready cadence as I vociferate, 'Battalion! Shoulder arms!' Nor is it till the line of white officers moves forward, as parade is dismissed, that I am reminded that my own face is not the color of coal."[28]

"My country 'tis of thee"

The regiment's first official act came just two months after Higginson's arrival: a ceremonial Emancipation Day celebration on January 1, 1863. On September 22, 1862, Lincoln had signed a preliminary Emancipation Proclamation declaring: "That on the first day of January, in the year of our Lord, one thousand eight hundred and sixty-three, all persons held as slaves within any State or designated part of a State, the people whereof shall then be in rebellion against the United States, shall be then, thenceforward, and forever free." The decision had detractors on both sides. To Lincoln's right were those who felt betrayed by the idea that the war was evolving from a war for Union to a war for Black rights. To Lincoln's left were those who felt betrayed by the idea that Lincoln would seek to free only those whom his armies couldn't touch, the enslaved populations of the rebellious states. For his part, Higginson resented the fact that his quiet world of drill was to be disrupted by dignitaries and reporters. "As the scene of the only effort on the Atlantic coast to arm the negro," he wrote peevishly, "I felt sometimes as if we were a plant trying to take root but constantly pulled up to see if we were growing."[29]

To understand the events of the day, however, one has to inhabit the mind of the local Black community. Day by day, publication by publication, act of resistance by act of resistance, generation after generation, Black Americans had finally brought matters to a head: A war for union was becoming a war for freedom. True, Lincoln had issued the Emancipation Proclamation merely on the basis of "military necessity." For all the local Black community knew, they could show up to the celebration only to be forcibly dragooned into the Union army as laborers. Among whites, the question was one Rivers never asked: "Would the Blacks show up?"[30]

As the new year dawned, the weather around Port Royal was "sublimely beautiful," according to a witness: "The old year . . . passed into the new with one of the most magnificent sunsets human eyes ever looked upon. A moonlight so clear and serene and to seem like day, followed, and ushered in the new era, cloudless, pure, and genial." And as the sun rose it became clear that the local Black community would show up . . . in the thousands.[31]

Unfortunately, little thought had been given to where they should stand. For Higginson, the oversight was profound. Black people had been displaced from the stage at the very event that was supposed to underline their equality and empowerment. As he later wrote in his diary: "The band of the 8th Me [Maine] regiment was here & they & the white ladies & dignitaries usurped the colored people" in and around the platform.[32]

This may be why Higginson was genuinely moved, grateful even, when his own prepared remarks were interrupted by a spontaneous Black performance of "America." Higginson had just cleared his throat and taken hold of the regiment's flag when someone in the crowd began a familiar refrain, in a cracked voice:

My country, 'tis of thee,
Sweet land of liberty,
Of thee I sing!

No one knows for certain who began singing first. Many years later Prince Polite, a renowned basket weaver on St. Helena, told the principal of the Penn School that the instigator was his grandfather. According to Polite, his grandfather was almost one hundred, with "hair white [as] cotton" but "eyes [that] could see as good as mine." Earlier that morning, the rest of the family had gone off, babes in arms, to "hear [the] paper" that would officially set them free. Barely mobile, Polite's grandfather waited until the rest of the family was gone, then announced: "Son, I was born free, and I'm going to die free." "His eyes, they burned like fire," Polite later said, "and there was no denying his look! I gave him his stick in one hand and in the other I put my hand so we started out to get our freedom."[33]

After a six-mile trek, during which his grandfather seemed to grow "stronger and stronger" with each passing step, the pair rounded a corner and could finally see the crowd. "I [have] never seen so [many] people before in my life," Polite would later remember. "I felt my heart almost burst when I saw all those Negro soldiers in their uniforms, and the bands playing and the flags a'flying!" Polite's attention was particularly arrested by the two Black figures atop the stage: Robert Sutton and Prince Rivers. "They were so big they made the Colonel look small," Polite thought, "though he was a sizable man himself." Polite was startled from such thoughts when his grandfather caught him hard by the shoulder and began to sing.[34]

"At first only one or two joined in," Polite later remembered. Then the dam burst. In the strange alchemy of crowd and moment, everything in the field reversed, the Blacks at the center and the whites at the periphery. "All of a sudden," Polite said, "we knew that that flag belonged to us and that for the first time we had a country of our own—and nothing could keep us from singing it out."[35]

As might be guessed, the spontaneous experience of a thousand recently enslaved Black people singing "America" had a profound effect on the assembled whites. Most of them had no idea that the Black population even knew the song. "Nothing could have been more unexpected or inspiring," noted the regiment's surgeon, Seth Rogers. "None of us had ever heard them sing 'America,' and the most infinite depth and tenderness of 'My country 'tis of thee Sweet land of Liberty,' was inspiring to the last degree." A correspondent for the *New York Tribune*, Frances Gage, was similarly shocked. "Col. Higginson," Gage reported, "had [just] received the flag [and] stood waiting [with] the golden tassels in his hands" when the singing started. "If he had written out a speech it was surely scattered to the four winds by this impromptu exercise," Gage said, "as the loud, soft, musical voices of hundreds of these men and women rolled out over the plain, or hung quivering upon the moss of a magnificent live oak over our heads. The aspect was sublime. Tears rolled down the cheeks of men as well as women [as] the last echoes of that beautiful (now more than ever beautiful) song died away."[36]

To Higginson's credit, he understood perfectly what had happened. Metaphorically, the Black soldiers had seized the stage, as they should, as he wanted them to. Whatever speech he'd prepared, he kept it short and handed the flag to Sergeant Rivers. "The Sergeant is a natural orator," reported *The Free South*.[37]

Flag in hand, Rivers gave one of the few speeches we have a record of. "Brother Soldiers," he told the assembly. "One request I make to you now. . . . When, on the battle-field, you see me fall under this flag, bury me . . . but let this flag float before the eyes of all."[38]

"Here Sergeant Rivers again planted his standard"

Boosted by Emancipation Day, the regiment's excitement was compounded by news of their first formal military assignment. From Port Royal, they were to travel down the St. Mary's River to spread the gospel of emancipation and probe the military defenses of North Florida. While far from the main theater of action in Virginia, the assignment suited them perfectly. The regiment would be taking the war not to the Confederate army but to slavery itself, a prospect the Florida men in the regiment faced with particular relish. Some of them still had friends and family enslaved on the very plantations they would move through.

To be sure, the journey would be perilous. The St. Mary's basin was "rebellious to the last degree," the river "crooked and sluggish and black," providing ample opportunity for ambush from shore. "We are more than ever satisfied that the blacks must help us in this war," noted Seth Rogers. "[The] question to solve is, how to penetrate far enough into the interior to free them."[39]

The flotilla set off on January 23, five days behind schedule, on the small steamers *Ben Deford*, *John Adams*, and *The Planter*, already made famous as the boat Robert Smalls had piloted to freedom and presented to the United States government. The river remains a beautiful one, almost Jurassic in its appeal, but from a military perspective, the advance was incredibly dangerous. "Again and again we had to turn points at right angles and we were never more than two rods from one or the other shore," noted Seth Rogers. "Often the sides of our boat were swept by the boughs of the mournful looking trees. The shores are generally low and marshy, and the moss droops so low as to give the appearance of weeping willows." The boats "ran aground so many times in the long, sleepless night that rebel pickets might have picked off" many of the men, but fortuitously it was several days before the rebels knew they had been invaded. The regiment's first objective was to help repair Fort Clinch on Amelia Island, the northernmost of Florida's barrier islands. This would require tons of lumber and brick, which meant taking the small town of Woodstock and its ample brickyard, north and west of Jacksonville.[40]

After running aground eight times in shallow water, the regimental flotilla finally dropped anchor before the little town of Woodstock an hour before daybreak. Rivers and his men disembarked, leaving their colonel squinting into the night. "I watched them push off into the darkness," Higginson later said, "got the remaining force ready to land, and then paced the deck for an hour in silent watchfulness, waiting for rifle-shots. Not a sound came from the shore, save the barking of dogs and the morning crow of cocks; the time seemed interminable; but when daylight came, I landed, and found [my men] pacing their beat before every house in the village, and a small squad of prisoners, stunted and forlorn as Falstaff's ragged regiment, already in hand." Curious about the place they now occupied, he and Rivers did a door-to-door sweep of the town. Their most memorable encounter was with a "Mrs. A.," who answered her door with a haughty: "To what am I indebted for the honor of this visit, sir?" Higginson then archly introduced her to her own former slave, Robert Sutton, now in federal uniform. "I believe," said Higginson, you are "acquainted with Corporal Robert Sutton?" "I never saw a finer bit of unutterable indignation come over the face of a hostess," Higginson later recalled, "as she slowly recognized him." Mrs. A. then "drew herself up, and dropped out the monosyllables of her answer as if they were so many drops of nitric acid. 'Ah,' quoth my lady, 'we called him Bob!'" Robert Sutton made no response. He was "too essentially dignified in his nature," said Higginson, "to be moved by words where substantial realities were in question." Instead, he "simply turned from the lady, touched his hand" to his cap, and asked Higginson if he would like to see the town's slave jail. "It was a master-stroke," Higginson later remembered. Here was "the whole drama of the war" in the tip of a hat. With that the regiment trooped off to bury Mrs. A.'s pretenses to civility at Woodstock's slave jail.[41]

Slave jails performed several functions in the compulsory labor system of the South. First, they operated as the way stations of the domestic slave trade—a sort of inversion of the Underground Railroad "depots." Second, slave jails were hubs in the magistrates and freeholders court system—the place where legal punishments were doled out on Black people, slave and free. Third, as William Wells Brown wrote in his own slave narrative: "In most of the slave-holding cities, when a gentleman wishes his servants whipped, he can send him to the jail and have it done." In short, the slave jails were places of concentrated evil where much of the "unpleasant" business of slavery was transacted. (For decades, for instance, the slave jail in Lexington, Kentucky, was overseen by Lewis Robards, who moonlighted as a slave poacher, swooping down on Ohio's free Black families and snatching as many children as he could find. Some were broken in his dungeon beneath the jail and sold to points farther south. Others joined his "select stock" of "yellow girls" who lived in a sumptuous upstairs apartment where their favors could be bought for a night or a lifetime.) "Slave-prisons," said William Wells Brown, "are part of the furniture which belongs to the American slave-trade. It is enough to make humanity bleed at every pore, to see these [places] of torture. Known to God only is the amount of human agony and suffering which sends its cry from these slave-prisons, unheard or unheeded by man, up to his ear; mothers weeping for their children—breaking the night-silence with the shrieks of their breaking hearts. We wish no human being to experience emotions of needless pain, but we do wish that every man, woman, and child in New England, could visit a southern slave-prison."[42]

After trashing the slave jail, the regiment moved on to the Woodstock brickyard. "Here Sergeant Rivers again planted his standard," Higginson later wrote, "and the men toiled eagerly, for several hours, in loading our boat to the utmost with bricks."[43]

Their first operation was a complete success, and all that remained was to make a clean escape. On the journey upriver, they had had the cover of darkness and the advantage of surprise. Now the regimental pickets could see mounted men beginning to congregate in the woods outside Woodstock. It was time to go.

As they cast off, Higginson hurried the men to "have the gun crews all in readiness." When the boat rounded the first two bluffs without incident, Higginson hoped they were in the clear and "lay down for a moment on a settee in a state-room, having been on my feet, almost without cessation, for twenty-four hours." Suddenly there swept down from the next bluff "a mingling of shout and roar and rattle as of a tornado loose; and . . . a storm of bullets came pelting against the sides of the vessel." Before Higginson could even get back on deck, his gun crews answered, strafing the top of the bluff. The Confederates' initial volley had killed their pilot, leaving Robert Sutton to man the wheel. Sutton stood as "philosophic as Socrates through all the din," Higginson marveled, "occasionally relieving his mind by taking a shot with his rifle through the high portholes of the pilot-house." "The steamer did not ground once on the descent," Higginson noted with satisfaction, and "we glided safely on."[44]

"The fate of the whole movement for colored soldiers rested on the behavior of this one regiment"

The Woodstock operation had gone so smoothly that in February General Saxton sent the regiment new orders: They were to steam up the

St. John's and take Jacksonville. This was a much taller order than the Woodstock mission had been. Jacksonville was the largest city in Florida, and the regiment wouldn't be raiding it for brick but occupying it permanently. "The main objects of your expedition," said Saxton, "are to carry the proclamation of freedom to the enslaved; to call all loyal men into the service of the United States; to occupy as much of the State of Florida as possible with the forces under your command; and to neglect no means consistent with the usages of civilized warfare to weaken, harass, and annoy those who are in rebellion against the Government of the United States."[45]

On March 7, Rivers and the rest of the regiment embarked on the steamers *Boston*, *Burnside*, and *John Adams* and set off for Fernandina. From there they'd have another convoluted dark river route thirty miles into "the heart of secesh." Standing on deck, Higginson once again felt "the dreamy delight of ascending an unknown stream, beneath a sinking moon, into a region where peril made fascination." "[H]ad I been some Aladdin, convoyed by genii or giants," he said, "I could hardly have felt more wholly a denizen of some world of romance." Proceeding silently, the men could occasionally feel "beneath the keel, that ominous, sliding, grating, treacherous arrest of motion which makes the heart shudder." Each time they braced for an explosion, fearing they had struck a mine. Each of the boats ran aground at least once and had to be laboriously freed. One accompanying vessel, the *Norwich*, became so hopelessly mired it had to be left behind.[46]

As at Woodstock, the regiment hoped to strike their target about dawn, but given the many delays, it was full morning by the time they rounded the last turn in the river and saw Jacksonville rising before them. More important, this was no Woodstock. "I should judge this to be a town of 4000 inhabitants," Seth Rogers later noted, with "excellent wharves and large brick warehouses more than half a mile in length. The town gradually rises from the river, back a third or half a mile . . . a New England look to everything, streets beautifully shaded by live oaks, now and then a *Cornus Florida*, the ground paved with its white petals,—peach trees in full bloom." As they steamed into the wharf, they waited for the alarm to sound or some previously alerted force to come out of hiding and engage. Instead, the residents went about their business with seemingly no idea they were about to be occupied. "Strange as it may seem," Seth Rogers noted, "the rebels were taken by surprise and the city was neither defended nor burned and we landed without a gun being fired."[47]

Taking Jacksonville had been one thing, keeping it another. Rivers and nine hundred men would need to police four thousand city dwellers while bracing for an attack from Confederate forces known to be operating in the area. Higginson later said he felt like the man who wins "the proverbial elephant in the lottery"—the metaphorical equivalent of the dog that catches the car. To compensate for his "deficiency in numbers," Higginson ordered his men to busy themselves anywhere and everywhere about town. He set up empty tents to swell the size of his camp. He ordered the gunboats to engage in ostentatious maneuvers up and down the river. And though it broke his heart, he barricaded the town by felling some of the giant linden trees that lined the city streets. "As the giants lay on the ground," Higginson said, "still scenting the air with their abundant bloom, I watch[ed] the children playing hide-and-seek amongst their branches [and] some quiet cow grazing at the foliage. Nothing impresses the mind in war like some occasional object or association that belongs apparently to peace alone."[48]

On March 19, Confederate forces sent a negotiator to Higginson's headquarters under flag of truce. Higginson was informed that if he and his troops did not immediately vacate, the Confederates would shell the town. This seemed to be an idle threat—would they really bombard their own town and its people? Still, Higginson felt better when reinforcements arrived on March 21 in the form of the Sixth Connecticut and the Eighth Maine. In an instant, the force occupying Jacksonville had doubled in size. To be sure, there were some racial tensions between his regiments, but "for the first time I saw two colors fairly alternate on the military chessboard; it had been the object of much labor and many dreams, and I liked the pattern at last."[49]

In the predawn hours of March 25, a single shell arced its way over the city with a slowness that seemed impossible and exploded near the center of town. Higginson feared it was the start of a general bombardment, but it turned out to be something personally worse—an attempt to assassinate him. The negotiation under flag of truce had merely been an excuse to get the range for a targeted strike on Higginson's headquarters.[50]

Gathering the troops, Higginson ordered Rivers to lead a "reconnaissance in force" to find the Confederate battery and relieve pressure on the city. Northwest of town they lit upon a level railway stretching through a lonely pine barren with what appeared to be puffs of smoke emanating from picket fires in the woods. As the smoke grew denser and closer, they realized an infernal war machine was bearing down the track. "I shall never forget," said Higginson, "that Dantean monster, rearing its black head amid the distant smoke, nor the solicitude with which I watched for the puff which meant danger."[51]

Blakely cannon were the so-called monster guns of the Confederacy. As Beauregard himself said, "These magnificent specimens of heavy ordnance were, apart from their immense size, different in construction from anything I had ever seen." The Blakely had originally been conceived for coastal defense against ironclads, but at Jacksonville the Confederates had managed to mount one to a reinforced railcar, creating a "mysterious locomotive battery"—a sort of tank on rails. Artillery was not yet the killing arm of the military that it would become during World War I, where it was responsible for most of the casualties. Still, the capacity of cannon to reduce men to what is irreverently called "pink mist" made such weapons, as Higginson said, more feared than "ten thousand rifles and all the Camanches [*sic*] on the plains." As the first shell arced toward them, then, Higginson watched anxiously for signs of panic in the men. Instead, Rivers and company jumped down the low embankment and bounced back up to return fire on the battery, now locked in place to prevent it from flying backward with the force of the recoil. With the next shell they repeated the maneuver and then began pursuing the Blakely, tearing up the rail track to ensure that the "great gliding serpent" could not again approach the city. It was only later that they learned a shell had found its mark among one of the white regiments, decapitating one soldier, cleaving another from shoulder to hip, and shearing the heel off a third.[52]

The day after the encounter with the Blakely, Higginson wrote his wife: "General Hunter is expected every day, and it is strange he has not come." Rivers and his men expected their efforts to take and secure Jacksonville to be crowned by a formal review. Instead, they received an official order recalling the whole expedition. Rivers was thunderstruck, the regiment crestfallen. "This is one of the saddest days of my life," Seth Rogers wrote home on March 29. "The evacuation of Jacksonville is the burial of so many hopes I had cherished for the oppressed that I feel like one in attendance at the funeral of a host of his friends."[53]

The order to evacuate was met with similar disbelief in the press, which for once was closely following the activities of the First South. "A more fatal order for the place, the interests of the people, and the Government, could not have been made," groused the *National Intelligencer*. "Every body was taken by surprise, and every body was exasperated, save perhaps a few who feared the negro soldiers would achieve a reputation. Was General Hunter crazy? Why occupy the place at all if not prepared to hold it?"[54]

Making matters worse, one of the white regiments set fire to the city during the abandonment. Most of the brick edifices survived, but the wooden section of the town went up quickly. More devastating to Higginson was the decimation of all the beautiful old trees—oak, orange, and sycamore—that lined the roads. Beneath a canopy of fire and nearly in tears, Higginson, in the words of his biographer, "groped his way in the thick blue smoke to pluck one last rosebud from the sooty garden of his former headquarters." With the fire about to take the wharf, the men piled into the boats and set off. "With heavy hearts," Higginson remembered, we "floated down the lovely river, which we had ascended with hopes so buoyant; and from that day to this, the reasons for our recall have never been made public."[55]

So why *was* Jacksonville abandoned? *Was* Hunter crazy?

On April 1, Lincoln had written to Hunter to congratulate him on the bright reports coming out of Florida. "I am glad to see the accounts of your colored force at Jacksonville," he wrote. "The enemy will make extra efforts to destroy them [Black troops]; and we should do the same to preserve and increase them." Even as Lincoln had written this, however,

Hunter had issued his recall. In his memoir Higginson speculated that "proslavery advisers" might have prevailed on Hunter's "impulsive nature," or more probably that Hunter believed they still had too few men to hold the city. "The latter theory," Higginson said later, "was strengthened by the fact that, when General Seymour reoccupied Jacksonville, the following year, he took with him twenty thousand men instead of one thousand,—and the sanguinary battle of Olustee found him with too few."[56]

The best theory for Hunter's change of heart, however, is that he had decided to recall the white troops to make a new push on Charleston. If successful, Hunter predicted, he would be lionized as the general who had captured one of the South's most storied cities and the birthplace of secession. Having committed his white troops to this new endeavor, he had no choice but to recall his Black troops as well, figuring they were not numerous enough to hold Jacksonville alone. Typical of his heavy-handedness, Hunter's calculus proved disastrous. Charleston was not taken, and instead of burnishing his reputation as the man who took Charleston, he tarnished it as the man who abandoned Jacksonville.

Even as the First South Carolina headed despondently back to Beaufort, certain that the cause of emancipation had sustained a mortal blow, Lincoln set in motion the forces that would formalize Black participation and scale up Black recruiting. Why?

For most antebellum whites, including Lincoln, the enslaved Black man represented a terra incognita, a smoldering powder keg. "We have the wolf by the ear," Jefferson famously said, "and we can neither hold him, nor safely let him go." No wonder, then, that when it came to the potential of arming Black troops, whites were of two minds: If I give a Black man a gun, will he ever pick it up? Equally: If I give a Black man a gun, will he ever put it down?[57]

"When armed," Kentucky Representative Robert Mallory warned Congress during a debate over Black troops, "they will be turned loose against those who have been heretofore their masters, and . . . when they

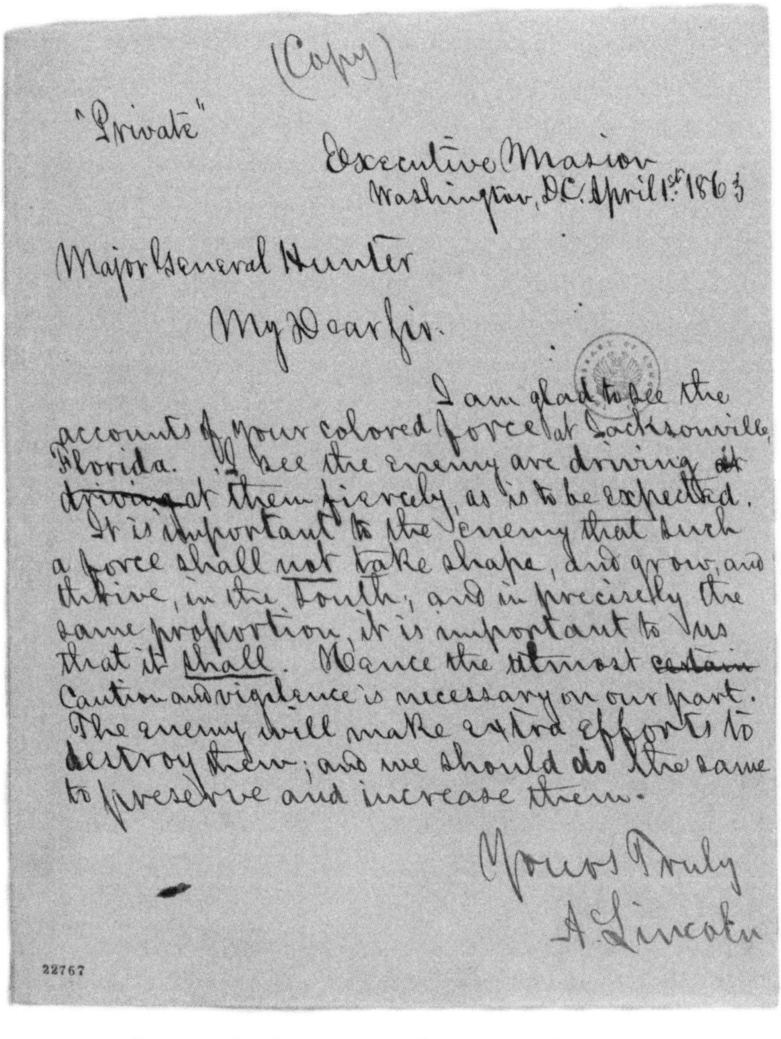

(Copy)

"Private"

Executive Masion
Washington, D.C. April 1st 1863

Major General Hunter

My Dear Sir.

I am glad to see the accounts of your colored force at Jacksonville, Florida. I see the enemy are driving ~~at~~ ~~driving~~ at them fiercely, as is to be expected. It is important to the enemy that such a force shall not take shape, and grow, and thrive, in the South; and in precisely the same proportion, it is important to us that it shall. Hence the utmost ~~certain~~ Caution and vigilence is necessary on our part. The enemy will make extra efforts to destroy them; and we should do the same to preserve and increase them.

Yours Truly

A. Lincoln

22767

On April 1, 1863, Lincoln sent a private letter congratulating the First South Carolina for its success in capturing Jacksonville, Florida. Image courtesy of the Abraham Lincoln Papers at the Library of Congress.

get the ascendency their practice will be the indiscriminate slaughter of men, women, and children, wherever they go." Lincoln was by no means immune to this thinking. What he, Secretary of War Edwin Stanton, and the rest of the administration most needed to see was an empowered former slave exercising restraint. What they most needed to see was a man like Rivers.[58]

In retrospect, Higginson came to see that, for all their disappointment, Jacksonville had been a turning point in the formal arming of Black troops. "There is no doubt that for many months the fate of the whole movement for colored soldiers rested on the behavior of this one regiment," he claimed. While it might be argued that Higginson had every reason to exaggerate the importance of his men, historians have made a convincing case that it was Jacksonville that turned the tide on Lincoln's decision to formalize the United States Colored Troops (USCT). The decision to scale up and actively recruit Black troops, for instance, came on March 24, the same day Lincoln appears to have read a column in the Washington *Evening Star* praising the conduct and capacity of Rivers and his men. In the editorial, the author admitted to having been skeptical of Black troops, but now he had come around:

> So far, their expedition into the interior has been a complete success, for they had, when last heard from, accomplished everything hoped for up to that time from them; and, besides, had so conducted themselves in the rebel country as to prove that . . . the apprehensions entertained by many that wherever they penetrated, indiscriminate rapine, arson, and murder of defenceless non-combatants would attend their footsteps were entirely groundless. On the contrary, it turns out that the United States has no more orderly and well-conducted troops in the service than this same negro regiment. It is due to the truth and the cause that these facts should be promptly realized by the country at large.[59]

Seth Rogers recurred to this same theme of restraint in his later assessment of the regiment's performance during the campaign. "We have had our soldiers three times under fire," he wrote home, "and *know* that they only care to face the enemy. We *know also*, that they can be trusted with the conquered foe. Not a single unbecoming act have I seen or heard of on the part of the guards, skirmishers or pickets. It was not for want of temptation, and I am led to wonder at their self-control."[60]

The fate of Black troops depended heavily on the First South Carolina, and the First South Carolina's success depended heavily on discipline. In ways we have never appreciated, then, the fate of Black troops rested most heavily on the shoulders of men such as Rivers. "As to actual discipline," Higginson had said, "it is doing no injustice to the line officers of the regiment to say that none of them received from the men more implicit obedience than Color-Sergeant Rivers."[61]

From the time he arrived at Port Royal on a stolen horse, Rivers had been the soul of the regiment. More than Higginson, Rivers was responsible for the self-restraint exhibited by the men. Rivers set the tone. Rivers led the way. "This is our time!" Rivers had exhorted his troops. "If our fathers had had such a chance as this, we should not have been slaves now. If we do not improve this chance, another one will not come, and our children will be slaves always." Rivers betrays here a theory of time, a deep understanding of how history proceeds. For all his genius, Charles Darwin had been wrong. Evolution is not gradual but occurs in punctuated equilibria, moments of rapid and profound change followed by long periods of stasis. As with biology, so with history. Every once in a while, time becomes elastic, politics becomes plastic, and then you push with all your might before everything locks down again. "It is extraordinary how completely the idea of gradual emancipation has been dissipated from the public mind everywhere, by the progress of events," marveled *The New York Times* in 1864. "Before the rebellion, it was accounted the very extreme of Anti-Slavery fanaticism to believe in the possibility of immediate emancipation without social ruin. . . . But all these gradual methods are now hardly more thought of than if they had been obsolete a century."[62]

Rivers, as much as anyone, had made this moment possible. "The destiny of the colored American," Frederick Douglass had said, "is the destiny of America." Destiny is not something that unfolds, however, but something that is seized. "It is almost impossible for us now to remember," said Higginson, "in what a delicate balance then hung the whole question of negro enlistments, and consequently of Slavery." Higginson was right. But it was Rivers who seized the moment, Rivers who tipped the scale.[63]

Up the Edisto

In July 1863, two significant military operations took place in South Carolina. One is more famous; both are more interesting when placed in a single frame.

The more famous was the Union army's failed maneuvers around Charleston, culminating in the heroic assault led by the Fifty-Fourth Massachusetts against Battery Wagner. Six hundred men of the regiment stormed a gigantic, evil sandcastle where 116 were killed, including Colonel Robert Gould Shaw, who was then stripped, robbed, and strung up before being dumped in a sandpit "with [the rest of] his n—s." Another 156 of Shaw's men were wounded or captured, a 42 percent casualty rate, higher than any regiment participating in the assault.[64]

It takes nothing away from the bravery of these men to ask the question of whether the assault was a good idea. Frankly, if it had been a good idea, they probably would have been blamed for not succeeding. Instead, they were rightly lauded for demonstrating, by their grit and sacrifice, that they'd been asked to do the impossible.

Is it smart or kind to ask soldiers to do impossible things when you know they will die doing them? The entire Charleston operation betrayed the myopia and misunderstanding that plagued Union high command. For years the top brass had seen the Civil War as a matter of taking forts and sacking cities, as if they were again storming the Halls of Montezuma. Only later would Ulysses S. Grant and Sherman usher in a new line of thinking: The job was to destroy the Confederate army and Confederate morale, which were so mutually reinforcing as to be essentially the same thing.

Now consider the other operation, occurring in the same place at the same time, which never got any press. On the afternoon of July 9, nine days before the assault on Battery Wagner, Rivers and the First South Carolina embarked at Beaufort aboard three boats: the steamer *John Adams*, the transport *Enoch Dean*, and the tug *Governor Milton*. The small flotilla steamed briefly into the Atlantic, turned north toward Edisto Island, then traveled inland up the Edisto River, with orders to penetrate the enemy interior as far as possible.

The army brass had given the operation the go-ahead because they were busy with bigger things. Maybe it would distract the enemy; certainly, it would distract Higginson; and maybe it would bring in a few Black recruits. They little understood that riverine runs into the Confederate interior had become the First South Carolina's specialty. Higginson and Rivers saw the Civil War not as the top brass did, nor even as Grant and Sherman did. What the top brass called a civil war they called a liberation movement.[65]

"In reading military history," Higginson wrote, "one finds the main interest to lie, undoubtedly, in the great campaigns, where a man, a regiment, a brigade, is but a pawn in the game. But there is a charm also in the free and adventurous life of partisan warfare, where, if the total sphere be humbler, yet the individual has more relative importance, and the sense of action is more personal and keen."[66]

The action up the Edisto was certainly "personal and keen." The flotilla had just steamed past Jehossee Island when it began taking fire from a land battery hidden in the trees. Jehossee Island was a single plantation, owned by perhaps the richest man in the state, former Governor William Aiken Jr. With seven hundred enslaved persons and more than a thousand acres under cultivation, Aiken's plantation had produced 1.5 million pounds of rice in 1860. All of this, as with most inland plantations, had been untouched by the war . . . until now.

Answering fire with fire, the Union gunboats lobbed shells into the trees until the Confederates fell silent. Peering through the clearing smoke, Rivers and Higginson saw what first appeared to be a mirage. "What were those black dots which everywhere appeared?" Higginson asked himself. "Those moist meadows [seem] alive with human heads." Then came a "straggling file of men and women, all on a run for the river-side . . . with their little bundles on their heads; then with larger bundles [trotting down] the narrow paths, kneel[ing] to pray a little prayer, still balancing their bundles [then] spring[ing] up, urged by accumulating procession behind."[67]

Higginson and Rivers quickly dispatched smaller dinghies to meet the refugees at the shore and carry them back to the gunboats. "Women brought children on their shoulders," Higginson remembered, "small black boys carried on their backs [their] little brothers." Every one of them wanted to shake hands with their liberators as they came aboard. The mood among the men, including Rivers, was ecstatic. This was *exactly* the kind of war they wanted to fight. "How weak is imagination, how cold is memory," Higginson later wrote, "that I even cease, for a day of my life, to see before me the picture of that astounding scene!"[68]

As the flotilla continued upriver, their boats bogged down under a receding tide and the Confederates' obstructive piles (heavy timber posts wedged into the river bottom). Worse, Rivers and his men began taking strafing rifle and battery fire from both banks. Keen to do more liberating work, they had no choice but to turn back. Continuing would risk not only the safety of the men but the lives of the women and children they'd just brought aboard. The boats had barely made the turn toward home when the engineer of the *Milton* was shot and killed. (Ultimately, the whole boat had to be abandoned and set ablaze.) Higginson's orderly was leaning against a comrade when the latter's head was blown off. Then Higginson felt a pinch at his side. It felt like the blow of "some prize-fighter," he said later, "doubling me up for a moment," and he sank upon his seat. Pawing at his clothes, he realized it must have been a glancing blow, leaving only "a large part of my side black and blue." Still there was "a sensation of paralysis which made it difficult to stand."[69]

The Edisto expedition liberated more than two hundred people, decimated rice fields, took two prisoners, humiliated a former South Carolina governor, and absconded with six bales of cotton. It also came at a cost: two soldiers killed, the loss of the *Milton*, and the wounding of Higginson himself.

Among the smaller victories, however, one of the refugees presented Higginson with a ceremonial sword, "expropriated" from the home of the very general who had ordered Colonel Shaw buried "with his n——s." "That I have retained," Higginson would later say, and "not without some satisfaction."[70]

Two versions of the Civil War were presented within miles and days of each other in July 1863. In one version, an entire regiment of Black

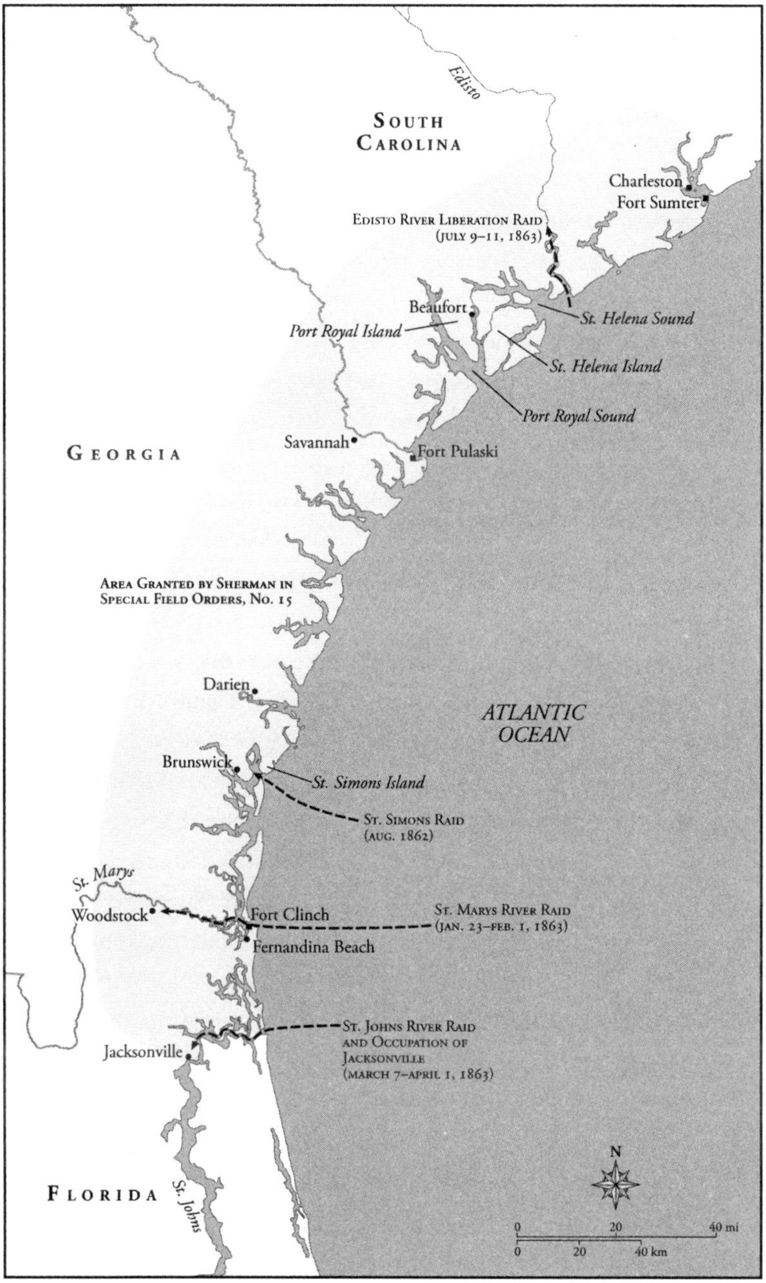

The First South Carolina specialized in riverine liberation raids that took the fight directly to slavery. Their efforts paved the way for the area in gray, the confiscated strip of land Sherman set aside to be given to Black families in forty-acre plots. Map by Mapping Specialists, Ltd.

soldiers became immortal assaulting an impregnable sandcastle. In the other version, an entire regiment of Black soldiers liberated half their number and came home in relative safety. Both versions were critical to Union victory. Only one got remembered.

"Before the war, how great a thing seemed the rescue of even one man from slavery," Higginson said later, "and since the war has emancipated all, how little seems the liberation of two hundred! But no one then knew how the contest might end; and when I think of that morning sunlight, those emerald fields, those thronging numbers, the old women with their prayers, and the little boys with their living burdens, I know that the day was worth all it cost, and more."[71]

"The first S.C.V. runs Beaufort"

Steaming back into Beaufort, Rivers and his men were in high spirits. Burying two comrades was hard. Adding two hundred souls to their community was priceless. In honor of their lost brothers, especially those of the Fifty-Fourth, they renamed their bivouac "Camp Shaw."

When referring to the regiment, Rivers and his men called themselves simply "the First South." Once upon a time, before secession and before the war, there had been a "Loyal South"—a "First South"—which had, yes, practiced slavery but also practiced patriotism. This South the enslavers had abdicated and abandoned, leaving it to Color Sergeant Rivers and his men to pick up the standard. As Higginson put it (somewhat offensively): "All the pride of my men was centered in 'de Fus' Souf.' The very words were a recognition of the loyal South as against the disloyal."[72]

"First South" was also a declaration of primacy. Rivers and company were the first of their kind, and they had every reason to be proud. Two years out of slavery, they had crushed Woodstock; destroyed a slave jail; raided North Florida; occupied Jacksonville; established the USCT; and liberated more enslaved people than any other regiment. As far as they were concerned, they deserved the moniker.

Returned to Beaufort to stay a while, they also had a chance to catch their collective breath and consider what their courage had won them. In their absence, Beaufort had become the epicenter of Reconstruction.

Black schools were open, as were Black businesses. With the town's leading menfolk back from another successful campaign, there was a sense that anything was possible. "The whole social position of the regiment is so different that officers as well as men feel it all the time," Higginson wrote his mother. "'The first S.C.V. runs Beaufort,' is now a common remark here [and] we have a recognized & leading place everywhere."[73]

Even as he remained focused on daily operations at Camp Shaw, Rivers caught this Beaufort spirit. Reunited with Elsie and his grown son Jack, he finally felt like he put down roots as a free man. And what he wanted most was land. "Till the black man can make his bale of cotton, and put his own name upon it," he had always felt, "he is still a slave."[74]

Fortunately, there was land to be had. In fleeing their homes and farms, Beaufort's white families forgot the simplest rule of American citizenship: Pay your taxes. In January 1863, three U.S. Treasury agents founded *The Free South*, a Beaufort newspaper that functioned partly as a beacon of resistance inside the South. (White Southerners might clamor for their rights, a typical editorial noted, but "a rebel has but two rights—a constitutional right to be hung and a divine right to be damned.") *The Free South* had a second, perhaps more primary and profitable, function—helping to foreclose on properties and bring them to market. Fully a quarter of the newspaper's columns were taken up with tax notices. Rivers purchased choice lots in Beaufort both for himself and for his son Jack; they even went into business together on a little liquor and retail store on Sixth Street.[75]

Unfortunately, the land boom quickly went bust. Rivers had gotten in relatively early, paying just above appraisal value, but by January 1864 the speculative boom had attracted land-hungry whites, driving up demand. Rivers himself may have been a partial victim in one particularly egregious case where a group of soldiers and freed people took up a subscription service to purchase the plantation on Hilton Head on which many of them had been enslaved, but they were outbid (by $500) by a white land speculator. To cool the market, and make it more fair, General Saxton worked with Radical Republican Senator Charles Sumner to create a new law that would give soldiers and especially Black soldiers a preference in the bidding process. Even Higginson considered joining in the fun, writing his mother that "all soldiers black or white have a chance to purchase & I have serious thoughts of investing a trifle, so as to be landholder in South Carolina."[76]

Ultimately Higginson decided against joining the land rush. For some months, he, like Rivers, had been considering his future. Gone were the constant worries about how he and his men would perform in the field. "My cares are lighter & the many anxieties which then oppressed me have vanished before the assurance of success beyond all dreams. Who could have foreseen a year ago the results now gained for the colored people & the nation—& due so largely, as I believe, to the success of [our] experiment." All of that success, however, cut both ways. Like his men, Higginson felt that he'd already accomplished a lot of what he set out to do. Moreover, having succeeded despite his superiors, Higginson found the top brass more insufferable than ever. Their incompetence and sense of superiority had been endurable when he needed them to give his men a chance. Having made the most of that chance, he found it much harder to return to a subservient role, watching as the higher-ups went on paying his men less and regarding them less.[77]

All of this particularly struck home in February 1864 when the First South Carolina was ordered back to Jacksonville as part of a larger Florida invasion. The men were ecstatic, but Higginson correctly predicted disaster. After packing up their camp and kits, Rivers and the men were just about to embark when news came to stand down. High command claimed there were too many cases of smallpox in the regiment, so they needed to stay behind. While his men were bitterly disappointed, Higginson was quietly relieved. Instinct told him the Florida invasion would prove a catastrophe—and so it did.

Led by Brigadier General Truman Seymour, 5,500 Union forces landed at Jacksonville and, meeting little resistance, quickly exceeded orders by marching on Tallahassee, which they thought sparsely defended by Florida militia. Instead, General Beauregard, operating out of Charleston, became aware of Union troop movements and sent five thousand reinforcements to Florida to meet them. Seymour and his men were about a third of the way to Tallahassee when they collided with the Confederates near Ocean Pond, a two-mile lake near the tiny town of Olustee. Having been outsmarted, Seymour proceeded to get out-generated. Still thinking he was facing ragtag Florida militiamen, he fed the battle slowly and was bled out quickly. Seymour's veteran troops had fought at some of the Civil War's most storied battles, but many of them would later say that Olustee was one of the gnarliest encounters of their lives. Fully 34 percent were casualties, making it one of the bloodiest battles of the war in terms of percentages. Many in the First South Carolina were crushed that they hadn't participated, but Higginson knew only too well that "as senior colored reg't we shld. hv. had a prominent place in the fight & suffered as badly as any." At the end of the day Higginson was not like Robert Gould Shaw. Shaw had, with staggering bravery and at staggering personal cost, volunteered his troops to lead a doomed charge on Battery Wagner and now lay buried in Charleston sand. As much as martyrdom might appeal to him, Higginson had been in the antislavery business too long to waste the flower of the Black population. "It is awful to go on a hospital transport & see wounded men, in that terrible stillness they have—& think they might have been yr. regiment."[78]

What plagued Higginson the most, however, was his own health. The injury to his side had healed, perhaps imperfectly. He had recovered from malaria, perhaps incompletely. He was left with what he called "my special trouble"—a chronic diarrhea that made it difficult to carry out basic duties and made horse travel a nightmare. At first he followed the advice of the regimental doctors and cleaved to what was called the "astringent treatment—brandy, blackberry cordial, [and] lemons." When that proved useless he followed his men's lead, switching to the "natural diet of the country, milk, hominy & rice." Still, nothing worked. As winter yielded to spring, Higginson wrote home that "it is the warmest day we have yet had . . . & [yet] a thousand soft arrows shoot through me & take all my strength away."[79]

On May 11, Higginson sat in his tent composing what was probably the most difficult letter of his life. Even for Higginson, the letter draft, which remains in his papers at Harvard, is chockablock with emendations and crossed-out words: "The Colonel commanding regrets to announce to the regiment that he is compelled by the condition of his continued ill health to give up its command for a few months ^ if not forever." A second line is almost unreadable for all the edits. "^Fellow soldiers [obviously added] Nothing can ever take from us [crossed out] you [crossed out] us the pride we feel in having been the pioneers in a great moment which might have proved a failure, but for our success." Here is the whole of Higginson's strength as a commander distilled to its essence: us-you-us. He didn't want to take credit for what his men had accomplished, but he wanted to be associated with it, because he believed in it so much and was so proud of it. "As to the war I feel that I hv. done my duty entirely," he wrote his wife, "[but as] to these people, I feel much more clinging yet, & it will be hard to leave them & [not] feel that I desert them."[80]

As expected, Higginson's resignation hit the men hard. In an attempt to soften the blow, he folded into the announcement the fact that the government (finally) intended to pay Black soldiers equally, a problem he had been working to solve for years. He also implied, and maybe even hoped, that he might return if he recuperated. He knew the odds were slim. "The regiment is all in mourning at the thoughts of losing so good a colonel," one letter importuned him. "They are living in hopes that you will regain your health so as to be able to rejoin them." The letter was written from Harriet Tubman.[81]

Of all the goodbyes, however, one was the toughest. "Dear Col.," Rivers wrote Higginson the day before his departure. "If you will be at home at half pass 4 o'clock I will call & see you. I have the honor to be Respectfully, your obedient Servant, Sergt Prince Rivers." We have no idea what the two men said to each other that night. Maybe Rivers tried to talk him out of quitting. Maybe they just laughed and talked of old times. Certainly, there are defilade positions of the heart that no man should get a bead on. Higginson believed he was doing the right thing by his men. "One invalided beyond a certain point," he noted, "makes a poor commander." Still, what Higginson had said of Rivers is germane: He was "inexhaustible." Higginson had the privilege of being exhausted. What he wrote in his journal says it all: "In May I went home invalided, was compelled to resign in October from the same cause, and never saw the First South Carolina again."[82]

Rivers had lost a first colonel to politics, a second to ill-health. More than ever, it was his regiment now.[83]

"Things have not glided on"

Even if it was his regiment, Rivers could not command it. He had already been promoted as high as allowable. Instead, the colonelcy fell to Major Charles T. Trowbridge, a logical choice. If Rivers was the first of the first among the Black troops—among the first to sign up and the longest in continuous service—Trowbridge was the first of the first among its white officers. A New Yorker, Trowbridge had been Hunter's orderly sergeant, tasked with organizing and drilling the Black refugees who fled to their camp at Port Royal, including Rivers. Leading Company A on its guerrilla-hunting expedition on St. Simons, Trowbridge had been the first officer to command Black troops in the field, which he did continuously from May 5, 1862, through February 9, 1866.

On the surface, Trowbridge seemed the perfect candidate to inherit command. He had come up organically through the ranks. He had been in continuous service at the head of Black troops for longer than anyone in America. Spanning both the Hunter and Higginson regimes, he was the institutional memory of the regiment. Higginson, moreover, respected him as a tactician and strategist. An engineer by training, Trowbridge had been integral to the design of the St. Mary's and St. John's campaigns, which had been a logistical nightmare of navigating the low, sluggish backwater that twisted and turned through the Jurassic hellscape of northern Florida. Promoted to major on the basis of his performance in the Florida campaigns, Trowbridge was promoted again, to lieutenant colonel, when he was named the new commander of the regiment. And why not? The First South Carolina was as much Trowbridge's "experiment" as anyone's, so it made perfect sense: He should command.[84]

For reasons that aren't clear, however, Trowbridge's transition to leadership created quiet discontent among the men. Partly, he had the problem any former sergeant would have: He was synonymous with discipline. He couldn't be aloof or inspirational, as Higginson had been, be-

Rivers's third commander, Charles Trowbridge, had a rocky relationship with his men as the First South Carolina transitioned from liberation raids to peace-keeping duties. Image from Rick Carlile Collection.

cause the men knew him best as a taskmaster, drillmaster, and enforcer. He also appears to have lacked Higginson's implicit understanding that, at the end of the day, the regiment's destiny depended not on its white officers but on its Black sergeants.

On August 14, during a period when they still thought Higginson might return, the bulk of the noncommissioned officers (which is to say the leading Black men of the regiment, including and especially Rivers) cosigned a letter to Higginson outlining their complaints against their new colonel. They understood that any deliberate move against Trowbridge would be insubordination, so they were incredibly polite: "Colonel:—We have the honor to lay before you a few facts, and present you with the request of the entire Regt." "Things have not glided on with that smoothness and justice, which so eminently characterized your conduct of our Regtl affairs," their complaint continued. "Abuses have been perpetrated which never could, nor never would have been attempted in any Regt composed of men from the Northern States."[85]

On two occasions, at least, Trowbridge had been present or done nothing when one of his white officers, Corporal George William Dewhurst, physically beat the men. First, Dewhurst slapped an unnamed Black corporal for verbally defending himself. Later, "as if encouraged by the impunity with which he maltreated" the officer, Dewhurst "struck the Orderly Segt. of Co. I with his fist (in the head) with great impetus, apparently with the intention of felling him to the ground!!!"[86]

One has to understand military hierarchy and discipline to understand the significance of these charges. This wasn't a mere matter of a white officer roughly treating a Black private. This was a white officer beating the highest-ranking Black men in the regiment in front of the soldiers they were meant to command. As the complaint noted, this was a "flagrant violation of the USA regulations" and a ruinous blow to morale. When the complaints were presented to Trowbridge, however, "the abuse was hushed up," and Trowbridge personally told the sergeant of Company I to "keep his mouth shut."[87]

For all Higginson's fussiness, he had the deepest empathy for his men. "We, their officers, did not go there to teach lessons, but to receive them," he famously said. "There were more than a hundred men in the ranks who had voluntarily met more dangers in their escape from slavery than any of my young captains had incurred in all their lives." This was precisely what Trowbridge didn't get. Though abolitionized by the war, Trowbridge hadn't been an abolitionist to begin with.[88]

In their complaint to Higginson, Rivers and the other Black sergeants said exactly this, demonstrating a canny understanding of the moral and intellectual journeys the whites around them were embarked on. "Again we aver that even men of education who have become abolitionized by the events of the present war are not the men to command colored Regts," their complaint notes. "As a rule it is very hard for such men to show that respect for, and entertain that kindly feeling toward, a Reg't composed of unlettered black men."[89]

Trowbridge was true to the cause, but he was only at the midpoint in his journey toward allyship. He didn't yet have what Higginson had, what his soldiers called "colored man heart." "We regret to say that from the non-commissioned staff down," Rivers and his fellow signatories wrote, "there is not a man in the Reg't who has the least confidence in him."[90]

We do not know how or if Higginson responded behind the scenes. Perhaps he wrote to Trowbridge. Perhaps he worked his contacts in high command. What he definitely did not do was respond directly, which made Rivers and the other signatories nervous. After a few weeks of silence, they sent a second letter seeking to soften the first. "Colonel," they wrote warily. "[We] have the honor to inform you that the letter that we forwarded to you some time since was intended for your own eye or ear only. Believing that we had the right under the 35 Art of War to complain of our grievances to our Col. Comd'g, we trust we have not misplaced our confidence when we say that we intended the letter aforesaid to be secret and confidential. . . . We do not wish to impair discipline; we wish for justice only." Once again Higginson declined to respond, which undoubtedly pained him. In his private diary, he admitted that Rivers and the other sergeants had every right to complain. "Having commanded black troops earlier than any of the rest," Higginson wrote, "and taken them at their lowest, [Trowbridge] does not feel the respect for their personal feelings that we do, mimics their own dialect to them, calls them 'boy,' patronizes them & in general seems like a good-natured overseer who will resent every tyranny but his own." Whatever else he was, however, Trowbridge was their colonel now, and the men would have to get used to it.[91]

The contretemps regarding Trowbridge's ascension was but one in a series of assaults on regimental morale. Around the same time, word came down that the First South Carolina was to be renamed as it was absorbed into the newly formalized United States Colored Troops. Henceforth it would be known as the Thirty-Third United States Infantry (USCT).

From the government's perspective it all made sense. As they began recruiting new USCT regiments, they began designating them in order: the First U.S. Infantry (USCT), the Second U.S. Infantry (USCT), and so forth. By the time they got around to folding in the existing regiments they had used up a lot of numbers. As Higginson observed: "It was one of those instances of injudicious sacrifice of esprit de corps which were so frequent in our army." In some cases governors were able to intervene to protect regiments from redesignation. The Fifty-Fourth Massachusetts, for instance, remained its storied self. As a regiment from a seceded state, however, the First South Carolina had no gubernatorial advocate, and while a name change may seem a minor matter, Rivers and his men felt it as a demotion and a blow to their identity. They were no longer the "First South."[92]

But the bigger blow to morale was the news that they were again leaving Beaufort. The men were thirsty for action, but for Rivers and the many soldiers from the local area, it also came as a gut punch. They would again be leaving wives and children just as they had begun putting down roots as free families. In rapid succession they'd lost their colonel, their name, and their home.

the "bondage of [a] soldier's life"

Whatever specific morale problems Rivers and his men were feeling, their broader sense of frustration was shared by the entire Union army. For most of the summer, the entire eastern theater had been stalemated. The Union's major eastern army, headed by Ulysses S. Grant, had lost sixty thousand soldiers that summer and was now bogged down outside Petersburg. The Union's major western army, headed by William Tecumseh Sherman, was less bloodied but equally bogged down outside Atlanta. For months Northerners had been reading nothing but casualty lists and hearing nothing but bad news. Given the political and military climate, Lincoln was sure he would lose reelection. Asked about his electoral prospects the lonely president pithily noted: "Well, I don't think I ever heard of any man being elected to an office unless *someone* was for him."[93]

More alarming for Rivers and the rest of the Black troops was the potential consequence of a Democratic victory. Lincoln's opponent, George B. McClellan, was running on a platform that declared, as Sherman put it, "the war was a failure and that it was better to allow the

South to go free to establish a separate government, whose corner-stone should be slavery." "Success to our arms at that instant was therefore a political necessity," Sherman concluded, "and it was all-important that something startling in our interest should occur before the election in November."[94]

And then something startling occurred. Atlanta fell in late August, and Sherman intended to "make Georgia howl." By November, he had begun his March to the Sea, and the Thirty-Third was ordered to protect his flanks. The men were ecstatic. The march would be the war's coup de grâce, and they would be present at the kill.[95]

Unfortunately, Sherman was notoriously averse to Black troops. While in Atlanta, he had written to his superior, Henry Wager Halleck: "I have had the question put to me often: 'Is not a negro as good as a white man to stop a bullet?' Yes, and a sand-bag is better; but can a negro do our skirmishing and picket duty? Can they improvise roads, bridges, sorties, flank movements, &c., like the white man! I say no. Soldiers must and do many things without orders from their own sense. . . . Negroes are not equal to this. I have gone steadily, firmly, and confidently along, and I could not have done it with black troops."[96]

Much of Sherman's accomplishments depended on Black troops, but he never acknowledged it. As Higginson put it: "Next to the merit of those who made the March was that of those who held open the door." The bulk of the troops protecting Sherman's left flank during the march were Black. This included Rivers and the rest of the Thirty-Third, who saw heavy action as they defended the final push into Savannah. "The fighting as [we] advanced was severe," wrote one of the regiment's white officers in December 1864. "Every one [is] saying the Blacks fought nobly. It was gratifying to me to witness the perfect democracy among the white and black soldiers. They are even in squads, black & white dueling together, sometimes under black sergeants." We cannot know whether he meant Rivers, but it certainly seems possible. If so, it would be one of the incredibly rare instances during the Civil War in which a Black man was effectively leading white men in battle.[97]

Much is made among historians of the innovations of Sherman's Savannah Campaign: leaving his supply lines, living off the land, bringing the pain directly to civilians. For the next century modern war would be made in Sherman's model.

Simultaneously, however, an equally profound military innovation was occurring in the Department of the South. Describing Rivers's camp at Hilton Head, the poet Charlotte Forten was struck by how fundamentally the war had remade race relations. She watched Black soldiers strolling through the front door of a major hotel as if it was nothing. Black and white soldiers, she said, "are seen walking, conversing, eating, drinking, playing & working and worshiping together as if all of a color." And all this in a place where, three years earlier, she had been told by white soldiers of every rank "that if [the army] continued with 'this n——r business'" of recruiting Black troops, "half the army in the department would lay down their arms." "Now the army of the department consists almost entirely of Blacks," Forten marveled, "and everybody respects them. . . . Nothing could be more gratifying to me than this." What Forten was glimpsing was a military innovation just as consequential as any that could be credited to Sherman. Here was another taste of the future, a future that would extend from the Department of the South to the Tuskegee Airmen to President Harry Truman's 1948 order officially desegregating the military to today's armed forces, which are 17 percent Black.[98]

At the very moment this military equality was achieved, however, it began to recede. As Sherman turned his army toward the Carolinas, Rivers and the rest of the Thirty-Third were assigned to provost and guard duty, first in Charleston, then in Savannah. Sherman accepted the surrender of the Confederacy's major western army at Durham Station. Grant captured Petersburg, forced the evacuation of Richmond, and accepted Lee's surrender at Appomattox.[99]

The war, as most of us understand it, was over. Most of the white soldiers went home to hug their families, mourn their dead, and tend their crops. Not the Thirty-Third. They were being reassigned to the Freedmen's Bureau to help oversee their former enslavers' transition to employers and their fellow freedmen's transition to citizenship.

Rivers had contracted to serve for three years or the duration of the war. Both terms were up. He was keenly aware of the larger political picture and certainly understood the importance of the new mission. There was no denying, however, that his men were running out of steam. As one member of the regiment put it bitterly, the majority of the Black soldiers had fought for three years and had little more than their uniform to show for it. They'd run away from their enslavers directly into the "bondage of [a] soldier's life." Now, when the rest of their fellow freedmen were off reconstructing their lives, the soldiers who'd helped win that freedom were still stuck in service, with "wives & mothers [who might be] a-perishing."[100]

The next year would be the most wretched of the regiment's military experience. It was also a pivotal year for Rivers, setting him on the path to his ascension as "The Black Prince."

"The guilty deserve the severest penalties of the law"

In July 1865, Rivers and the rest of the Thirty-Third were ordered upriver from Savannah, Georgia, to Hamburg, South Carolina, to prepare for their new role as upcountry peacekeepers. Rivers knew Hamburg well from his days as a coachman, when it had been the leading transit hub of the Carolina interior. Now it seemed like an overbuilt ghost town. The regiment was not encamped there long, however, before they were ordered farther north and west to police the counties of Pickens and Anderson.

South Carolina's piedmont had always been poor in comparison to the Lowcountry. The war had made things immeasurably worse. The manhunt for Jefferson Davis alone had sprawled across the whole region, demolishing what little infrastructure there was. "The Railroad was for miles destroyed," Trowbridge noted, "bridges burned, and all kinds of forage and provisions had been consumed, so that it was little better than a desert." As plantation liberators, Rivers and company thought they had seen every face of slavery. This piedmont version, however, seemed infinitely more depressing. The freedmen they encountered seemed broken, desperate, and "destitute of clothing." Meanwhile the hatred of local whites glowed more intensely in defeat. Pulling up outside Anderson, the regiment was met by the Anderson town council.

Their first words to Trowbridge were simply, "Please don't bring them n—s into our town."[101]

Into the town they went. The whole point of the regiment now was to oversee "fair" labor contracts that would compel the freedmen to remain on their current farms while compelling former enslavers to pay "fair" wages. For Rivers, as for the rest of the Thirty-Third, it was grueling, thankless work, totally at odds with the identity they had crafted for themselves. No longer a force of liberation, they were enforcers of a compromise that tasted sour in the mouth.

At one plantation, Rivers and the Thirty-Third witnessed a scene so "revolting" Trowbridge himself longed for his "term of service in this horrible place to end." On a recon to a farm just outside Anderson, the regiment demanded that the planter call those he had enslaved into line. When Trowbridge asked the man if "his people were all present" the man replied, "There is one more in the house, I will get her out." "Stepping inside the door," Trowbridge said, "he soon returned dragging by the hand a lovely, delicate girl about nineteen years old as white as any woman I ever saw. He roughly ordered her to take her place in line, and as she passed by where I was standing she said: 'Father, I never knew that I was a n—r before.'"

"Is that your child?" Trowbridge asked the man.

"She is one of [the] house n—s," the man said flatly.

"I finished my duties on that plantation with all possible haste," said Trowbridge, "leaving this human monster and his wretched people with feelings of indescribable disgust and utter loathing."[102]

Of all the grotesqueries Black soldiers faced in their postwar service, it was their powerlessness in the face of scenes like this that ultimately drove them to despondence. At the beginning of the war, Rivers had said: "Now we soldiers are men—men for the first time in our lives. Now we can look our old masters in the face. They used to sell us and whip us, and we did not dare say one word. Now we aren't afraid, if they meet us, to run the bayonet through them." The Thirty-Third was no longer in the bayonet business. They were in the "peacekeeping" business.[103]

The worst was yet to come. Liberating plantations, even occupying Beaufort, Jacksonville, or Savannah, had been something the Thirty-

Third was good at. Now it was charged with pacifying multiple counties in a region that seemed in an amorphous state of rebellion. Shortly after the regiment's arrival in Anderson, Trowbridge sent Company D forty miles north to Walhalla after hearing from multiple sources about "lawlessness and confusion in the place." Such assignments multiplied until "outlying companies," including Rivers's Company A, were "stationed throughout the remote portions of the district." The broad distribution gave the Thirty-Third eyes and ears in many communities, but it also made them vulnerable.[104]

On entering Walhalla, Company D had taken "up quarters in the principal hotel and set to work making themselves as comfortable as possible." The head of the company, a white lieutenant named Jerome Furman, was a twenty-five-year-old former sergeant in the Fifty-Second Pennsylvania who had accepted promotion and transfer to the First South Carolina in August 1863. He was also an open-faced kid, and a true believer in the Black cause. On August 26, Furman stood in the warmth of the hotel's front porch after his evening meal when he was approached by a tall ex-Confederate with blue eyes and red hair who said earnestly, "We are glad to have you come into our town for we are absolutely without any kind of government. The town is full of desperate characters; we are living in constant fear of our lives and the presence of United States troops will no doubt soon restore order and be a blessing to us." According to Trowbridge's later report, the stranger's "mode of speech and cordial manner threw the officer completely off his guard and he foolishly accepted an invitation to take a walk with his newly made acquaintance." A few steps into their conversation the tall man "drew his revolver, shot [Furman] in the back, and as he fell, put the muzzle . . . to [Furman's] head . . . and discharged two more bullets into his brain, and then disappeared into the darkness."[105]

When word of the assassination reached the rest of his men, Trowbridge, along with Rivers's Company A, flew to Walhalla "as fast as the cars would carry" them. Forcing the town's mayor into the room with Furman's corpse, Trowbridge informed him: "As this officer has been murdered I shall hold you responsible for his death, giving you ten hours to produce the murderer, or I will burn the town." He then told the mayor to go to the town hall, ring the bell, assemble the townsfolk, and tell them what he'd said. The locals suddenly became compliant, informative, and sweet as molasses. They convinced Trowbridge that the man he was after was the notorious outlaw Manse Jolly, who did not belong to the town. They were not entirely lying.[106]

Four days after Furman's burial in Walhalla, another of the Thirty-Third's white officers was bushwhacked and murdered in Augusta. The victim was Alexander Heasly, former captain of Company E, who had been honorably discharged only a month earlier to take a position with the Freedmen's Bureau. The circumstances of Heasly's assassination were at once vastly different and yet somehow just as informative as the Furman case. Heasly had ulterior motives in seeking his discharge. He was infatuated with Sarah Jane Blakely, a "fair young mulatto woman" who lived in a small house behind her former enslaver's mansion in Augusta. Three nights before the murder, Heasly got into a heated exchange with another young white man, Frank Hight, a twenty-one-year-old ex-Confederate from a leading Augusta family who claimed to have a prior and superior claim to Blakely's attention. After some "high words," Hight apologized and departed. Three nights later, however, Heasly and Blakely were again at her home when they heard noises in the yard. Heasly was inclined to investigate, but Blakely thought she glimpsed familiar shapes through the window and cautioned him to stay. Some hours later Heasly took his leave and Blakely walked him to the gate of the larger house when "three persons rose up from a log of wood on which they were sitting, and, without any provocation or words, fired at the captain and wounded him fatally. He was also stabbed, to make their deadly work more sure." According to the *New York World*, who had a correspondent embedded in Augusta, "a more cowardly and disgraceful murder has never shocked our community. . . . It was committed in the very heart of the city, before midnight, on a man who had done no harm except to win the favors of a fair young mulatto from those who had hitherto enjoyed them. . . . The guilty deserve the severest penalties of the law."[107]

There is no way to know what was going on between Blakely, Heasly, and Hight, particularly because we have so little of the story from Blakely's perspective. Judging by her actions, she clearly preferred Heasly, feared

Hight, and was in an incredibly precarious position. Heasly's friends claimed "that he was about to marry the girl and take her to his friends at the North." If true, this makes the events of that night even more tragic for Blakely as she had just witnessed her fiancé's murder at the hands of a man who might have been a former lover, client, or serial sexual abuser. As the correspondent for the *New York World* noted, however, in Augusta the revelation of Heasly's romantic intentions, "even if true, lessens rather than increases the sympathy with the deceased for many believe it more degrading to be the husband than the paramour of a negro."[108]

The news of a second assassination in four days sent a shock wave through the regiment. Scattered, vulnerable, and seething, members of the Thirty-Third were afire with impotent rage. Many of them, including and especially Rivers, had been in the field months beyond their terms. They missed their homes and families. They still had ambivalent feelings about their commander, and they were beginning to resent their government for neither training nor empowering them to engage in a guerrilla war against Southern civilians.

In the wake of Heasly's murder, Trowbridge's counterpart in Augusta, General James Steedman, declared that the only way to bring peace to the region was to seize every gun, rifle, and pistol in the theater along with all the ammunition. He was probably right, but this was deemed impracticable or inadvisable by his superiors. Instead, the Thirty-Third was ordered back to Charleston. They were mustering out; they were finally going home.

"this wretched, unhappy, rebellious country"

The extraction of the Thirty-Third from upstate South Carolina would prove challenging. Trowbridge first sent dispatches to his far-flung troops, rallying them on Anderson, where he hoped a train would take them forever out of this "wretched, unhappy, rebellious country." Manse Jolly and his compatriots had other ideas. Tired of retail bushwhacking, Jolly concocted a brazen scheme to "annihilate the whole regiment." Just as the regiment's train was passing over a bridge, a guerrilla pulled the pin on the engine car, which quickly sped away, leaving the soldiers coasting to a stop in closed boxcars on a high, narrow trestle. The bushwhackers then set the trestle ablaze and fired into the cars at will.[109]

The plan might have worked but for the quick thinking of a soldier detailed to protect the engine crew. Putting the muzzle of his gun to the engineer's temple, he demanded they go back. Amid the firefight, the engine was relinked to the cars, and the regiment sped to safety, arriving in Newberry physically and spiritually exhausted. Thinking the worst was over, Trowbridge ordered Rivers to guard the train depot while he took the bulk of the men to a nearby grove to get some rest ahead of their long countermarch back to Charleston.

Four hours later, however, a westbound train jumped the track and came to rest aside the Thirty-Third's own eastbound train at the Newberry depot. It is possible that Rivers and company had purposely set a block on the track to prevent enemy pursuit or reinforcement, which would certainly make sense. This is supported by one eyewitness who noted: "I suspect the train had been thrown off by an obstacle placed on the track by negro troops camped nearby." Regardless, the new arrivals skidded to a halt, creating a combustible situation. Faced with Black troops holding the depot, most of the whites quietly tottered off to Newberry. Others determined to sleep in their cars while the train was put back on the track.[110]

What happened next is not clear. According to the Democratic press, one of the newly arrived whites, Calvin Crozier, was the beau ideal of Southern chivalry, boldly protecting two women from the gross insults of a boisterous Black soldier who demanded to sleep in the same car with them. In the version preferred by the regiment and its partisans, Crozier was a cunning guerrilla who had stowed aboard the train at Anderson, waiting until nightfall to engage in yet another murderous act of bushwhacking. In both versions, Rivers plays the pivotal role in a case that became a national cause célèbre, forcing even President Andrew Johnson to take a side.

The known facts are these. At Alston, South Carolina, two women embarked on a westbound train for Newberry. One of the women was a young mother, traveling with two children. The second was a younger, unmarried woman, hailing from the North. An unnamed railroad employee first approached a white Union sergeant, Dr. —— Pillsbury, to see if he would be willing to act as escort and see to the ladies' baggage. Overwhelmed with the transfer and care of several sick soldiers, Pillsbury declined. In his stead, he suggested Calvin Crozier, a Confederate parolee headed home to Galveston. Why he suggested Crozier is lost to time. Crozier was a twenty-five-year-old former member of the Seventh Kentucky Cavalry, dressed in full Confederate uniform. Captured on a raid with John Hunt Morgan in Syracuse, Ohio, Crozier had spent the last two years of the war imprisoned at Camp Douglas before being paroled to head home, making it as far as North Carolina before falling ill and convalescing for a few months before resuming his journey. Embarking at Orangeburg, Crozier had been in quarrelsome humor, engaging in "badinage with a Union Sergeant" under Pillsbury's charge in a conversation "so warm" Pillsbury "stopped it and reprimanded Crozier for his language." Fifteen minutes later Crozier came up to Pillsbury and "in a gentlemanly manner apologized for any offence he might have committed." This apparently had been enough for Pillsbury to suggest that Crozier would prove a worthy escort for the ladies. Crozier accepted the charge, little knowing he would be dead forty-eight hours later.[111]

The train from Alston to Newberry arrived later than expected, derailing at Newberry Station, where Rivers and company were standing guard as the remainder of their regiment bivouacked in the nearby grove. The white occupants of the train were undoubtedly alarmed at derailing after dark into a company of "colored" soldiers. They also probably did hear, as several witnesses report, "colorful" language outside the cars as Rivers's men continued to process their harrowing escape from Anderson. Here, however, the story of Crozier's partisans also derails. Realistically, no soldier in Rivers's company would ever have opened the door to Crozier's car, much less with a determination to sleep there. Rivers had been charged with overseeing the depot, which meant that he and his men could not sleep without risking court-martial and execution.

And it is precisely here that the evidentiary chain also turns against the myth of Crozier as a defender of white womanhood. While most of the new arrivals set off to find accommodations in Newberry, Crozier and the ladies remained because one of the women didn't have funds for a hotel. Sometime near midnight, Crozier alighted from the car on "private business" (meaning, most likely, he had to pee). Here one of two things happened. Either Crozier encountered a wakeful picket, Private Gloster Mills, and an altercation ensued, or Crozier encountered a sleeping picket, the same Gloster Mills, and stabbed him in the back of the neck. Either way, the violence occurred beyond the cars and beyond Rivers's sight in a depot that was otherwise quiet. The only known eyewitness to these events was the railroad repairman working to reset the engine, Jacob Bowers. Bowers thought he glimpsed "two men engaged in a fight" near the brush line just beyond the depot. The moon was fairly bright, so he may have seen a fight, but if so it was a lopsided one. Crozier didn't have a scratch or bruise on him, while Gloster Mills received two savage gashes to the face and a four-inch-long cut at the back of the neck that penetrated all the way to the spine, "severing muscles and parts." Did Bowers see a fight? Or did he just see Mills rising up after being bushwhacked? Either way, Bowers described the two figures as they emerged from the gloom. "One of them ran past me," he said, "and the other went in a contrary direction, calling out that he was cut." The second figure was obviously Mills, running toward the grove to find the regimental surgeon. The first figure was Crozier, running away from the grove and into the night, hoping to escape.[112]

Rivers's pickets quickly captured Crozier and hauled him back to the depot. Here a violent argument erupted between Rivers and his men, who demanded that Crozier be executed on the spot. This breakdown in discipline was uncharacteristic of the regiment, but the context is important. These men had spent the last two months under constant threat of harassment and bushwhacking. They'd finally turned toward home before spending an entire day fending off sabotage and arson, barely limping into Newberry, before Crozier popped out in full rebel regalia to half decapitate an adored private. Mills was just a teenager, the youngest and smallest in the regiment. Everyone loved him. Everyone also assumed his wounds were mortal, making this the third assassination the men had endured in a week. When Rivers told his men to stand down, they replied that unless Crozier was killed, "they would put a bullet through [their] sergeant." We do not know what Rivers said in reply. We only know that he took Crozier by the arm, turned his back on his men, and marched his prisoner down to the grove to find his colonel.[113]

Tensions were high as Rivers presented Crozier to Trowbridge. Most of the regiment was awake and seething with anger. Trowbridge was at the breaking point too. Glaring at Crozier, he "asked him what he stabbed that man for," and Crozier replied, "I did not intend to kill the damn n—r, I gauged my knife with my thumb and finger when I stick it into him." This was enough of an admission of guilt that Trowbridge was inclined to agree with his men: Just shoot him. The nature of Mills's wounds was incredibly suspicious. How exactly does a man engaged in a seconds-long fight manage to get stabbed that deeply in the back of the neck? As a precaution, Trowbridge sent one of his sergeants, perhaps even Rivers, down to the headquarters of Lieutenant Colonel Rockwell Tyler, commander of the district, to beg him to come at once. Awakened in the wee hours and apparently ill, Tyler misjudged the seriousness of the situation and instead sent one of his adjutants. The adjutant returned to Tyler to report "that a member of the 33d U.S.C.T. had been brutally stabbed and that Lt. Col. Trowbridge had said that his men were in a high state of excitement owing to a number of his officers & men having been killed by citizens in that section of the country, and the train which the regt came down on having been fired into that day and that he had the murderer in his possession and that unless the murderer was severely punished his men would burn the town." Tyler told the adjutant to inform Trowbridge that "the town must be saved at all hazards." Trowbridge took this to mean what he wanted it to mean: "Shoot him."[114]

Having done what he regarded as his due diligence, Trowbridge stalked over to Crozier and told him he "had decided to shoot him within one hour, and if he had any preparations to make, to make them." Crozier drafted a note for posterity that said, "I die for my country," but the guards wouldn't allow it. On a second attempt, Crozier wrote simply: "I forfeit my life for stabbing a U.S. Soldier."[115]

At dawn Crozier was marched to the ironically named Halcyon Grove, where he was "shot by a guard detailed for that purpose." Trowbridge's surgeon confirmed Crozier's death and the body was dragged a short distance to a hastily dug grave that was apparently too small. Later claims that the body was desecrated by someone jumping or dancing on top of it to stuff it into the hole cannot be confirmed or denied. The only eyewitnesses were members of the regiment, who wouldn't have invented such a story or repeated it if it did happen. More likely, white folks in Newberry made up the story when they discovered Crozier crumpled into a cramped, shallow grave.[116]

Having dispensed the summary judgment demanded by his troops, Trowbridge still didn't believe that his men had calmed down enough for him to take them through Newberry. Instead, he marched them a dozen miles around the town to rejoin the track where the train waited to carry them back to Charleston and their long-delayed mustering out.

Trundling down the track, the men of the Thirty-Third had ample time to reflect on their extended tour of service. Emotionally, they were a long way from the Beaufort grove and the sunny promise of Emancipation Day. Since then, they had liberated plantations, destroyed slave jails, occupied towns, recruited Black men to the Union cause, and helped justify the creation of the United States Colored Troops. There had been low moments as well: endless garrison and guard duty, epidemics, unequal pay, friction with whites, including their own colonel, and a final campaign that could only be described as an abject failure. For two months they'd done little to pacify, and everything to inflame, a white population hell-bent on consigning their fellow freedmen to slavery in all but name.

There was exactly one highlight during the Thirty-Third's sorry effort in the upstate: Rivers's political practicality during the Crozier affair. In all versions of the story, Rivers is the fulcrum and the hinge. According to Crozier partisans, Rivers had suggested to Crozier that he at least claim to be innocent and thereby get a fair trial. (This Crozier refused, preferring, apparently, martyrdom and immortality.) On the other side, at least according to Trowbridge, Trowbridge had executed Crozier in part to protect Rivers, because otherwise the regiment would have torched Newberry and fragged their ranking Black sergeant for his failure to summarily shoot Crozier in the first place.

In a story in which both sides agree on almost nothing, it is important to focus on what they do agree on. In both stories, Rivers stood alone. Without Rivers's leniency, Crozier could have no claim to martyrdom; he had chosen execution, which he could do only because Rivers had offered him a way out. And yet without Rivers's leniency, Trowbridge could have no claim to being the protector of the regiment, since he'd based his decision, at least in part, on the necessity of safeguarding his primary

Black sergeant from the wrathful force of a regiment whose discipline had all but shattered.

The French call the ability to see how a battle will play out, before it ever happens, the *coup d'oeil*—the sweep of the eye. The best Civil War generals could stare into a battlefield the way a chess master stares into a board: These losses on that hill would make possible this breakthrough, turning the tide of the engagement. Rivers had that same eye for politics. Of the thousand men in the regiment, including its white officers, including its colonel, Rivers alone understood that executing Crozier had been an epic mistake.

Shortly after the Thirty-Third returned to Charleston, President Andrew Johnson sat perusing a letter on his desk. "I enclose for your attention," the letter began, "the published account of the death (may I not call it murder?) of my son Calvin Crozier. I trust your Excellency as Chief Magistrate of our great Nation, in justice to me, in honor of our common country, and for the credit of the U.S. Army will have an investigation of this matter and hope the Officer Commanding this atrocious band may be brought to answer and pay the penalty due for having suffered so great an outrage." The letter was signed "R. G. Crozier."[117]

The entire point of guerrilla war is to frustrate your enemy into making a political error. In virtually their last act in their last engagement, the Thirty-Third had made a major political error. Rivers had been right. They should have left Crozier with the head of the military department, where he could have gotten a fair trial. They should have moved as quickly as possible to Charleston to muster out, go home, and fight a better fight on better ground. Instead, they'd been suckered by an ignoramus into creating the first martyr of the Lost Cause.

"if there should ever be a black monarchy in South Carolina"

Arriving in Charleston in mid-September 1865, the Thirty-Third were (again) assigned to garrison and guard duty while they dully awaited word on when they would finally muster out. Instead, they were electrified by the news in early November that their lieutenant colonel had been arrested. Trowbridge was quickly released on his own recognizance and told to find legal counsel in the city. On November 7, he would face a court-martial on the charge of murder.

Pulling strings behind the scenes was Andrew Johnson's handpicked provisional governor of South Carolina, Benjamin Franklin Perry. Like Johnson, Perry had been a steadfast Unionist before the war, editing South Carolina's only Unionist newspaper, the *Southern Patriot* (later the *Patriot and Mountaineer*) from 1851 to 1858. (Once the state seceded, however, Perry famously said, "You are all now going to the devil, and I will go with you.") Like Johnson, however, Perry was also a legendary racist. "The African, has been in all ages, a savage or a slave," Perry claimed, "and it is in vain to think of elevating him to the dignity of the white man."[118]

In executing Crozier, Trowbridge had given men like Johnson and Perry an incredible gift. Here was a chance to prove to the nation that Black militias could never be trusted. For several months, Perry and his partisans had been building their case against Trowbridge, and there is no denying he had made significant mistakes. First, he had taken his surgeon's word that Mills's wounds were mortal. They weren't. Multiple witnesses had seen Mills walking around Newberry, bandaged and busted up to be sure, but very much alive. Then there was the problem that Trowbridge hadn't even bothered to gather evidence from witnesses, including the two white women on the train. He hadn't convened a formal military tribunal, nor sought formal counsel from his officers. He hadn't truly conferred with the head of his military department, Rockwell Tyler, instead interpreting the nebulous words of Tyler's adjutant to mean "Shoot him." And then, after the fact, Trowbridge had left Crozier's crumpled body in a shallow ditch, thereby allowing the citizens of Newberry to gather up the corpse and bury it with great pomp and circumstance in the town's Rosemont Cemetery, all but securing the young man's claim to martyrdom. Most egregiously, Trowbridge had failed to understand the political hay the opposition press might make of his summary execution of Crozier, who, despite his rebel regalia, had been a private citizen who hadn't actually killed anybody. The lineaments of the entire affair fit too perfectly into the story Johnson and Perry wanted to tell: If Reconstruction went too far, if Black people were given too many rights, if they were armed, white men would be gunned down in any attempt to protect white women's honor.

At the court-martial, Trowbridge did an admirable job explaining the incredible pressure the regiment had been under during its entire tour in upstate South Carolina. His own life had been threatened on multiple occasions. The very day they left Anderson, his "landlady [had told him] the particulars . . . of a private plot to murder me." "While I was embarking my troops on board the train at Anderson," Trowbridge noted, "I heard remarks from the crowd that were standing around that that regiment of Negroes would never get out of the Dist. alive." The constant refrain coming in from Trowbridge's informants was that guerrilla bands were everywhere. Logically, he had seen Crozier as yet another bushwhacking ne'er-do-well. He was no "private citizen." He was yet another guerrilla in the Manse Jolly mold, and he'd gotten exactly what he deserved. Trowbridge even assured the board that "I have since learned unofficially that Gloster Mills is dead."[119]

The members of the court-martial board were inclined to agree. They found "Lt. Col. C. T. Trowbridge . . . Not Guilty and the court does therefore acquit him." Further up the military chain, however, pressure was brought to bear, especially by the commander of the military district of Charleston, Brevet Major Charles Devens. "The findings in the above case are disapproved," he said. "Calvin Crozier was executed summarily by Lt. Col. Trowbridge for the murder of Private Mills, 33d U.S.C.T., who was not only not murdered, but is to day alive and well. It was in my opinion a most unjustifiable act and indicates a weakness in yielding to momentary clamor and excitement unworthy of a brave and judicious officer." Possibly on his own initiative, possibly at the behest of Perry or Johnson, Devens had charged Edward C. Culp, a former officer in his regiment and now acting inspector general, "to proceed to Charleston and Newberry, and take all evidence that could be found and thoroughly investigate the whole affair." Culp's report was incredibly damaging to Trowbridge. "But little evidence seems to have been taken down by Lieut. Col. Trowbridge," Culp reported,

> not any evidence was taken from persons at the train, who were cognizant of the facts; even of the young ladies who certainly knew all about the affair, and who remained in Newberry long enough to have given any testimony required. No meeting of the officers of Regiment was convened, or it would certainly have been known by one of the four officers whose testimony is taken in affadavits. . . . All outrages perpetrated upon the Regiment were far from that section of the Country. Lieut. Col. Tyler was certainly in fault for not giving the matter more attention, when a man's life was in the balance. There is no evidence to show that Crozier was a desperate character; on the contrary, Dr. Pillsbury testifies that he was of gentlemanly deportment. . . . There was much excitement, no doubt, in the Regiment, and which was increased by the knowledge that several of their number had been shot by the citizens; but I have no knowledge of any offence for which a man can be executed without some trial. From the evidence adduced it appears that Calvin Crozier was shot by order of Lieut. Col. Trowbridge to satisfy and allay the excitement among the enlisted men of the 33rd USCT, certainly a very poor reflection upon its discipline.[120]

In his second court-martial, Trowbridge was acquitted again, this time by a board specifically instructed to grapple with the fact that Mills hadn't died. Once again, however, Devens voided the recommendation and substituted his own: Trowbridge should be summarily dismissed as unfit to wear the uniform of the United States. By this point it was clear that Trowbridge's case had become deeply enmeshed in the larger battle between President Johnson and the radical Republicans. It wasn't just one man on trial but Black citizenship and Black service as well. In an effort to protect both his regimental successor and his own legacy, Thomas Wentworth Higginson worked furiously behind the scenes, firing off letters in the hope of finding someone who could lean on the president. On December 13, for instance, he wrote to Senator Henry Wilson, one of the lead architects of the Fourteenth Amendment, to see what leverage he might have. "I have the honor to call your attention," said Higginson, "to the enclosed copy of a note addressed by me to Col. Robert Johnson, son and private Secretary of the President, with whom I have some acquaintance. I do this because I believe that a strong effort will be made by 'Governor' Perry & others to have Lt. Col. Trowbridge expelled from the service, in spite of his acquittal by Court Martial & their reaffirmation of that acquittal. I wish therefore to lodge the matter in your mind, should it be necessary to bring it up hereafter."[121]

Ultimately the Trowbridge case would be decided by Joseph Holt, judge advocate general for the entire Union army. Holt had been a Kentucky Democrat before the war, but like Lincoln he had learned to despise slavery and treason as a two-headed monster. Lincoln had originally been opposed to appointing Holt, preferring a more moderate candidate. His secretary of war, Edwin Stanton, however, foresaw that the ability to review courts-martial might prove pivotal as the Lincoln administration sought to transform the army from a conservative (and therefore Democratic) instrument into a radical and Republican one. He had been right. On April 3, 1866, Holt handed down his decision: "Upon a full and careful consideration of the facts in this case, as elicited from the voluminous papers submitted, this Bureau cannot concur in the recommendation for Col. Trowbridge's dismissal. . . . The Bureau recommend that in view of the acquittal of Col. Trowbridge by a competent court, and the circumstances attendant on the case, which rendered his action justificable, if not praise-worthy, the suggestions of General Devins . . . be disregarded."[122]

Before that decision came, however, news arrived that the Thirty-Third were finally disbanding. On February 5, 1866, they received word that "all Officers of the 33d USCT who are responsible for Quartermasters Stores will at once turn them over . . . as the Regiment is about to be mustered out of service." And on February 9, Rivers and the rest of the men were standing in formation on the beach at Charleston, staring into the harbor where the war had begun.[123]

The scene itself was stirring. The regimental flag, presented to Rivers in a Beaufort grove on Emancipation Day, snapped in the wind for the last time. Under a nearby dune lay the common grave of Colonel Robert Gould Shaw and the hundred men of the Fifty-Fourth Massachusetts who had given their last full measure in the heroic assault on Battery Wagner. Whatever problems had beset the Thirty-Third toward the end of their tour seemed suddenly small against the enormity of their long experience, now coming to a close. Trowbridge himself drew dark energy from the threat of formal dismissal hanging over his head, and the speech he gave that day was one for the ages. All that he and his men had achieved, he said, they had done in service, and sometimes in defiance, of a largely thankless nation. In addressing the men, he called them not by their army name, but by the name they preferred: "The First South." He spoke not of what the Union army had done for America, but of what these particular Black men had done for America. He spoke especially to and for men like Rivers, who had joined up before there was an army to join. The resulting remarks were so poignant Higginson reprinted them in full in his own memoir:[124]

> Comrades,—The hour is at hand when we must separate forever, and nothing can ever take from us the pride we feel, when we look back upon the history of the First South Carolina Volunteers,—the first black regiment that ever bore arms in defence of freedom on the continent of America. On the ninth day of May 1862, at which time there were nearly four millions of your race in a bondage sanctioned by the laws of the land, and protected by our flag, on that day, in the face of floods of prejudice, that well-nigh deluged every avenue to manhood and true liberty, you came forth to do battle for your country and your kindred. For long and weary months without pay, or even the privilege of being recognized as soldiers, you labored on, only to be disbanded and sent to your homes, without even a hope of reward. And when our country, necessitated by the deadly struggle with armed traitors, finally granted you the opportunity again to come forth in defence of the nation's life, the alacrity with which you responded to the call gave abundant evidence of your readiness to strike a manly blow for the liberty of your race. And from that little band of hopeful, trusting, and brave men, who gathered at Camp Saxton, on Port Royal Island, in the fall of 1862, amidst the terrible prejudices that then surrounded us, has grown an army of a hundred and forty thousand black soldiers, whose valor and

> heroism has won for your race a name which will live as long as the undying pages of history shall endure.[125]

All veterans have a relationship with their military service. Some relationships are like the persistent memories of a bad breakup—episodes of a former life you are always struggling to forget. Other relationships are like the persistent memories of a lost love—episodes of a former life you are always struggling to remember. Most relationships sit in the psychic space in the middle, and so it was for Rivers. Proud of his service, he would treasure forever his pivotal role in the creation of the First South. In the upcountry, however, he had glimpsed the new face of white supremacy as the entire battlefield shifted from defeating slavery to achieving equality. In 1862, Higginson had said, "If there should ever be a black monarchy in South Carolina, [Rivers] will be its king." For the first time in his life, Rivers was finally free to pursue his own ambitions. Thirty-five years in bondage, five years in the army, he had seen much and knew more. "This is our time!" he had told his men. Rivers knew the window of opportunity would not remain open forever; now was his time to put his stamp on the world.

In October 1865, another member of the First South had written to Higginson to ask about his contacts in Washington. If Higginson could get him out of the service, the soldier promised to self-deport to Haiti, where he longed to be anyway. "I now have no faith," he said, "in the moral ability of either the Government or the people, to give justice to the colored man." This soldier's experience had been the same as Rivers's, the same grueling, extended tour, the bushwhacking, and the bad faith on the part of the federal government. "After fully considering our civil status in this country from *my* standpoint," the soldier concluded, "I have come to the conclusion that we can *never* be any thing here."[126]

Surveying the landscape, Rivers thought he saw another way through.

THE LEGISLATOR

It is in justice that the ordering of society is centered.

ARISTOTLE

Rivers returned to find his hometown subsumed in "ominous silence." During the war, Beaufort had been the seat of the "First South"—a bustling embodiment of the "new birth of freedom." A year later, Rivers felt the tide starting to turn.[1]

Today, many Americans think Reconstruction began after the Civil War. Rivers feared it might end with the Civil War. The Black folks around Beaufort had only ever known one version of Reconstruction—a version that began in 1861, put men like Rivers in uniform, ended slavery, and brought opportunities in education, entrepreneurship, property and office holding, and access to health care. With the speed of an assassin's bullet, everything changed. "Secesh are coming back thick," noted Laura Towne, a teacher at the nearby Penn School. "They are crawlingly civil as yet but will soon feel their oats."[2]

They had every reason to feel their oats. "Whatever [else] Andrew Johnson may be," Frederick Douglass said upon meeting Lincoln's successor, "he certainly is no friend of our race." (Johnson's opinion of Douglass was more severe: "I know that damned Douglass; he's just like any n——r, and he would sooner cut a white man's throat than not.")[3]

The new president's vision for Reconstruction (he preferred "Restoration") began and ended at the Thirteenth Amendment. "There is no such thing as reconstruction," Johnson said. "These States have not gone out of the Union, therefore reconstruction is unnecessary." Black people in the South, Johnson thought, should neither be slaves nor citizens but, effectively, serfs, bound to land and bound to labor.[4]

In late 1865, Johnson unilaterally vacated Sherman's Order 15, which had confiscated almost half a million acres of the Southern seaboard with the declared intention of giving it to the freedmen in forty-acre parcels. (Families working the land could also apply to the government for a mule to help improve it, giving rise to the widespread understanding that reparations would include "forty acres and a mule.") Sherman may have made the offer cynically, seeking to sever the train of freedmen traveling in his wake during the Savannah and Carolinas Campaigns. Lincoln and the radicals in Congress, however, had intended to honor his promise, charging Rufus Saxton with settling and titling the land as quickly as possible.[5]

Rivers himself had put in a claim, hoping to secure at least a parcel of his enslaver's old plantation on the Coosaw River.[6]

This had been the state of things when Lincoln sat laughing with his wife in a box at Ford's Theatre, watching a terrible play he had already seen. We can barely imagine how different this country would be if African Americans currently owned half of the Atlantic Seaboard for thirty miles inland, including the cities and environs around Charleston, Savannah, St. Simons Island, and Myrtle Beach. Instead, Johnson revoked the order, opening the question of whether the government would honor any of the land titles given to freedmen.[7]

To be sure, Rivers and his family still had property in Beaufort, based not on one of Sherman's "promissory titles" but on titles they'd bid on and bought at legal tax auctions. Even so, the mood in Beaufort as Rivers returned to town was "very sad and troubled." "We hear reports and rumors that make us quake," Laura Towne said. The rumor that "Beaufort and Hilton Head [were] to be closed as Government depots" turned out *not* to be true. The rumor that General Saxton was to be demoted and sent elsewhere *was* true. More worrying, Saxton's replacement, Robert Kingston Scott, was widely understood to support the idea that "the Sea Islands be returned to the former owners when they shall have paid the negroes for the improvements [to their property]." Meanwhile, a massive purge of the Freedmen's Bureau, including Laura Towne's own brother, left the agency crippled. The replacements they sent from Washington, Towne complained, were "often more pro-slavery than the rebels themselves, and only care to make the blacks work."[8]

Rivers watched glumly as many Black families made what deals they could with their returning former owners. "The spring found them seeking employment in the fields," noted the local paper breezily, "instead of depending as in years past, upon the precarious livelihood of town jobs." This formulation utterly misrepresents the forces at play. The precarity of the "town jobs" was a function of an economy in which the legal titles of Black people were under siege, and Beaufort began to wane as a seat of Reconstruction. As Laura Towne put it more astutely: "The people receive the rebels better than we expected, but the reason is that they believe Johnson is going to put them in their old masters' power again, and they feel that they must conciliate or be crushed."[9]

Rivers was not the sort of person to "conciliate or be crushed," and he was in no hurry to meet his old enslaver again. In the second-most consequential decision of his life, he decided to quit Beaufort.

Why?

Part of the reason may have been personal. For many Black families, the immediate aftermath of slavery had been an epic moment of reunion. After decades of displacement, they were all finally free to pick up the pieces and chart their own course as families. They were also in the grips of post-traumatic stress. Inevitably, some Black families reunited only to find themselves estranged. Decades of distance, the drama of the times, divergent memories, and differing goals—there were endless challenges in trying to put back together what time had torn apart.

These reunions and reckonings were especially fraught for Black soldiers. Mostly illiterate, they had often been out of touch with their families for extended periods and came home changed men, having seen more of the world.[10]

While he had been stationed in Beaufort, Prince and his wife Elsie had made everything work. When Rivers left Beaufort for his final tour in the upcountry, however, a seam opened up in the family that apparently couldn't be mended.

When an event warps the English language, we know it has significant gravity. There is a reason the Black community invented terms such as "before-the-war wife" and "before-the-war husband." Rivers and Elsie had been on divergent paths even before he joined up. Raised in the "white folks' house," Rivers was literate, widely traveled, and, according to his former commander, destined to become the "king" of South Carolina. Elsie's experience of enslavement and emancipation had been sadder and more circumscribed. She was an illiterate field hand. She and Prince had lost ten of their twelve children before the war even began. Understandably, her primary drive in the aftermath was to hold on to her remaining children as tightly as possible.

According to Rivers's daughter, Pattie White, "after Pa came out the Army he never returned regularly to my mother." We can't know exactly what this means or why the two split, but we see signs of alienation on both sides. In one deposition, Pattie noted that "my father had children by plenty of other women," and there is no question that Rivers was a Casanova. On Elsie's side, several witnesses claimed that she might already have been living with one Renty Simmons before Rivers returned to Beaufort in 1866. A later pension application simply notes that "the very best colored witnesses testify that [Prince] and Elsie never resumed marital relations after soldier's discharge from the army," which seems fair to both sides. Whatever the reasons or timeline, Elsie married Simmons and spent the rest of her life with him on Cain's Neck, a remote exurb of Beaufort. Rivers charted a different course.[11]

Rivers may have had political reasons to quit Beaufort as well. As a Black sergeant, and especially as the regiment's provost sergeant, he had always secured his men's "implicit obedience," as Thomas Wentworth Higginson put it, but not always their love. In 1863, while stationed in Beaufort, Rivers's men had looked to him for help in pooling their resources and investing in property. As the war dragged on, however, the relationship between him and the men became strained. Rivers's primary obligation was to maintain discipline in a regiment that was becoming increasingly frustrated and starting to lose steam. This gulf had only widened during the Crozier episode, where Rivers had thwarted his men's thirst for extralegal justice. In retrospect, his conduct made him the most reasonable man in the regiment, but many of the men didn't see it that way, and some of them may have nursed grudges all the way home.[12]

Then, too, there may have been tensions between Rivers and other of Beaufort's leading Black men, especially Robert Smalls. Both men had similar biographies—one had stolen a horse and ridden it to freedom, the other had stolen a boat. Both were associated with the Thirty-Third, Rivers as ranking sergeant and Smalls more vaguely attached to the regiment as a pilot. Both were now veterans and effectively neighbors, having bought properties on the same road in the tax sales of 1863.[13]

In the years after the war, however, Smalls's legend continued to grow. The story of his daring seizure and ride to freedom aboard *The Planter* made him a household name. (It had also given him considerable seed capital—$1,500 in prize money that would be worth $50,000 today.) Between his capital flows, Northern contacts, and heroic backstory, Smalls was a rising man who would eventually join the U.S. Congress. In 1866, just as Rivers was thinking about moving away, Smalls purchased a two-story building to open a new Black school. He also partnered with a Philadelphia businessman to open a Black general store.[14]

Even as Smalls's political power grew, Rivers could feel his own legend sinking into obscurity. Speaking of a different Robert (Sutton, not Smalls), Higginson had once said: "If Sergeant Rivers was a natural king among my dusky soldiers, Corporal Robert Sutton was the natural prime-minister." Higginson might have made the same comparison between Prince Rivers and Robert Smalls. Rivers understood better how power worked on the ground; Smalls was the more natural politician. "The entire 1st South Carolina volunteer regiment were more than ever heroes in the eyes of the people," noted Edith M. Dabbs in her *Sea Island Diary*, but "it is doubtful if any one man was ever as outstanding a symbol as Robert Smalls." Whether the town of Beaufort was yet too small to support two local legends is a question for future historians to consider.[15]

What can be said is that by the time Rivers returned to Beaufort, many of the local economic and political opportunities had been soaked up by men who hadn't been diverted into an extended tour in the army. For five years Rivers had fought to protect the "First South," assuming he would return to Beaufort forever. Back in the city, however, he found his dreams receding with the sea. With every sweep of the eye, he saw a son established, a daughter married, a wife taking up with another man, and his own political fortunes sinking.

Rivers never made a precipitous decision in his life. Whatever he did, he did for a reason. Whatever his personal circumstances, whatever petty beefs there may have been among the great men of Beaufort, we should assume that what he most clearly saw was the coming political storm. "Only let us know for sure—*for sure*, mind you," Rivers had said, "that the white people mean right . . . and I *know* we will fight."[16]

As the South collapsed into guerrilla violence, Rivers knew that, taken as a group, the white people did not mean right. In the political battles he saw coming, he believed Black people could benefit from white allies, but they couldn't depend on them. Protection for Black communities would require bolder thinking and bolder action by Black leaders.

Signing his property over to his son, Jack, to manage, Rivers took leave of Beaufort forever. Why control a piece of property, he had decided, when you could control an entire town?

"Bloody Edgefield"

Key to Rivers's decision to relocate was the Military Reconstruction Act, which passed Congress on March 2, 1867 (over Johnson's veto). Dividing the South into five military districts, Congress demanded that any state seeking readmission to the Union would first have to draft (and then ratify by popular vote) a new state constitution guaranteeing voting rights for *all* men, including African Americans. Rivers saw this as a historic opportunity. In the early days of the regiment, he had been a titanic force in recruiting Black soldiers. These same skills would help him register and mobilize an army of Black voters for the new war he saw coming.

The question was: where to begin organizing?

The terrain on which Rivers chose to make his stand was some of the rockiest he could have chosen: Edgefield County, South Carolina. "Bloody Edgefield" had earned its reputation for violence in the colonial period as a place where hair-trigger tempers sent white elites to the dueling grounds and white rubes to wrestling grounds where an eye for an eye was literal gospel. Introduced to an Edgefield courtroom in its heyday, a visiting circuit judge interjected: "Before God, gentlemen of the jury, I never saw such a thing before in the world! There is a plaintiff with an eye out! A juror with an eye out! And two witnesses with an eye out! What a state of society you must have in this part of the country!" Parson Weems had called Edgefield "Pandemonium itself, a very district of Devils." "What South Carolina was to the nation," one historian has concluded, "Edgefield was to South Carolina."[17]

So why in all the world had Rivers determined to set up shop in Edgefield County?

First, he knew the people. For years Rivers had sojourned in Edgefield as he and his enslavers fled the malarial season on the coast. Local Black residents knew Rivers as a man widely traveled, bringing news from afar. Moreover, in Edgefield Rivers's legend as a Black commander of troops had grown unimpeded by Beaufort rivalries and grudges.

Second, he knew what his people needed. When Rivers returned to Edgefield in 1867, he brought with him a gospel from the coast that bypassed cavil and cut to the bone. Black locals were busy fighting for better sharecropping contracts when they should have been fighting for better schools *staffed by Black teachers* or better hospitals *staffed by Black doctors*. More than anything, they should have been fighting for Black opportunities to farm their own land. Rivers's vision for Reconstruction had been informed by his Beaufort experience but extended beyond it in its independence from Northern white aid. All he demanded of federal authorities was that they keep the playing field level and fair. He would do the rest.

The first step of Rivers's plan was to become "register" for Edgefield County, which is to say the man charged with registering new voters. The Republican Party had staked its future (and the future of Black rights) on the franchise. What they most needed were organizers in the South, especially in places such as Edgefield, where Black people represented more than 60 percent of the population.

To become register, Rivers would need to apply to the military commander of the Second District, Major General Daniel Sickles. With one leg, droopy eyes, and a droopy moustache, Sickles had weathered so many scandals he seemed like a political cockroach, omnipresent and unkillable. How he managed to survive is one of the greater mysteries of the mid-nineteenth century. He had gunned down his wife's paramour on an open street corner. He had introduced a prostitute to Queen Victoria. He had covered up the leak of Lincoln's 1862 State of the Union address. He had created a massive salient in the Union line on the second day at Gettysburg that almost resulted in disaster. And yet somehow, in 1867, Rivers's entire future depended on Daniel Sickles, a man whom a fellow New Yorker described as "one of the bigger bubbles in the scum of the [legal] profession, swollen and windy, and puffed out with fetid gas."[18]

The Military Reconstruction Act had passed in March and by early April, Sickles's office was inundated with applications for positions as county registers. Among the candidates for Edgefield County was James Johnston, a white New Yorker who sought to play on Sickles's sympathies as a Tammany man. "I am a native of New York," Johnston noted, "and when a lad residing in Albany often had the pleasure of delivering telegrams to the Hon. Daniel E. Sickles and others of the Rock-ribbed Democracy."[19]

Rivers chose not to importune Sickles directly, instead working through intermediaries. "I have known Sergeant Rivers for several years and can assure you that he is peculiarly fitted to perform the duties of a register," wrote J. E. Bryant. "If you have read the *Atlantic Monthly* for a year past and have read Colonel Higginson's articles published in it you have read considerable of Sergeant Rivers as Col. Higginson has seldom written an article for that magazine during the past year but that he has alluded to him. The Colonel regarded Prince as the ablest colored man in his regiment. I know considerable of the colored men in Edgefield District and think that Sergeant Rivers is the best colored man in the District for register. I trust you may feel at liberty to appoint him." Samuel B. Spencer sent a similar endorsement with a long list of cosigners: "Sir, the undersigned do in accordance with your order send the bearer of this Mr. Prince Rivers as our man for the register and we are happy to say General that we feel perfect confidence in Mr. Rivers and we hope you will accept him as our representative to your notice and in the behalf of our cause."[20]

For whatever reason, Sickles acceded to popular will, probably outsourcing the decision to his underlings in Edgefield. Regardless, by summer 1867, Rivers had been appointed register and was again a rising man. Physically commanding and biographically inspiring, he quickly consolidated a new base of power and by November, he was elected one of Edgefield's representatives to the state constitutional convention.[21]

"Nothing quite like this [has] ever been tried before"

Gaveled in at the sumptuous Charleston Clubhouse, the majority Black delegates—elected in a majority Black state—went to work redrafting the laws that all South Carolinians would live under. "Nothing quite like this had ever been tried before," historian Lerone Bennett noted in 1976, "and nothing remotely approaching it has happened in America in all the years since." As a show of racial solidarity, the Black majority unanimously elected a white ally, Albert Gallatin Mackey, as president and chair. Mackey was gracious in turn: This Convention, he said, demands "the commendation of every lover of liberty and respecter of human rights. . . . It is the first Constitutional convention in this State, in the selection of whose members, the ballot box, the true palladium of rational liberty, has been made accessible to every man."[22]

The work before the convention was as portentous as when George Washington gaveled in the Founding Fathers at Philadelphia. Against the backdrop of a country scarred by four years of war and three years of failed Reconstruction, Rivers and company hoped to strike "every vestige of serfdom . . . from our institutions in so emphatic and unambiguous a way, that no doubt can be entertained of our determination that this relic of barbarism shall never again, in any form, pollute our soil."[23]

Over the succeeding month, Rivers and the rest of the radicals rolled out a raft of initiatives striking massive blows for progressive reform. In addition to full legal and civic equality (including interracial marriage), they proposed a uniform system of free public schools (including an interracial state university), as well as the abolition of property qualifications for voting and the abolition of debtors' prison. All of these measures passed, leading W. E. B. Du Bois to later pronounce the convention a more radical experiment than the Paris Commune of 1871.[24]

Rivers wanted more, however. All political offices in the state, he and his colleagues said, should be vacated and new elections held in which

Black people would have an equal chance to participate. In addition, the state should pay the freedmen back wages from the Emancipation Proclamation and establish a land bank with the potential capacity to pay much larger reparations.

Both ideas were carefully considered. The Emancipation Proclamation had specifically freed enslaved people in areas then under rebel control. To William Henry Seward, Lincoln's secretary of state, this made the proclamation seem ridiculous, "emancipating slaves where we cannot reach them and holding them in bondage where we can set them free." (He famously dismissed the proclamation as a mere "puff of wind," meaning a legal fart.) But Rivers and the radicals followed the proclamation to its logical conclusion. If South Carolina's enslaved population had been legally free from January 1, 1863, they were owed back wages for all the days they had worked between then and the date of their first labor contract. Either the state or the federal government needed to pay up. Forget forty acres and a mule. Rivers and the radicals thought it should be one hundred acres and several thousand dollars.[25]

Even as the convention met, opposition forces were rallying to bury the new world before it was born. The *Charleston Mercury* led the way with a series of deeply grotesque "Sketches of the Delegates to the Great-Ringed-Streaked-and-Striped-Convention." The title was intended to convey at once the image of a political circus and mongrelizing of the races. When complete, the sketches were collected into a single convenient edition—a political "hit list" of sorts—along with an ensemble photograph of every radical member who, presumably, deserved to die.[26]

According to the paper, Delegate "W.J. Whipper" was "a genuine negro, black and kinky headed, who, in the days of slavery, would be esteemed a likely fellow for a house servant."[27]

Albert Clinton was "a backwoods negro of whose antecedents we have not been informed."[28]

James Henderson, "alias Johnstone alias almost anything," was "a half-and-half [who] severely handles his wives on provocation; yet, when a dangerous man comes about him, he is said to add discretion to the list of his virtues and betake himself to the bushes."[29]

And Prince Rivers was "frightfully black, ignorant and impudent [and] talks like a low country 'gulla-n——r.'" "Since his discharge from the army," continued the paper, "[Rivers] has been devoting himself . . . entirely to politics, and is a very consequential member of the Union League. [He] appears to be a bird of passage, here, there and everywhere, except in his proper sphere, with curry comb and horsebrush, or the box of some genteel carriage."[30]

We don't know if Rivers read the portrait. Was he hurt by it? Certainly, it was designed to wound. The threat to return him to the carriage, the easy digs at his accent were also attempts to foster scorn and derision among whites. Another example of this seemingly casual, deliberately calculated cruelty was some doggerel in the *Daily Phoenix* set to the rhythm of Edgar Allan Poe's "The Raven." In one stanza, a correspondent for the *Charleston Courier* has snuck into the convention and is documenting the most ridiculous delegates:

> Note the "previous question" Johnson, mark the huge Augustus Thompson,
> Catch the fire of lisping Langley, echo Elliott's awful roar,
> List the stalwart P. R. Rivers knock the English tongue to shivers,
> While the modest Jervey quivers, struggling hard to take the floor;
> Then with note and sketch abundant, welcome to the *Courier* door,
> Enter there forevermore.[31]

These portraits are so obviously racist and hurtful one hesitates to quote them, and yet they often contain unintended revelations. Rivers *did* speak with a Gullah accent. He had been a carriage driver. Like any caricature, the game was in taking his distinctive qualities and holding them up to ridicule. That comic process can also be unwound, however, to find the original kernels of truth.

Take, for instance, the word "stalwart." The attribution of the word to Rivers is almost lost in the ribaldry, but it can also be taken as a grudging sign of respect. This is an aspect of the man we already know—his precise manners and military bearing. The *Mercury* paid another backhanded compliment in noting that Rivers "had shown his wisdom thus far by holding his tongue. Will he have the wit to continue to do so?" (The *Edgefield Advertiser* had a similar impression of him, saying "P.R. Rivers, seated at his table, looks wondrous wise, but wisely keeps his reflections in his own cranium."[32])

If Rivers was a more reticent legislator, he was also more pragmatic.

To his mind, his Republican allies in the North were naive if they thought the franchise alone would be enough to protect the formerly enslaved from their former enslavers. Real change would need to be rooted more deeply in the soil, or it would be swept away. "God help the people of South Carolina," another radical member said presciently, "if they allow the power they now have to again slip out of their hands."[33]

The radical member who said this was Solomon George Washington Dill, an ex-Confederate delegate from Kershaw County. Early in his career, Rivers had depended deeply on Hunter and Higginson, men who had given him his first lessons in whites who meant right. These men had been Northern born, however, raised in an abolitionist tradition. More surprising to Rivers was the discovery of a minority of white Southerners who also meant right.

Through the whole first month of the convention, Dill had sat in perfect silence, just as Rivers had, both men feeling a little a-sea. On the thirty-ninth day of the convention, Dill rose to argue in favor of a motion that all public offices should be vacated, reelected, and made answerable to all the people, white and Black alike. "I have consumed as little time on this floor as any man in this house," Dill admitted, but "I am tired of seeing the people of South Carolina robbed of their rights."[34]

From that moment forward, Dill became one of the most outspoken proponents for progressive reform, voting with Rivers on everything. When the editors of the *Mercury* called Rivers a "Gullah n——r" and denigrated the entire proceeding as an interracial farce, Dill pounced. "The *Mercury* calls us a ring-streaked-and-striped Convention," he told his colleagues. "I admit it is all that; but who made it ring-streaked-and-striped but just such men as conduct the *Mercury*? It would not have been ring-streaked-and-striped if such men as manage the *Mercury* office and newspaper had been exterminated long ago. They put the stripes into it."[35]

Dill knew exactly what he was saying: If the editors of the *Mercury* didn't like race mixing, maybe they shouldn't have raped those they enslaved. At this, a delegate named Randolph leapt up to demand that Dill be ruled out of order. Dill was just getting started, however.

What did it mean, Dill asked rhetorically, that "such men as conduct the *Mercury*" both raped their slaves and compared them to animals?

Weren't such men, by their own racist logic, guilty of bestiality? "I know as much about the men who call us ringed-streaked-and-striped as any body," Dill said, "and if I choose to tell, I could astonish you with a revelation of secrets that would account for some of these streaks." The implication was clear; Dill would name names; he would stop at nothing to create a new politics for the state. "I want to get [us] out of the old channel," Dill said, "and I intend to fight to the day of my death."[36]

That day came soon. Dill was assassinated shortly after the convention, on June 4, 1868, as a volley of mob gunfire poured into his house. Dill was shot in the spine. His Black bodyguard was shot in the head. His wife was shot in the leg. A bullet narrowly missed his infant son.[37]

Dill's death impressed Rivers. Here was a man willing to die for racial solidarity. Dill's death also impressed on Rivers the need to create an interracial sanctuary. The *Mercury* was probably right: Rivers knew little of, and cared less for, parliamentary procedure. He was never a politicker or speechifier. He had a different set of skills. He led by example. He led by *doing*. In the army, he had always been in charge of logistics. His questions always ran: How do we make the camp run more smoothly? Or, more generally, how do we create a disciplined interracial community?

As a politician, Rivers's questions, instincts, and abilities still ran the same in the same line, except this time he was thinking of something much bigger than an army camp.

If Rivers didn't say much, it was because he was busy doing much. This is where the *Mercury*'s other charge rings true. Rivers really was "here, there, and everywhere"—working tirelessly behind the scenes to create a refuge for his people.

To understand how he did it, we have to begin in an unlikely place.

"Probably there is no other town . . . where more or larger commercial vicissitudes and successes occur"

Prior to the cotton gin, South Carolina's midlands and upstate were considered inferior farmland. None of the colonial cash crops—tobacco, rice, indigo, long-staple cotton—could grow there for a century, so most of the money (and most of the enslaved) remained on the coast.

The cotton gin changed everything. Long-staple cotton grows where it's very wet and warm. The fibers aren't that much longer (perhaps a quarter inch), but the resulting cloth is stronger, softer, and more durable. All of that matters if you're making bedsheets for snobs. None of it matters if you're trying to clothe the masses. The bigger issue had always been the seeds. Short-staple cotton, which grew well in the arid upstate, had never been a practical or profitable crop, because it took a laborer a whole day just to remove the seeds from a single pound. The cotton gin removed one of the greatest bottlenecks in the history of agriculture, and the resulting upstate cotton boom left inland planters scrambling for infrastructure that could carry their new crop to market.

In the early days of the boom, the upstate's cotton was carried by wagon road from the South Carolina interior to Augusta, Georgia, where it was floated and poled downriver to Savannah. This arrangement was good for Georgia's economy but bad for South Carolina's. South Carolina's planters had to pay a bridge toll at the Georgia line, and all cotton ended up in Savannah for transport rather than in Charleston.

In 1820 a German émigré, Henry Shultz, had a bright idea. Why not locate a town on the South Carolina side, across the river from Augusta? The current was stronger on the South Carolina bank, creating a deeper channel for steamboats. Shultz named this new town Hamburg, after his native city, and quickly convinced the state legislature to help underwrite his efforts with favorable loans, state infrastructure projects, and a five-year tax exemption on "all lots of land, Negro slaves, stock in trade, and all other taxable property."[38]

Hamburg quickly became the state's central inland cotton market. Within two years there were seventy-eight buildings in Hamburg, including "a warehouse 50 x 300 feet for cotton and tobacco—a public house 50 x 70 feet," new storefronts, a new bank "magnificent in appearance," and a massive new wharf. The roads were as wide as the town's ambition—one hundred feet everywhere except Market Street, running along the river, which was 150 feet wide.[39]

Equally critical to Hamburg's success was the completion of the rail connection to Charleston. Most people think the B&O (the Baltimore & Ohio) was the largest common carrier in the antebellum United States. When completed in 1833, however, the Charleston & Hamburg Railroad was the longest rail line in the world. In the city's heyday, sixty thousand bales of cotton moved through Hamburg annually (with a value of $2 million). On one day in April 1847, the Hamburg depot shipped to Charleston "900 bales of cotton, 3,000 bushels of corn and wheat, 50,000 pounds of bacon from Tennessee, and 600 bales of yarn." "A few years since an unsightly marsh sending forth its pestiferous exhalations," gushed one newspaper, Hamburg "is now covered with stately buildings and is a great emporium of trade." "Probably there is no other town of equal size in America," concurred another paper, "where more or larger commercial vicissitudes and successes occur."[40]

Seeing antebellum Hamburg as a hub of agriculture, however, misses the other aspect of its significance. The most valuable "product" that poured through Hamburg in the antebellum years was not cotton but human beings. Early in the nineteenth century, the Georgia legislature had banned the interstate slave trade—not because slavery was cruel but because the trade would inevitably bring more Black people into the state. This allowed Hamburg to find its true economic sweet spot as an inland transport hub for the sale of enslaved people. "There are two large houses there," reported a correspondent for the *Anti-Slavery Bugle*, "with piazzas in front to expose the 'chattels' to the public during the day, and yards in rear of them where they are penned up at night like sheep, so close that they can hardly breathe, with bull-dogs on the outside as sentinels. They sometimes have thousands here for sale, who in consequence of their number suffer most horribly." Traders pitched tents and slept in wagons on Hamburg's side of the bridge, awaiting Georgia buyers who had to wait only a year for their purchases to be legitimated by their state.[41]

In 1972, historian Richard Ralston coined the term "Second Middle Passage" as a way of conveying the devastations to the Black community of America's domestic slave trade. In this second wave of the larger African diaspora, two million men, women, and children were sold "down the river" from the older tidewater states to the newer Cotton Kingdom.

Historian Tiya Miles tells the harrowing history of Ashley's sack, a simple cotton bag given from an enslaved mother, Rose, to her nine-year-old daughter on the occasion of her daughter's unexpected sale. Heartbroken at having to say such a sudden goodbye, Rose repurposed the bag as a psychic med kit, filling it with a dress, some pecans, and a braid of her hair. She told Ashley the bag would be filled with her love always. Rose never saw her daughter again. Ashley kept the sack filled with her mother's love always.[42]

To understand the devastation of the Second Middle Passage, you'd need to multiply this story by two million, and then understand that thousands of those stories unfolded on the streets of Hamburg. The town had more slave traders than any city in the upstate. The leading purveyors included Benjamin Davis, who blithely advertised in all caps "ONE HUNDRED AND TWENTY NEGROES FOR SALE," including "SEVERAL SMALL BOYS WITHOUT THEIR MOTHERS." Then there was Oliver Simpson, who advertised fresh "supplies *every fifty days*" and advised prospective buyers to call "at No. 2, near the Bridge, and examine for themselves." Then there was Richard M. Owings, who kept an enslaved mixed-race mistress named Madame Sophia, and wrote his Charleston supplier that he was interested "at all times" in buying "all likely and handsome fancy girls [that] can be got at reasonable prices." Even the local judge, Abner Phair Robertson, "kept a n——r trade office over in Hamburg."[43]

At its antebellum height, Hamburg was a place so steeped in mammon and sin that even its own citizens cried foul. In 1842, they circulated a petition decrying "the practice of many evil-disposed Negro traders exhibit[ing] their Negroes for sale on the Lord's Day within the corporate limits of Hamburg, to the annoyance of the peace and good morals of the said town." Their petition went nowhere.[44]

The reason it went nowhere is simple. Hamburg owed its massive success less to being a cotton market than to being a slave market located just across Georgia's state line. *The Anti-Slavery Bugle* said as much in 1848 when it noted: "Hamburg, South Carolina was built up just opposite Augusta, for the purpose of furnishing slaves to the planters of Georgia. Augusta is the market to which the planters of Upper and Middle

Georgia bring their cotton; but if they want to purchase negroes, they step over into Hamburg and do so."[45]

If there was ever a town in need of Reconstruction—and redemption—it was Hamburg.

"leaning tomb stones [and] bad epitaphs"

We don't know when Rivers first encountered Hamburg. We know that whenever malaria or monotony threatened his enslaver's family, Rivers was tasked with carrying the Stuarts to Edgefield or further inland to their retreat in Flat Rock, North Carolina. Both trips would have taken him through Hamburg at the height of its antebellum significance.

What interested Rivers more, however, was witnessing Hamburg's steep decline.

Henry Shultz's idea that Hamburg could compete with Augusta as a commercial rival proved a figment of his imagination. Shortly after Hamburg opened its rail line to Charleston, Augusta embarked on an equally ambitious program of internal improvements. Chartered in 1845 and completed in 1847, the Augusta Canal became one of the most successful infrastructure projects undertaken in the antebellum South. The waterpower generated by the various step-downs in the Savannah River allowed for a flourishing of gristmills, sawmills, paper mills, and textile manufacturing. At the same time, the "monied aristocrats of Augusta" made sure that the city was connected by rail to Chattanooga, Atlanta, and Savannah, creating one of the leading logistical hubs in the entire Southeast.[46]

As Augusta ascended, Hamburg edged into precipitous decline. Wagon traffic dwindled in the age of trains. Hamburg's significance as a slave market collapsed when Georgia repealed its ban on the interstate trade in 1856. Once the town lost its economic purpose, Hamburg's property values collapsed, its population dwindled, and Henry Shultz died intestate before he could see his bustling city become an overbuilt ghost town. Hamburg "looks like a country grave yard," said one witness, "with leaning tomb stones filled with bad epitaphs."[47]

Year after year, Rivers had guided his carriage through Hamburg, surveying increasingly vacated buildings and overgrown streets. What he saw was not a "country grave yard" but a historic opportunity.

Reconstruction was a contestation over power: the right to labor, negotiate, participate in commerce, serve on juries, and vote. It was also a real estate problem. Immediately after the Civil War, Southern whites began building city halls and town squares, erecting Confederate statues, and staking their claim to power as something that literally grew out of the ground.[48]

Black people were disadvantaged in this new "space race." They had almost no wealth and little heritable property, especially real estate. "We feel it to be very important that we obtain HOMES," wrote one Black community to the Freedmen's Bureau. "[We need to own] our shelters, *and the ground*, that we may raise fruit trees, concerning which our children can say—'*These are ours.*'"[49]

There are reasons the church dominated the postbellum lives of Southern Black folk. Partly it was spiritual. In the aftermath of slavery, there was much to celebrate and much to mourn. Just as often, the church dominated Black life because it was the only building they owned. Thus, of necessity did Black churches become schools, banks, day care facilities, recreation centers, incubators of Black leadership, and hubs of Black cultural life.

What Rivers saw in Hamburg was the capacity to multiply this effect a thousandfold. Hamburg wasn't a single church but a whole town. This wasn't just depressed real estate but *a lot* of depressed real estate. These were buildings with good bones, situated on wide streets that stretched all the way to the coast and deep into the Southern interior, beckoning Black pilgrims like a road to Mecca.

The most consequential of those pilgrims was Rivers himself. The possibility of converting Hamburg into a Black sanctuary had probably come to him at least as early as his upcountry tour in 1866, if not well before. All we know for certain is that shortly after he mustered out of the army, Rivers purchased two key properties on the town's main street, Lots 1 and 2, and a farm outside of town on Little Horse Creek. Hamburg had been founded once as a white man's dream. Rivers was determined to found it again.[50]

Leaving Beaufort had been one of the most difficult decisions of Rivers's life. For all its massive achievements as an epicenter of Reconstruction, Beaufort had been a coastal garrison town, protected by an army that was led and staffed by whites.

Hamburg, Rivers foresaw, could be the hub of a new Black world.

"The Power of Aiken County"

Abandoning one epicenter of Reconstruction to establish another, Rivers by 1868 had land of his own, a home of his own, an office of his own, and, most important, a dream of his own. The *Charleston Mercury* may have dismissed him as a political gadfly, but there was a pattern to his activity and a focus to his vision. In his second term in the statehouse, he again said almost nothing, but the raft of legislation he sent downriver spoke volumes: "A Bill to Incorporate the Rivers' Guards" in Hamburg; "A Bill to Incorporate the Knights of the Circle Tie" in Hamburg; "A Bill to Incorporate the Hamburg Warehouse Company"; "An Act to Construct and Keep in Repair a Certain Public Road" (that ran through Hamburg); and the "Act to Charter the Town of Hamburg" itself.[51]

Even when Rivers wasn't in Hamburg, his mind was there. His effort was there. Some of the laws he sponsored were obscure or mundane; all were emblematic of his understanding of how to organize power. Take, for example, the simple matter of Hamburg's town charter. Today we might associate an "unincorporated" town with a bedroom community or a remote enclave for the arts. For Rivers, the term "unincorporated" was synonymous with impotence and peril. From a legal perspective, unincorporated towns are effectively neighborhoods. They function by tradition, not by separate law. They can hold association meetings, host barbecues, even open a quaint post office of sorts. But they can't collect taxes, furnish services, establish ordinances, or elect local officeholders such as a mayor or sheriff.

Rivers did more than resurrect a ghost town when he reincorporated Hamburg. He remade Hamburg as a legal entity with rights of self-governance other towns, and the state itself, had to respect. More than

The only surviving image we have of Rivers was a photo taken during his days as a South Carolina state legislator. Image from the Collection of the Smithsonian National Museum of African American History and Culture.

this, he had redeemed a notorious former seat of the Second Middle Passage. Quickly elected mayor (technically "intendant"), Rivers became one of the first Black mayors in the United States, and Hamburg became one of the country's first Black-led towns, antedating the more famous examples of Mound Bayou, Mississippi, and Eatonville, Florida, by sixteen years.

Incorporating Hamburg was just the first step, however. Rivers's next legislative move was even bolder: creating a new county he could wrap around Hamburg like a legal blanket.

The idea for the county was not entirely new. For very different reasons, Hamburg's white citizens had agitated for a new county for years before the city collapsed.

Understanding why requires a short lesson is South Carolina geography and governance. Hamburg was situated on the Edgefield side of the boundary between two of South Carolina's largest counties—Edgefield and Barnwell. Typically, both had located their county courthouses at their rough epicenters, resulting in long travel days for Hamburg's cotton merchants and slave dealers, who often had business before the court. Beginning in 1827, and periodically thereafter, Hamburg's white business community petitioned the state legislature to create a new county *between* Edgefield and Barnwell, as that would allow them to build a new courthouse in or near their new cotton boomtown. Their petitions had always been tabled, usually at the behest of the influential Edgefield contingent, who feared not only the loss of influence but the loss of revenue from Hamburg's weary travelers as they made their way to the Edgefield courthouse.

For Rivers, the question of a new county had nothing to do with travel times and everything to do with Black liberation. Both Edgefield and Barnwell were majority Black. *In theory* this made them potential

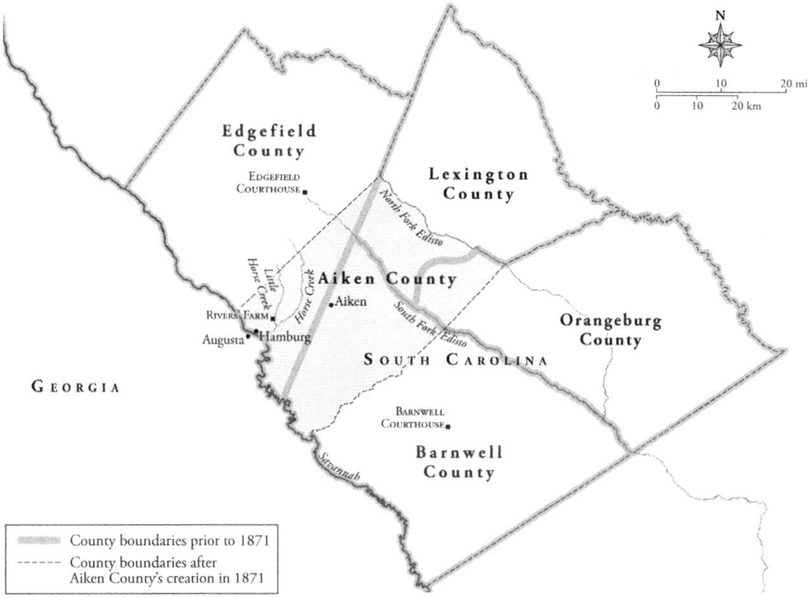

Rivers was instrumental in helping to establish Aiken County, South Carolina, formed from pieces of Edgefield, Lexington, Orangeburg, and Barnwell Counties. Map by Mapping Specialists, Ltd.

centers of Black power after the Fifteenth Amendment gave all Black adult males the right to vote. In reality it made them places where a powerful minority of whites were desperate to maintain their customary control.

Rivers understood that much of that control came from the whites' stranglehold on county offices. The bureaucratic whip hand of the slave regime had always been the Big Four—the coroner, the sheriff, the trial justice, and the head of the local militia. All were either county-level offices or required county-level control to be effective. As Rivers saw it, the only sure way to protect Hamburg was to consolidate the Big Four under Black authority, and the only way to do that was to start a new county from scratch.[52]

Ultimately the new county of Aiken was cobbled together from parts of Barnwell and Edgefield but also Orangeburg and Lexington. (The hope was to spread the pain so no single county had a special reason to feel aggrieved.) The county took its name from William Aiken Sr., the railroad magnate who had pioneered the Hamburg to Charleston line. (Ironically, Aiken had been killed by his own infrastructure project before it was completed. In 1831, at the Charleston depot, a sudden noise from one of his trains startled his horse, throwing him from his carriage. He landed awkwardly and died the next day.)

More important than the name of the new county, however, was the reason for its formation. The preamble of the county charter, which Rivers had a hand in creating, is worth quoting at length:

> Whereas, it is evident that the laws and ordinances of the State of South Carolina and county of Aiken have, within the past few years, been flagrantly violated, and the peace and quiet of our community violently disturbed, and the life, liberty and property of our citizens seriously endangered; and Whereas, it is alleged that the constituted authorities have failed to meet satisfactorily the requirements, either from neglect of duty or inability to cope with the lawlessness which has been so prevalent; Whereas, it is alleged that the constituted authorities have failed to meet satisfactorily the requirements, either from neglect of duty or inability to cope with the lawlessness which has been so prevalent; and Whereas, it is alleged that it is a notorious fact that within the last few years dastardly murders and other crimes have been committed within the bounds of our county, and the perpetrators of the crimes have either been permitted to go unpunished and free, or in some cases have received inadequate and insufficient punishment; Therefore, we, the undersigned citizens of Aiken county, deem it necessary that all law abiding citizens who favor the suppression of those evils and desire to protect the morals, good order and good name of our city, county and State, shall meet together, combine and organize for that purpose, and we, the undersigned citizens of Aiken county, do hereby combine and organize ourselves into an organization for this purpose.[53]

Aiken County was explicitly chartered as a legal sanctuary. Rivers and the other signatories designated themselves the "Aiken County Law and

Order League." What they most wanted was simple protection from violent crimes (perpetrated almost exclusively by whites). And they believed the best way to guarantee that protection was to anchor it deep in local Black power.

Rivers was not alone in the fight to create this new county. Two other men, Samuel Jones Lee and Charles D. Hayne, deserve to be numbered among Aiken County's "founding fathers."

Born to a free Black mother in 1844, Lee claimed to be the son of a Samuel J. Lee of Charleston. Historians have speculated he was more likely the son of Samuel J. McGowan, owner of the plantation on which he was born. At sixteen, Lee had accompanied McGowan into Confederate service as a manservant, where he was photographed armed and wearing the uniform of McGowan's Fourteenth South Carolina. Lee took a superficial shot to the ear while riding beside McGowan at Second Manassas and a more serious shot to the leg at Hanover Junction.[54]

After Appomattox, Lee removed to Hamburg, where he became a vocal proponent of Black rights. Like Rivers, he was elected to the statehouse as a representative for Edgefield County in 1868. In his first legislative session, Lee opposed the formation of a new county as he felt bound to the historic interests of Edgefield. In the next session, he changed his tune. Later Lee would serve as the first Black speaker of the South Carolina statehouse, and his skills as a parliamentarian were certainly critical in whipping votes in support of the idea for a new county.

Charles D. Hayne was the same age as Lee, born to a free Black mother and a white father who owned a lumberyard in Charleston. Of the three men, Hayne had gotten the strongest education, and before the war he earned a steady living as a tailor. Like Lee, Hayne had also "served" in a nebulous capacity in the Confederate army (likely also as a compelled manservant), though he was never photographed in a rebel uniform. After the war he worked as a teacher with the Freedmen's Bureau.[55]

By 1867, Hayne had settled in the sleepy town of Aiken, then in Barnwell County, where he was elected to serve first in the South Carolina

House of Representatives and then as one of the earliest Black state senators. More learned, wily, and adaptable than Rivers or Lee, Hayne had a knack for securing committee appointments—especially the chairmanship of Ways and Means, the financial arm of the legislature and the committee that could trade favors. Hayne had been the one to draft the final successful proposal for creating the new county, and he was likely the one who did the most to secure the site of the county courthouse for his hometown of Aiken rather than Hamburg.[56]

While they shared much, the differences between the men offer instructive lessons in the political distinctions, options, and turmoil within the Black community during Reconstruction. Of the three, Rivers was the oldest. (He was in his late forties; Lee and Hayne were in their early thirties.) Rivers was also the darkest and the least formally educated, the only one born enslaved, and the only Union veteran.[57]

Given their backgrounds, Lee and Hayne could get things done without necessarily inviting a violent backlash from the intransigent white majority. Legible as negotiating partners to the white opposition, they could also negotiate separate treaties for themselves. Ultimately, Lee would remove to Charleston, where he became an immensely successful lawyer. Similarly, Hayne would work in common cause with white Democrats to tar his fellow Black legislators with corruption charges while securing his own position as the long-serving postmaster of Aiken. Such decisions and outcomes take nothing away from their significant accomplishments, but they also highlight Rivers's unique position as a Black leader.

Rivers's political experience had been forged as a color-bearer and provost sergeant for his regiment. His political vision, instincts, and abilities all ran in one direction: toward creating a well-oiled, well-disciplined Black community that included a minority of white allies. For him, creating an army camp had been but a stepping stone to creating a city and then a county of freedom fighters built on the same model.

Given his background and biography, Rivers had no possibility (and no interest) in negotiating a soft landing into mixed-race "respectability." He had none of the advantages or opportunities of Lee or Hayne. Born enslaved, he had no formal education, spoke with a strong Gullah accent, and was a legendary Union veteran from one of the highest-profile regiments in the USCT.

Coding as fully Black, Rivers couldn't (and wouldn't) be peeled off from the larger Black freedom struggle. Metaphorically, he had lashed himself to the mast and burned all the boats. Neither as strong a parliamentarian as Lee nor as strong a politician as Hayne, he alone became known as "The Power of Aiken County."

The Right Hand of the Legislature

In the only surviving image we have of Rivers, he is depicted—along with Charles Hayne and Samuel Lee—in one of the stranger scrapbook mash-ups ever to grace American politics. Captioned "RADICAL MEMBERS of the First State Legislature After the War," the image depicts the sixty-three Republican legislators cut out from their individual cartes de visite (or, in some cases, their caricatures) and then assembled into a single image. While there is much we do not and cannot know about this image and its origins, there is much we do know and more we can infer.[58]

First, we know who likely made it. The oldest version of the image is copyrighted by J. G. Gibbes, likely James Guignard Gibbes, son of Dr. Robert Wilson Gibbes, a South Carolina College (now University of South Carolina) assistant professor of chemistry and geology, who served two terms as mayor of Columbia and as surgeon general for the state of South Carolina. The Gibbeses' ancestral home and textile factory on the Saluda River had been burned during Sherman's sack of Columbia, giving the younger Gibbes a personal as well as political motivation for creating the image.[59]

Second, we know the image took considerable ingenuity to assemble. How difficult must it have been to acquire the images of so many first-term legislators? For Rivers, as for many of these men, this may be the only photograph of them ever taken. Perhaps Gibbes paid off a Columbia photographer to acquire these images? Perhaps he traded for them amid the so-called cardomania of the age—the new rave for collecting and trading military carte de visites? Regardless, we can say this: Whoever put this together was highly motivated.[60]

Motivated to do what? The purposes were clearly derogatory, defam-

This image of the "radical" members of the South Carolina legislature circulated widely in multiple forms and likely functioned as a political "hit list" for Red Shirt Democrats during Reconstruction. Image from the Collection of the Smithsonian National Museum of African American History and Culture.

atory, and potentially far worse. While the original "cut-and-paste" sheet is lost, we know the image was then photographed and disseminated throughout the state for years afterward in various sizes, from larger broadsides to foldable cardboard-backed images small enough to fit into a wallet. Virtually all of the versions use the term "RADICAL MEMBERS of the First State Legislature," which is enough to signal political opposition. None of these men considered themselves "radicals."

Then there are the two white men at the center of the photograph, each festooned with a handwritten caption. South Carolina's lieutenant governor, Lemuel Boozer, is decorated with the words "40 acres & a mule." A former slaveholder, Boozer was a steadfast Unionist and opponent of secession who became a true resistor during the Civil War, helping Union prisoners to escape before erecting a freedmen's school in his backyard. At Boozer's burial, one of his Democratic opponents grudgingly admitted that he almost admired him. "He and I were antipodes in politics," the friend said, "but I regarded his identification with the Republican party of this State as an act of signal moral heroism. . . . To be dissevered from the friends of his youth, of his manhood and advanced years; to drop the hands of his own Carolinians and grasp those of strangers; to aid in seizing the government of the dear old State from the possession of her own children to be confided to the guardianship of aliens, was indeed almost to tear his body and soul asunder. But still he did it."[61]

The other major white figure at the center is Franklin Moses Jr., an ardent secessionist from an elite Jewish family who raised the Confederate flag over Fort Sumter before dramatically reversing course. Denounced by family and friends as a racial turncoat, Moses gradually embraced the possibility of a Jewish-Black alliance, first as a matter of political expediency and finally as a matter of conscience. In 1933, a historian called him "the most perfect scalawag, perhaps, in all the South." By 1868 Moses was both speaker of the statehouse and the organizer of the state militia, charged with protecting the rights of Black voters.[62]

The central position of these two white men, personae most non gratae to state Democrats, confirms the collage as the work of the political opposition. Another version of the image includes a caption that makes that opposition explicit: "These are the photographs of 63 members of the reconstructed South Carolina Legislature, 50 of whom are negroes or mulattoes and 13 white. 22 read and write (8 grammatically), the remainder (41) make their mark with the aid of an amanuensis. Nineteen (19) are tax-payers to an aggregate amount of $146.10, the rest (44) pay no taxes, and the body levies on the white people of the State for $4,000.00."[63]

While this is conjecture, there are reasons to believe the image was intended to do more than arouse political indignation. It may also have served as a "rogues' gallery," "mug book," and "hit list." Is it really a coincidence that seven of the men in this collage were assassinated? Or was the collage created in part to inspire and serve the purposes of assassination?

Regardless, it is significant that Rivers sits on the main row, immediately to the left of Boozer, as the symbolic right hand of the legislature. Including all the men the Democratic opposition most hated, this image also reveals all the men the Democratic opposition most feared. Clearly, they were scared of Rivers.

They had reason to be.

THE MAYOR

Take from the altars of the past the fire—not the ashes.

JEAN JAURÈS

After three terms as a state legislator, Rivers decided to quit. Hamburg had its charter; Aiken was a county. Rivers served as Hamburg's mayor, trial justice, and general of the militia; he acted as coroner and appointed the sheriff. He controlled the Big Four and had created something never before seen in America: a functioning interracial democracy.[1]

Rivers had other reasons to rally around home. "I married Mr. Rivers on 22 Dec 1870," wrote his second wife, Louisa, near the end of her long life. "My husband was a stalwart man [that word again], fully six feet in height, broad shouldered and robust, complexion black."[2]

We don't know precisely how and when Rivers met his second wife. Louisa was a dressmaker, light-skinned, beautiful, and significantly younger, in her early twenties while Rivers was forty-seven. (As Louisa bluntly said of her new husband, "He was almost as old as my father.") Even so, the two made sense together. According to a white witness, Louisa was "a highly respectable colored woman [who] enjoys the distinction of being in the highest walks of colored life at the Capital City (Columbia, S.C.). She is a dress-maker of ability and sews for the best white people." If Rivers was marrying up, so was Louisa. However humble his origins, Rivers was now a rising political power in a dawning new age for Black people in America.[3]

The ceremony took place in Columbia. The Reverend E. J. Adams, legendary Black minister of the Charleston Episcopal Church, performed the service. Adams was a movement preacher in the model that would later produce Martin Luther King Jr. In 1867, Adams had greeted the prospect of the Fifteenth Amendment with a fiery speech in support of the Black franchise. "These are revolutionary times," he proclaimed. "For many years a contest, terrible in its nature, has been waged between despotism and republican principles, between freedom and slavery, until finally we behold the genius of republican liberty bearing its escutcheon upon the threshold of the capitol of every nation, waving its banner in triumph over every continent, sea, and ocean."[4]

Adams's imprimatur on his marriage would have meant a lot to Rivers politically but also personally. His first marriage had been consummated in slavery and consumed by profound loss. If there was even a preacher at his first wedding, Rivers would have heard the words "until death *or distance* do you part." Such language was an implicit recognition of the omnipresent possibility of sale and the certain sense that even the most intimate ties could be sundered by an enslaver's will.[5]

Ultimately, Rivers and his first wife had succumbed to a different kind of distance, foundering on the shores of freedom itself. Elsie was now Mrs. Renty Simmons, living in her beloved community in the familiar surroundings of Cain's Neck. Their daughter Pattie was now married, and both were new grandparents. In 1868, Jack and his wife Caroline had welcomed into the world a first son, whom they named Prince.[6]

Listening to his vows, Rivers must have felt as though he had lived ten lifetimes in ten years. From a carriage driver fleeing to freedom, to a soldier moving from city to city and tent to tent, to a politician struggling to establish himself and something lasting for his people, Rivers finally had something he'd always dreamed of—a stable household.

As Adams pronounced the simple words "until death do you part," Rivers must have felt the promise of a new beginning. He had outlived much and had much living left to do.

After the wedding, Louisa and her school-aged sister, Sarah, moved into Rivers's new home on Little Horse Creek, and they all settled into a domestic routine: Louisa at her sewing and Sarah at her schoolbooks. Every morning, Rivers took his own carriage into town to study the plat map of Hamburg spread across his new desk in a new trial office in a town he had resurrected from the grave.

In these moments, Rivers's vision for Hamburg comes into focus. What he wanted was as gossamer as it was simple—domestic normalcy.

Once a slave, I am now the law

Even as he achieved his dream, Rivers was immediately beset on all sides. White editors variously decried Hamburg under his leadership as "a province of Africa," an "Africanized town," and a "perfect Sodom." "Once the great cotton mart of Western South Carolina," noted the *Georgia Weekly Telegraph*, Hamburg now "rejoices in a sable Mayor by the name of Prince Rivers and an equally shady board of councilmen." "Poor old God-forsaken Hamburg," echoed the *Edgefield Advertiser*. It is "now the abode of a greater number of consummate radical thieves, plunderers, and 'curs of low degree,' in proportion to population, than ever cursed any other spot on the broad face of this green earth of ours."[7]

The portrait of Hamburg as a "perfect Sodom" is ludicrous on its face. *Before* Rivers's arrival, law and order had been looser; the town had no mayor, no sheriff, no charter, no ordinances. Rivers's entire experience as a soldier was in bringing order to a Black community, and his arrival in Hamburg meant exactly the opposite of what his editorial adversaries described. How then can we explain the fact that incessant imputations of Hamburg's lawlessness began at the exact moment when law and order took hold?

Imagine what white supremacists saw when they drove through Hamburg. Left and right they saw scrums of men, Black and white, laughing, jawing, and talking politics. They saw clutches of women, Black and white, hanging laundry on their own lines. The whole scene must have seemed so inherently "wrong" it had to be illegal.

A thriving, boisterous, bumptious majority-Black community, Hamburg during Rivers's reign was never a den of criminals. Rather it represented a conceptual "crime" against white supremacy, a flouting of the "natural" laws that separated the races and ascribed Black residents to subservient roles.

The projection of lawlessness onto Hamburg was instead a psychological reflex and a media strategy. The imputation of offenses against law and order could always be used to justify the restoration of "law and order" by any means necessary. This racist formula, as enduring as it has proved effective, also serves as a historical guide: Whatever the opposition press most demonizes, it most fears.

At the height of his power, Rivers became widely known as "The Black

Prince," "The Power of Aiken County," and the "Masoniello of South Carolina," an allusion to the common fisherman of Italy who led a rebellion to become viceroy of Naples. Such epithets sound grand. What did Rivers do to earn them?

In 1871, the Augusta City Council passed an ordinance levying a five-cent toll on all foot passengers who crossed the bridge across the Savannah River into town. "This at once precipitated matters," joked the *Augusta Chronicle*. "A large proportion of the foot passengers across the bridge are impecunious colored vagabonds from Hamburg, and, as may be imagined, it made the hot blooded, chivalrous Africans boil with indignation to think that when they wished to reach the gin-mills of Augusta they would either have to swim the raging Savannah, or else pay over to a rebel city government the nickels won by honest industry at draw-poker or the string game."[8]

In response, Rivers posted a notice on the Hamburg side of the bridge stating "that any Augusta cow which wandered into his dominions would be arrested and not released until a tribute of five dollars was rendered."[9]

Rivers's bovine proclamation was a rare, perhaps singular, example of his sense of humor. Characteristically, he was also dead serious. Consider the message he was sending: "Petty legal bullshit on the Augusta side of the bridge will be met by petty legal bullshit on the Hamburg side, and there is nothing you Augustans can do about it because I make the law. Oh, and by the way, yes, my new proclamation does sound something like the laws you enacted about runaway slaves." Even in arresting miscreant Georgia cows, Rivers managed to underline the entire point of his career: "Once a slave, I am now the law."

This is what makes monikers such as "The Black Prince" so informative. Obviously, Rivers never called himself "The Black Prince." The opposition press invented the title. Why? Because they found the simple but indefatigable performance of the law, in the hands of a Black man, haughty and imperious. A similar compliment / not-a-compliment lies buried in another of his cognomens: the "head of the dusky Ku Klux." Were Rivers and his goons actually out night riding and terrorizing Klan members in acts of extralegal justice? We might wish they were, but Rivers was too steady for this. Rather, he simply declared that if Klan members broke the law, they could expect to answer to the law.

Adherence to the law was Rivers's entire vision for Hamburg, the reason he had created a sanctuary county wrapped around a sanctuary city. He had almost no faith in the federal government's active interest in reconstructing the South, but he had every reason to believe that the United States was and would remain a nation of laws.

Adherence to the law was also the foundation for Hamburg's success, both among the Black majority and among its minority of whites. No community wants less policing. They want better policing. As Rivers knew, most of Hamburg's whites just wanted peace and prosperity, which is precisely what he brought to the town. At the height of Reconstruction, Hamburg was 80 percent Black, 20 percent white, and 100 percent politically stable.

The percentage of whites is particularly significant. The historian William Barney has noted that Reconstruction survived as long as it did not rely merely on the backs of the 40 percent of the South's population that was Black and voted Republican but on the 20 percent of the remaining whites who voted the same way. The math, Barney said, was simple: 40 percent plus 20 percent (of the remaining 60 percent) would always produce an electoral majority of 52 percent. In any functioning democracy, 52 percent will win every election.[10]

As he consolidated control in Hamburg, Rivers pulled the majority of the town's whites to his side. The *Georgia Weekly Telegraph* may have lampooned the "equally shady board of councilmen" who served as wardens during Rivers's first term as mayor. (The use of "shady" was deliberate, seeking to synonymize criminality and color.) The truth, however, is that several of Rivers's "shady councilmen" were white. Indeed, just as the town was 20 percent white (technically 24 percent), both the council and the Hamburg militia were 20 percent white.

What Rivers had accomplished in Hamburg was precisely what the opposition press most hated and feared: a functioning interracial democracy deep in the heart of Dixie. Majority Black and Black led, Rivers's city also served the interests of the minority of whites who determined to make common cause with their Black neighbors.

As Hamburg became a Black mecca, the city's whites had the means to leave if they wanted to. Evidently, they didn't want to. Take, for instance, the case of Louis Schiller, born in Prussia in 1841. His father, Abram, had immigrated with his family to Hamburg shortly after Louis's birth, perhaps drawn to the German-sounding name of the town. At twenty, Louis had volunteered to serve the Confederate army in Company C, First South Carolina Cavalry. Mustered in on September 18, 1861, Schiller served through the war, but he was apparently miserable the whole time, suffering not least from chronic hemorrhoids, an (understandably) understudied aspect of being a Confederate cavalryman.

After the war, Schiller, like Solomon George Washington Dill, had a change of heart. What had the Confederacy's commitment to racism and slavery tangibly brought to him and his family? Nothing but misery and death. Schiller could easily have moved to majority-white Augusta across the river, as some of Hamburg's white families had done. Instead, Schiller not only stayed but served as Rivers's advisor and compatriot, a city councilman and secretary to Hamburg's interracial militia.

Then there was Frank Arnim. Like Rivers, Arnim was a former delegate to the South Carolina convention in 1868 who then became a state senator. Arnim had made a small fortune as a federal revenue collector after the war, "seeking out illicit stills and whiskey" in Edgefield County. As might be imagined, this made him persona non grata among the whites in Edgefield, but he used the proceeds from his position to purchase a former plantation just outside Hamburg that became known as Arnim Town. The opposition press derided him a "Prussian adventurer . . . as ignorant of the English language as English law," but, like Rivers, Arnim was a true Unionist. (He even named one of his sons Fremont, after the first Republican presidential candidate in 1856.)[11]

Several of Hamburg's leading whites were German born (and Jewish), effectively making them outsiders as well. But many were not. Hamburg's leading white citizens included William Hill Sr., a South Carolina merchant; Joseph Rosamund, a South Carolina cotton buyer; Robert Philip, a Scottish wheelwright; Thomas Dunnigan, an Irish farmer; Alexander Simmons, a Prussian merchant; T. D. Ransom, a Connecticut life insurance salesman; A. S. Newhouse, a New York carpenter; and Cornelius Holland, a South Carolina physician.[12]

Each of these white households had ample resources and time to flee Hamburg as it became a sanctuary city for Black people. Instead, they

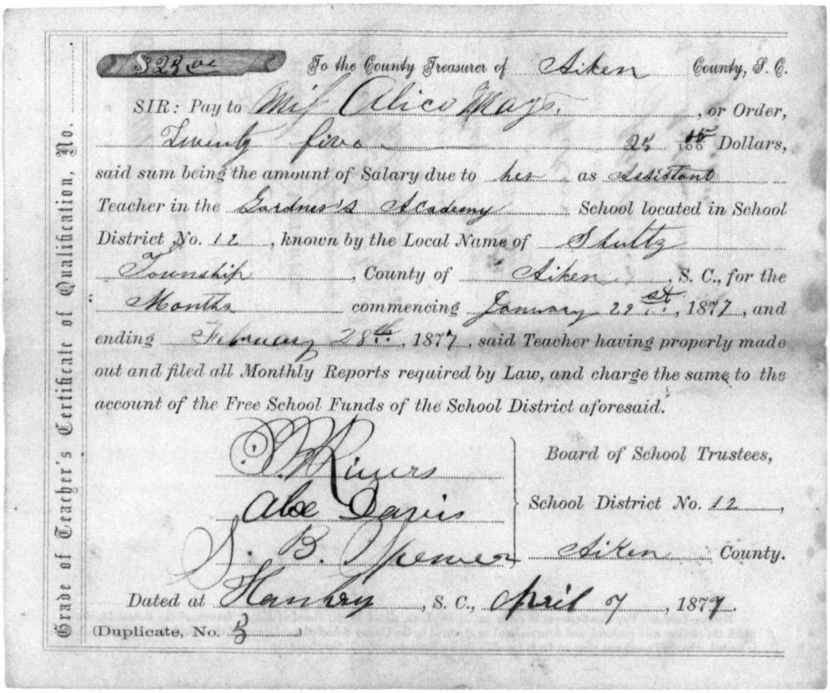

$25.00 To the County Treasurer of Aiken County, S. C.

SIR: Pay to Miss Alice Mayo, or Order,

Twenty five 25 00/100 Dollars,

said sum being the amount of Salary due to her as Assistant Teacher in the Gardner's Academy School located in School District No. 12, known by the Local Name of Shultz Township, County of Aiken, S. C., for the Months commencing January 21st, 1877, and ending February 28th, 1877, said Teacher having properly made out and filed all Monthly Reports required by Law, and charge the same to the account of the Free School Funds of the School District aforesaid.

P. B. Rivers
Abe Davis
S. B. Spencer

Board of School Trustees,
School District No. 12,
Aiken County.

Dated at Hamburg, S. C., April 7, 1877.

(Duplicate, No. 3)

Grade of Teacher's Certificate of Qualification, No.

As mayor of Hamburg, Rivers oversaw every aspect of town governance, including teachers' pay. Image provided by the Aiken County Historical Museum, Aiken, South Carolina.

stayed to create a full-service town where citizens white and Black could buy insurance, get a wheel repaired, educate their children, purchase dry goods, sell cotton, minister to a sick family member, or grab eggs from the local grocery. Far from a "perfect Sodom" dominated by "curs of low degree," Hamburg during Rivers's tenure was relatively bucolic, majority female, full of families looking for "domestic normalcy."

"This Fourth of July is yours"

Nowhere was this spirit of the ascendent new Hamburg more evident than during the town's centennial celebration in 1876. Prior to emancipation the Fourth of July had meant little to Black Americans. During the American Revolution the British had offered the enslaved population a better deal (freedom for service), and in subsequent years the United States consolidated around slavery while Britain moved toward enforcing abolition. To Frederick Douglass, white people celebrating independence in front of those they enslaved was nothing but a cruel joke. "This Fourth of July is yours," he famously declared, "not mine."[13]

After the war, everything reversed, at least in the South. Black Americans celebrated the holiday in earnest even as whites turned against it. "The Fourth of July [has] ceased to be of the slightest interest to the white people of the south," noted the *Richmond Enquirer* in 1868. "Like a worn-out pair of breeches, it has fallen into [Black] hands." Such bitterness was particularly acute in South Carolina, where the *Edgefield Advertiser* claimed that the only appropriate attire on America's birthday was the "sack-cloth of humiliation."[14]

In Hamburg, the centennial festivities opened with a reading of the Declaration of Independence, as President Grant had decreed for all towns. Speeches followed and then came the closing ceremony—a parade—which during Reconstruction meant a series of precision drills executed by the local militia. Thanks in part to Rivers, who served as general of the militia in addition to being the mayor of the town, the men had recently reorganized and elected a new captain, Dock Adams. Adams had served in the Civil War and captained a militia company in Augusta before relocating to Hamburg. Under his regime, the militia had drilled regularly to improve, sometimes in the moonlight when few were watching, often in their "barracks"—a brick edifice known as the Sibley Building. Now they were parading down Hamburg's main street, with hundreds of men, women, and children gathered to watch them. As Louis Schiller later remembered, "They were most equal to any company, white or colored, no matter where they came from. [Adams] had them well-drilled, and that was the great fault."[15]

Around dusk, two young white men clattered across the Augusta-Hamburg bridge and pulled their wagon to the side of Hamburg's main thoroughfare, where they sat contemplating the scene. Tommy Butler sat on the right. He was twenty-one, a bit of a loafer; he enjoyed cursing and was good at it. Henry Getzen sat on the left. He was twenty-six, quieter but more violent. When he had married Tommy's sister, he had been adopted as one of the "Butler boys." Both had been too young for Civil War service. They had inherited some of its bitterness and none of its resignation. They were on their way back to the Butler plantation, a trip that always took them through Hamburg. The two had had occasional words with some of the residents, but they'd never seen anything like this parade. Probably, Tommy couldn't have said what he hated most about it. Certainly, he hated that the militia had guns and that they marched so well. Probably he hated that they were happy and that the hundred Black men and women who lined the road to watch them were happy too. After about half an hour, Getzen cracked the reins and steered the wagon directly into the marchers.[16]

Soft Eyes

Let us pause for a moment, with the young white men in their wagon and Hamburg in full swing. We needn't be in a hurry to get to the denouement. It will come soon enough. Soon all that Rivers loved, and much of what he accomplished, will tumble down in a day. For now, we should remember Hamburg in this moment, at the height of its significance and happiness. No victim is synonymous with their lynching or murder. This isn't what their loved ones remember when they think of them gone. So why not remember this parade as the true redemption of Hamburg? Why not take a beat to let the revelers revel and celebrate the Fourth of July as their new birth of freedom?

There are scholarly reasons to slow down as well. The Hamburg Massacre has always been understood in the context of voter intimidation and violence in a turbulent election year. Certainly, that is how the United States Senate understood it when it released its compendious 2,500-page report two years later. And that is certainly what the Hamburg Massacre became—a signal to the "all-outs," white militias, and rifle clubs that violence could work and the government would do nothing.

Even so, we need to treat the scene with what detectives call "soft eyes." If all politics is local, so is all political violence. Whatever the Hamburg Massacre became nationally, its origins and nature were local and specific. For a decade, Rivers had worked to wrap a county around a city, creating one of the more stable sanctuaries during Reconstruction. From can see to can't, he had used subtlety and cunning to make it all work, never taking his eye off the known unknowns. He knew he was sitting on a powder keg. It would insult his intelligence to suppose that he didn't. So, what happened? How did all blow apart? How did he not see it coming?

The answer is simple: Whatever one's political acumen, there is one universal truth—no system can be idiot proofed when idiots are such geniuses.

This, then, is the story of the Hamburg Massacre, a story set in motion by two idiots, full of sound and fury, signifying everything.

A Tale of Two Cities

The Hamburg Massacre had its origins in two local beefs, one between two cities, the other between two men. Let's start with the first.

Augusta and Hamburg had been at odds for decades. The antagonism antedated Rivers's ascension to mayor and antedated the Civil War. Hamburg had been literally founded on spite when Henry Shultz located his rival cotton city on the mudflats across from Augusta. During a drought in 1839, a sandbar formed in the middle of Savannah, scuttling Augusta's riverboat traffic. Rubbing salt in the wound, Shultz planted crops in the sandbar to turn a profit at Augusta's expense and draw attention to their plight. When his ersatz farm inevitably drowned, Shultz said simply: "Money will buy rice and turnips for me to eat, but money will not buy water for them to run their steamboats on."[17]

By the time Rivers became mayor, there was no commercial rivalry between the two towns. Indeed, from an economic perspective, Augusta had beaten Hamburg out of existence. Even at its height as a sanctuary city, Hamburg had a tenth of Augusta's population and a scintilla of its wealth.

If Hamburg was no economic threat to Augusta, it was also no political threat. While the two towns were neighbors, Augusta was in another county and another state. Moreover, as Rivers consolidated power in

Hamburg he always conciliated, moving judiciously, carefully, *legally*. As Augusta's leading white newspaper grudgingly noted, Rivers's "influence with the negroes is very great, but it has always been on the side of peace and good order."[18]

All Rivers's careful work was upended the summer before the massacre when he was implicated in a plot so obscure it's impossible to say he was even involved. His name made national headlines for several weeks in late August as newspapers breathlessly reported the details of what is variously called the "Freedmen's Land Revolt" or the "Great Georgia Negro Insurrection" of 1875. The basic charge was that Rivers masterminded a massive, if ultimately foiled, plot to slaughter all the whites in nineteen Georgia counties. Did he?

Understanding the lineaments of the plot requires first understanding the contrasting political situations in South Carolina and Georgia. As South Carolina created a functioning Republican administration and centers of Black power such as Hamburg, Georgia's Black population was quickly routed as white supremacists recaptured the government. On October 23, 1871, Georgia's Republican governor, Rufus Brown Bullock, abdicated and fled the state, rightly fearing that he was about to be impeached and indicted. In quick succession, Democrats seized control of both houses and elected a staunch opponent of Reconstruction, former Confederate colonel and Confederate Congressman James Milton Smith, as governor. By early 1872, Georgia had been "redeemed."

Redeemed. Never in the history of American politics has there been so inappropriate a term. Reconstruction history is dominated by terms coined by white supremacists. We talk of "carpetbaggers" (the Northern-born jackals who came South to pick clean the bones of a defeated Confederacy). We talk of "scalawags"—a term for the diseased cows farmers culled from a herd—as a synonym for the Southern-born race traitors who sided with their Black brothers in voting Republican. And we talk of "redemption" as the moment an ex-Confederate state defeated the Union army, the Freedmen's Bureau, and all forces propping up an interracial democracy. For the South's Black population, "redemption" was catastrophic. Across the Black belt, former planters began overcharging sharecroppers for seeds and tools and stiffing them on their shares of the crop. Once these Black sharecroppers were in their debt, whites made sure they stayed there, laboring until the debt was paid. The only other option for Black workers was to run off or welch, leaving them at the mercy of courts that routinely sent them into chain gangs and the convict lease system.[19]

Rivers watched with horror as Georgia descended into "redemption." In the shadiest version of its new debt peonage system, Georgia planters would drive to the jail in Macon or Atlanta to secure the release and pay the fines of prisoners, then take them back to their farms, where they could work them, practically, forever. The result was a labor system cheaper than slavery and cheapest with human life. Crooked cops would pick up Black men on bogus charges, judges would overfine them, and then everyone got a kickback from the planter when he came to pick up his new laborer. The system was called slavery by another name, but in many ways it was worse. In this system, Black people who were deemed "indebted" or "fractious" were routinely sentenced to whippings, forced labor, and chain gangs. In this system there was no incentive for planters to care for the lives of their laborers. Any dead worker could be buried and replaced by a simple trip to the local jail. Unlike under slavery, workers had no family to return home to. They simply lived to labor on "the farm."[20]

The key to making the new system work was all-white juries. Understandably, historians have placed great emphasis on the value of the franchise, but in many Black communities, jury representation was the only thing that could, for years, prevent their husbands, fathers, brothers, and sons from being dragooned back into the loneliest kind of slavery.

The only glimmer of hope for Georgia's Black population was the Civil Rights Act of 1875. Signed into law by President Grant, the new act pledged the United States government to protect Black citizens' equal access to public accommodations and, more important, their equal representation on juries.[21]

Enter Joseph Morris, a self-styled militia general who probably did see himself as Georgia's equivalent to "The Black Prince." (Whether Morris did or didn't, as reported, formally seek Rivers's counsel and support, or whether Morris merely took inspiration from Rivers's achievements, is impossible to determine.) Regardless, by the early 1870s Morris had "assumed a certain air of authority over and demanded the obedience of the colored population" of his native Burke County, Georgia (according to the deeply biased Democratic press).[22]

We can understand Morris's appeal. His argument was simple: The Civil Rights Act of 1875 had promised Black citizens equal representation on juries, but how would that be enforced? In Georgia, militia laws were so rigged that older units (meaning those organized before 1861) would be the first to be recognized, the first to receive uniforms, and the first to receive ammunition and arms. To contest this, Morris created an extralegal system of Black militias charged with enforcing federal laws the white militias wouldn't. Predictably, this created a furious reaction, both among the white militias and within the opposition press. Conjuring up images of Africa and insurrection, the *Georgia Weekly Telegraph* claimed that Morris's militiamen were established "with all the paraphernalia of password, grip, and sign, and meet, regularly and often, at midnight, by the sound of the drum or the dismal conch, to perfect themselves in the drill with deadly weapons, or to form and mature schemes of warfare upon the whites." "Heaps of explosives," continued the breathless coverage, are "ready to take fire from any passing spark."[23]

This was exactly the kind of provocative press coverage Rivers had worked for a decade to avoid. Nevertheless, Morris leaned in. On May 19, 1875, he led 150 of his men to the Burke County Courthouse, demanding Superior Court Judge William Gibson accept a slate of Black jurors for the upcoming term. Gibson was a former Confederate colonel, wounded once at Malvern Hill and then again at Gettysburg, where he was left on the field, captured, and finally paroled. Gibson had zero sympathy with Morris (or with Georgia's Black population). He quickly denied Morris's request and ordered him arrested. (The formal charge—carrying a concealed weapon—was a bit of an inside joke. Virtually all white militiamen, regardless of whether they were formally recognized by the state, carried concealed weapons. Like many local judges, Gibson sought purposely to remind the Black population that the law could and would be arbitrary and punitive.)

Not to be dissuaded, Morris then wrote the sheriff of neighboring Washington County, Reuben Mayo, demanding to hold a mass meeting on the Black jury question at the county courthouse in Sandersonville on July 19. Again, Morris could not have selected a less sympathetic white. A former Confederate lieutenant, Mayo had two years earlier demonstrated extreme prejudice against Black people in an officer-related shooting that left an unarmed man dead in the street. According to the *Sandersonville Herald*, on September 29, 1873, Mayo had escorted a "young Negro man" named Floyd Brinson from the county jail to the county courthouse to be tried for stealing. The judge sentenced Brinson to thirty days on the local chain gang and remanded him back to the jail to await transport. Apparently the thirty days on the chain gang didn't scare Brinson more than the idea of being put back in the Sandersonville jail. The paper admitted that Brinson had been "jailed for some time," and one can imagine that the conditions were stifling and brutal. Regardless, according to the paper, "when [Brinson and Mayo] reached the jail yard, the Negro refused to enter, and said he would not go in there again." Grabbing Brinson by the arm, the court's bailiff started to shove Brinson into the jail, but Brinson "struck him in the face, jerked loose, and ran." Mayo drew his gun, yelled for Brinson to stop, and then opened fire. Brinson was shot in the back, the bullet entering just to the left of the spine, below the ribs, then ranging upward toward the heart. Brinson collapsed on the street and died within ten minutes. An all-white jury declared Mayo innocent and "found the killing to be justifiable."[24]

Morris may or may not have known this history when he demanded to assemble at the Sandersonville courthouse, but the result was predictable. Mayo refused permission, and local white militias began hanging around the courthouse. Even so Morris pressed ahead, announcing that the meeting would take place as scheduled and further that it "would honor the presence of Major General P. R. Rivers and his staff."[25]

It is difficult to imagine Rivers accepting such an invitation (assuming it was even offered). Certainly, as July rolled around, Rivers must have felt that Morris had gotten himself into exactly the stupid position Rivers's own careful political work had been designed to forestall. Morris's intentions were righteous. Like Rivers, Morris had been born enslaved and taught himself to read and write. Like Rivers, Morris was a charismatic figure. Here, however, the comparison ends. Unlike Rivers, Morris had not served in the Civil War, had not served in the state legislature, had not been appointed a trial judge, and did not serve as a general of the state militia. Instead, operating entirely without legal cover, he had ham-fistedly pissed off a duly elected sheriff in his own backyard. Too late, Morris saw the writing on the wall. With white militiamen prowling around Sandersonville, Morris skipped the assembly and went to ground.

Significant damage had already been done, however. In the opposition press, Morris and Rivers had been linked to each other and to a much larger group of extralegal militiamen agitating for Black rights. Whatever they had been planning at Sandersonville had been quashed. But who knew what they planned next? And where was the outlaw Morris?

Into this atmosphere of intrigue and suspicion dropped a letter, purportedly from Morris's militia secretary, Cordy Harris. Harris's letter read as a formal order from "Gen. Morris and his Staff and Gen. Rivers and his Staff" and directed all Black militiamen to "start killing the whites on Aug. 20th." "Kill every one you find," said the order. "Kill with axes, hoes, pitchforks, and get gunpowder and shot as you kill."[26]

Harris's supposed order became a casus belli for white militias as newspapers across Georgia treated the insurrection plot as the second coming of Saint-Domingue. Eighty Black militiamen were swept up and spirited off to the Sandersonville jail. Then on August 1, the Washington County court indicted the "triumvirate of scoundrels" responsible for the plot—"Prince Rivers, Joe Morris, and [Cordy] Harris"—and ordered their arrest.[27]

Cordy Harris surrendered quickly. Under questioning, he complied fully, implicating Rivers as the mastermind of the plot. (White law enforcement was so impressed with Harris's survival lying and capacity for telling it what it wanted to hear, heedless of veracity, that it determined he wasn't a threat and let him go.)

Joseph Morris did not fare as well. At large for a month, Morris was caught on September 20 trying to sneak into the Atlanta office of Henry P. Farrow, state district attorney for Georgia. In fairness to Morris, Farrow probably was the only white in Georgia who could help him. A former Confederate colonel, Farrow had always been a reluctant rebel. A vocal Unionist up to 1861, he eventually succumbed to social pressure and served efficiently as head of the Confederacy's Department of Niter and Mining. (Farrow even achieved a degree of infamy as the man who ordered the ladies of Selma to save their "chamber lye" to aid the Confederacy in the making of nitre. As one bit of doggerel put it: "We thought the girls had work enough in making shirts, and kissing / But you have put the pretty dears to patriotic pissing.")[28]

After the war, however, Farrow returned to the fold of the "secret Yankees" in Atlanta. First as state attorney general (before the Republican Party's collapse) and then as district attorney for eight years (during and after the party's collapse), Farrow remained a critical white holdout supporting Ku Klux prosecutions and Black rights in Georgia.[29]

Once captured, Morris was jailed and hauled before the court to be tried on his weapons charge. It was a sweet moment for the white opposition. In ways ironic and awful, an all-white jury sentenced Morris to hard labor in the state's notorious convict lease system. His specific assignment—laboring for Henry Stephens at Stephens Pottery—was probably not a coincidence.

In 1908 an overdue state senate investigation of Georgia's penitentiary system cited Stephens Pottery as one of the worst abusers of the convict lease system in the state. "The beds were dirty and unsanitary," noted the penitentiary committee's report, "the food of poor quality and poorly prepared, and the work was too hard, as the men were rushed to the limit of their strength." The pottery's convicts labored over hot kilns and dig pits to make "fire-brick, sewer pipe and other terra cotta products from the local clay." It was dirty, brutal work, but Morris didn't have to endure it for long. Days after his arrival, he and several convicts set out with a single guard to cut wood for the kiln. In the midafternoon they were surrounded by twenty armed men who "demanded possession of the 'General' and disappeared into the forest."[30]

In ways that are sad to contemplate, Morris's inevitable end highlights the wisdom of Rivers's more cautious, more politic approach. One could wish that a heroic, uncompromising attitude in the face of racial injustice would always end in triumph, but it more often ends in terror. There is a theory about drowning victims that seems especially appropriate: If two people are plunged into water, one might save the other. As the number of victims multiplies, however, the chance that they drag each other down multiplies also. None of the victims do it purposely. In their desperation, they seize on the possibility that someone will save them.

Morris had clung to Rivers, to his success, as a drowning man does, linking his name to "The Black Prince" as if the Black Prince could save him. But for all his heroism, Morris hadn't done anything like Rivers's hard work. This is not to slight Morris. He played his hand, perhaps as well as he could. It is only to note that Rivers was dealt a better hand and played it more shrewdly. Linked to Morris and his failed "insurrection," Rivers responded as he always did—by playing a deeper game.

As soon as he saw his name in print, Rivers sent word to the Augusta newspapers, denying any knowledge of Morris or Harris. He was (probably) telling the truth. Certainly, he knew *of* these men, but there is no evidence he'd ever met them or ever attended a Black militia meeting in Georgia. Perhaps Morris had issued the invitation. If he did, we have no record of it, and certainly Rivers would never have accepted it. Why would he? His entire career, his entire theory of power, focused on his city, his county, his state. Whatever Rivers had done, whatever he had accomplished, he had done and accomplished it all *legally*. With customary modesty he told the Augusta papers that it "takes all my time to give attention to my corn and cotton."[31]

Across the state, few white newspapers believed him (especially because it was politically convenient to disbelieve him). Nearer to home, however, the newspapers respected and feared him enough to tell something closer to the truth. "The negro demonstrations in Washington county are so devoid of sense and method," admitted the *Georgia Weekly Telegraph*, "that it is hard to believe that serious mischief is intended." Even as they lampooned the order to "kill the whites [as] a grotesque piece of practice on the public," however, these papers clung to the faith that any threat to law and order, no matter how bogus, is always a chance to score political points. "It is certain that this scheme of universal murder, however stupid as well as fiendish and brutal," said the paper, "has been gravely discussed and arranged in the negro clubs in conformity with these 'orders.'"[32]

Rivers knew Morris had been in the right politically. Every person has a constitutional right to free assembly. Morris's entire career had been a tactical mess, however. Without Rivers's legal cover, Morris had raised his head and taken his shot at the racial establishment only to become a cautionary tale for anyone who would do the same. Suitably terrified, eighty of Morris's Black militiamen—the supposed "plotters" of the "Great Negro Insurrection"—were eventually released from jail. Rivers survived the imbroglio as well, his indictment effectively vacated, not least because, on the state and county level, he was legally untouchable. "Rivers positively denies, in a card, that he had anything to do with the plot," reported the *Georgia Weekly Telegraph.* "Citizens of Augusta who know him well believe that he tells the truth."[33]

Even so, Morris had cost the movement more than his life. In borrowing against Rivers's success, he had dragged Rivers into a fight he did not need or want to make. Worse, he set the entire region against the very idea of Black militiamen.

Rivers's militia was interracial, reflecting the population of the county and the city. More important, it was fully sanctioned by law. Thanks to Morris, however, white Augustans had become more paranoid than ever about the very sight of Black men with guns. We can understand Morris's frustration as his state descended into redemption, forcing him to find extralegal solutions. We can understand Rivers's frustration as well. Morris was a bold player, but like Dill before him, he had played his hand poorly. It was one thing to die for the cause; it was another thing to live for it.

As Morris met his brutal end in a forest near Stephens Pottery, Rivers had Hamburg under perfect control. Wounded and weakened by Morris's failed "plot," Rivers eventually smoothed everything over. Then he immediately had to turn to another local beef he could never have seen coming.

"[The] old negro-hunter"

Just above Hamburg lived an old racist Once-ler named Robert Butler Sr. Born into money before marrying into more, Butler had always seen himself as a rising man of the antebellum order. In 1850, his plantation was valued at $50,000, the vast majority ($43,700) representing the value of the people he enslaved, including "19 children under the age of 15, 8 men and 9 women between the ages of 15 and 60 and 2 men and

2 women over the age of 60." Such numbers may seem modest, but they made Butler the equivalent of today's millionaire.[34]

Most of Butler's money came from training dogs for a specific purpose. In the antebellum economy, there was an immense fortune to be made in running down fugitive slaves. Sojourning in Alabama to study the sublimity of its flora and fauna, the renowned British naturalist Philip Henry Gosse came away thinking the antebellum South an absolute perversion of nature. "Bloodhounds, of high breeding and of great ferocity," he said, "are taught to follow the human trail in this manner: A negro is sent into the woods, and told to climb up into a tree; when sufficient time has been allowed him, the hound is set on the scent, and is soon at the foot of the tree, which he will not leave till the party come up and release the poor slave. If any accident prevent him from mounting the tree in time, his life will probably pay the forfeit, for these ferocious dogs not infrequently kill their victims."[35]

Butler took to the work of slave catcher with a missionary zeal. In Hamburg's heyday, there were always hundreds of dislocated enslaved people moving through the city to points farther south. Throughout Edgefield, Butler became known as "the old negro-hunter," the man you went to when your property got itchy feet. As one Hamburg resident said of Butler: "He has made his living, all he has made, by hunting negroes."[36]

Butler accumulated capital enough in his peculiar profession to begin construction on a massive new home he called The Star of Edgefield. As it neared completion, he invited the local press in to do a feature on his "plantation aesthetic." "Elevated several hundred feet above the Savannah River," enthused one reporter, "the houses and church steeples of Augusta [are] clearly visible from the house's windows." "From 'Butler's Hill,' echoed another witness, "the view is magnificent. Uplifted more than three hundred feet above low-water mark, he will look across the Savannah Valley, with all its splendid improvements at this point, to the far Georgia hills reposing in the haze of distance. He may peer down upon Augusta, as if 'up in a balloon.'" As one historian has put it, "Such a home served a social climber like Butler as the symbolic foundation for his claim of membership in an upper order."[37]

Just as antebellum Hamburg edged into precipitous decline, however, so did Butler. His slave-catching business dwindled after 1856, when Georgia lifted its ban on the interstate slave trade, effectively closing Hamburg as a major way station of the Second Middle Passage. Immediately after, Butler's wife passed away, leaving him rudderless and perhaps drinking too much.

More devastating to Butler's personal standing was the "lamentable affray" that occurred in 1864 between himself and the popular Confederate colonel, John D. Twiggs. The scuttlebutt in the family is that Butler was carrying on an affair with Twiggs's wife. This cannot be confirmed. What is known is that in September 1864, Twiggs secured a sudden furlough to return home to visit his family in Hamburg. In explaining his hurried departure from the regiment, local newspapers referred vaguely to an "insult" recently visited upon "his wife and little children and his aged father and mother-in-law" at the hands of the Butler clan.[38]

What is clearer is this: Immediately after returning home, Twiggs took his buggy and rode up to the Butler estate, just above town. Along the way, he crossed paths with Butler himself, also in a buggy, along with his son, Robert Butler Jr. Whatever the "history" between the two men, things devolved quickly on the open road. Twiggs shot first, "inflicting a mortal wound" on the seventeen-year-old Butler Jr. sitting at his father's side. Butler Sr. then unloaded on Twiggs, "killing him instantly."[39]

Like a stone in a pond, all violence has a way of rippling out, creating a wave of significance that may break on the shore of history and disappear forever or reorder the entire timeline. Unfortunately for Rivers, Twiggs's death was the latter.

South Carolina's papers spilt considerable ink lamenting the death of Colonel Twiggs. Twiggs was popular in a way that Butler deeply wasn't. Just a few months before Twiggs's death, the *Charleston Mercury* had gushed about his "dash and daring" during a bold cavalry raid in which Twiggs and company had captured or killed twice their number of Yankees. "Twiggs was a gentleman and a soldier of the highest and most irreproachable character," reported the *Edgefield Advertiser* after his death. "He has fallen!" wailed the *Mercury*, "not amid the roar of cannon and the clashing of glittering sabres, where the patriot soldier is wont to dare to do and to die—no, he fell defending his home . . . from insult." The

Charleston Courier was similarly veiled: "Unpleasant occurrences very aggravating to Col. Twiggs had previously taken place during his absence from home," reported the paper, "and it is supposed that he went around to resist further insult to his family."[40]

Confined to jail after the Twiggs encounter, Butler was quickly cleared of all charges. Like children in a troubled marriage, local (white) juries tended to look the other way when their betters fought. Then too there was little appetite for a public trial that might imply that Confederate wives were sexually insecure at home.

If the legal consequences for Butler were minimal, however, the personal and psychological consequences were significant. In rapid succession he had lost his wife, his namesake, and his entire social standing, leaving him alone with a brooding son and son-in-law.

Several months later Butler suffered another blow so devastating he seems never to have recovered. A month after Robert E. Lee's surrender at Appomattox, a detachment of Iowa soldiers was foraging for food near their camp east of Hamburg when they happened upon Butler's "impressive peach orchard." They were about to make a meal of it when they discovered "a kennel of bloodhounds trained to pursue enslaved people." By then, Butler himself had accosted the soldiers, cursing them generally and threatening to sic his dogs on them. The soldiers retreated to camp, but the entire incident sat poorly with them. Rumors circulated that Butler had used these same dogs to pursue federal escapees from prisoner-of-war camps, which is undoubtedly true. According to Private Ephraim Blake, the soldiers spent two days stewing on the problem before deciding to act. "We resolved these dogs must die," he later wrote, "and Butler too if he monkeyed with us."[41]

Thus, on May 22, 1865, the morning after a heavy rain, the soldiers trudged the two miles back to the peach orchard outside "The Star of Edgefield." With bullets and tri-sided bayonets, they dispatched every dog in the pack while Butler stood lacing them with curses but powerless to stop them. "When the battle was over in the peach orchard," wrote one Iowa officer, "the ground looked as if it had rained . . . a plain shower of blood hounds."[42]

The death of his dogs broke Butler in some new way, curdling what remained of his humanity. Demanding retribution, he lodged a formal complaint with the soldiers' brigade commander, claiming the dogs had been worth $23,000 (almost half a million dollars today). The commander demurred with respect to damages but agreed to have his soldiers line up so Butler could review them and point out the guilty parties. As Butler began walking down the line and inspecting the soldiers' faces, however, many of them began barking and howling like dogs, laughing at his grief and humiliating him completely. Butler quickly fled, but several soldiers caught up to his buggy and were about to loose his horses and roll him over a steep hill before officers intervened. As one Iowa captain noted, "[F]ew regret the death of [Butler's] dogs. Neither would his death be lamented by us."[43]

Long accustomed to pouring oil over troubled racial water, Rivers was uniquely adept at moving between Black and white worlds. As a coachman, he had quietly ferried whites to their destiny while biding his time. As a federal sergeant, he had quietly translated the orders of white officers while biding his time. Only when circumstances became elastic did he exhort his people: "This is our time!"

Even then, Rivers had moved shrewdly, brick by brick, erecting an edifice that could stand the test of time. For all his careful plotting and planning, however, he could never have foreseen the danger Robert Butler represented. Certainly Butler was on his radar. As mayor of Hamburg, Rivers couldn't escape knowing the racist, old dead-ender rattling around in a too-large house perched on the hill overlooking the town. Even so, Butler must have seemed like any old crank, marinating in resentment (and alcohol) until deeply pickled.

Very occasionally, any old crank can turn the tables on history and set everything (awful) in motion. Stewing in grievance and isolation, mourning a dead wife, dead son, dead dogs, dead livelihood, and dead way of life, Butler was a powder keg, ready to blow.

"I am but one man"

In 1871, the *Augusta Chronicle and Sentinel* had predicted "another war brewing" in the endless squaring off between Augusta and Hamburg. "Affairs seem rapidly approaching a crisis," reported the paper, "and we had better begin to prepare for war. [We have forces] more than sufficient to crush the haughty Rivers in the event that he proclaims hostilities. If war does come, we will never stop until the Hamburg government is overthrown, and our victorious forces have entered the enemy's capital in triumph, and then we will annex the little burg and keep it straight."[44]

Instead, something remarkable had happened. Rivers hadn't "proclaimed hostilities." Instead, he had consolidated control and created a model community. Grudgingly, the opposition press admitted that he had managed everything so impossibly well they largely dismissed his alleged involvement in "The Great Negro Plot of 1875."

All of this changed in a crack of the reins, as the "Butler boys," Tommy Butler and Henry Getzen, hurled into Hamburg's Fourth of July parade.

Just before impact, Getzen pulled the wagon up short. The militia company's captain, "Dock" Adams, spoke first:

"Mr. Getzen, I don't know for what reason you treat me in this manner."[45]

"What?" said Getzen.

"Aiming to drive through my company."

"Well, this is the rut I always travel," Getzen said. Getzen may have been right, but Market Street, the main thoroughfare through Hamburg, was 150 feet wide. Owing to disuse, it was more like a big field than anything else, with low grass covering all but some ruts down the middle. Certainly there was ample room for a wagon to pass on either side of the marchers. Getzen was of a mind to make trouble, however. In his mental world, whites went straight and Blacks went around. He revealed more than he intended when he said, "This is the rut I always travel."

"That may be," replied Adams, "but if ever you had a company out here I should not have treated you in this kind of a manner. I would have gone around and shown some respect to you." Adams thought he was being polite. But, in bringing up the specter of Black and white people reversing roles, he touched something like the very root of Getzen's anger.

"Well, this is the rut I always travel," Getzen stammered again, "and I don't intend to get out of it for no damn n——s."[46] Tommy added a few choice curses of his own as murmurs spread through the marchers and the surrounding crowd. Some wanted the militia to stand its ground. Adams called for silence. "Open order!" he commanded (the militia equivalent of "Make a hole!"), and the marchers parted as reluctantly as the sea. As the Butlers' wagon lurched forward, Getzen and Tommy leveled pistols at the crowd, threatening to shoot anyone who tried to bayonet their horse. The commotion brought Hamburg's sheriff, Jim Cook, to the scene on the run. Trailing their wagon, Cook shouted at the Butlers to stop and threatened them with arrest, but they kept driving.

In a light rain, Adams urged his men back to their barracks. Their centennial was over.[47]

The following morning, July 5, Getzen, Tommy, and Robert Butler Sr. all returned to Hamburg. Rivers met them at his office on Market Street and tried to keep a straight face as they swore out a complaint against Adams and his men for obstructing a public road (that is, holding a parade). They had to know that Rivers was general of the very militia they had come to execrate.

Rivers was disinclined to give them any satisfaction. They had, after all, ruined his town's centennial and were now exploiting the situation to drag his militia captain into some legal weeds, where they hoped to beat him half to death. We have to remember, though, that they had to come to him. He remained the law, a fact they implicitly recognized by showing up in his office.

Even so, Rivers could already tell he would need to split the baby. He was probably inclined to, anyway. Rivers had the natural conservatism of a military man. Most of his experience, both as a sergeant and as a trial justice, had been in disciplining Black people. The Butlers' conduct was predictable, pathetic. Adams's conduct was problematic, but tractable. If Adams had comported himself poorly, Rivers would dress him down. Otherwise, he would send the Butlers packing. After the meeting, Rivers had his constable write out a summons for Adams and his officers to appear at an informal hearing the next day with the Butlers.

Adams was enraged upon receiving the summons. The legalities beyond him, he knew only that he was being called to defend conduct that was unimpeachable given the circumstances. His officers were even more livid. Their company had finally come together. They felt a justified pride in their accomplishments and a justified outrage that their centennial had come to such an ignominious end. They weren't ready for a fight, but they were inclined to one.

Hoping to avoid a confrontation, Adams took his summons to Henry Sparnick, a local Hamburg attorney deeply sympathetic to Black individuals. Sparnick told Adams the summons was not legally binding, but he should probably go anyway. The surest way to defuse the situation was to bury it in legal niceties, which is obviously what Rivers preferred. Sparnick also offered to attend the inquiry and give what counsel he could.

The hearing itself got quickly out of hand. Called to testify first, Getzen shamelessly lied, contending an unruly Black mob had deliberately and repeatedly blocked his way and threatened him and Tommy with violence. Getzen done, Rivers allowed Adams to do the cross-examination, which was probably a mistake. Nervous in front of the court and nursing a thinly masked disdain for the ludicrousness of the situation, Adams couldn't help but throw fuel on the fire. His questions were so effective at punching holes in Getzen's story that Getzen became enraged and had to be calmed by his father-in-law. Unfortunately, however, Adams persisted in asking his questions with so much tart, topspin, and legal ignorance that Rivers was forever interrupting him with judicial objections. Exasperated, Adams finally admitted that he didn't "respect [Rivers] no how" and sat down to sulk. This earned him another rebuke from Rivers, and a threat of contempt, and when Adams responded by openly cursing the court, Rivers ordered him arrested.[48]

At this, Adams's first lieutenant, Allen Attaway, also lost his cool. Pacing before a gathering crowd outside the trial office, he called Rivers a "white-livered son of a bitch" and said he'd "be damned if he didn't wade in blood up to his [ass]" before his captain would be arrested. "I carry no arms," Attaway exclaimed, "but we have got arms. The white men have ruled the black men long enough. . . . The next white man who [rides] in front of [our] company [won't] have any report to make. . . . [I will] see that his head [is] shot off so [fucking] clean . . . he [will] have nothing to tell." Whatever lesson Rivers was hoping to teach Adams, it was beginning to backfire. Thinking cooler heads would prevail with time, Rivers suggested the hearing reconvene in two days, at four o'clock on July 8.[49]

At roughly half past 2 p.m. on a blistering July 8, General Matthew C. Butler rolled up outside Rivers's trial office in a small buggy. Butler was South Carolina royalty. His father and grandfather had both been congressmen. His uncles included a senator, a governor, and Commodore Matthew C. Perry. Widely regarded one of the more dashing rebels ever to mount a horse, Butler had been steadily promoted during the Civil War, mustering in as a captain and out as a brigadier general. Butler had suffered setbacks too. He had lost his right foot at Brandy Station, and the war had ruined him financially. In his own run for Congress (in a bid to be the equal of his father and grandfather), he had been defeated by a Black man. According to local legend, Black people had also burned down his house as a personal "f— you" for his years as an enslaver.

Utterly unreconstructed, Butler was an unstable compound of gentility and rage. "With all of his beautiful manners," an acquaintance noted, "when he wanted to he could be the most cold-blooded, insolent human being that mortal eyes ever beheld."[50] Alongside the general was Robert Butler Sr. Though both were Butlers, the exact relation was too distant for either to know it. Tommy and Getzen had arrived also, with a few other toughs on horseback. All of the men were armed. General Butler did not step down from his buggy but instead called into the office where Rivers's constable, William Nelson, sat at his desk with his feet propped up on the door frame, fanning himself.[51]

"Where is Rivers?" demanded the general.[52]

"At his house, I reckon," said Nelson, "but he will be here directly."

"I have come here as counsel to these people," the general said, gesturing to the Butlers. "Go and tell him to come here to me."

"I am not Mr. Rivers's office boy," said Nelson calmly. "I am a constable, and I am here tending to my business. He told me that he would be here at four o'clock, and he won't come any quicker by my going after him."

"Do you know who you are talking to?"

"I am talking to General Butler, I believe."

"Well, God damn you, bring me some paper here." (Butler, it should be said, was renowned for his "highly sulphurated vocabulary.")[53]

Nelson didn't move. Rivers had told him to set up the office and so he had. "Here is the office," he said, "and here is the chairs, and here is the

Brigadier General and South Carolina Senator Matthew Calbraith Butler is best remembered as the architect of the Hamburg Massacre. "With all of his beautiful manners," noted one acquaintance of Butler, "when he wanted to he could be the most cold-blooded, insolent human being that mortal eyes ever beheld." Image courtesy of RR Auction House.

paper and pen and ink, sir, and there is the chairs for all the attorneys that wants to do business here to come in and sit down."

"God damn you, bring it to me, sir."

"I won't do it. Come in, sir, and sit at the table."

Butler jumped down, as did Getzen, who trained his gun on Nelson. Nelson still sat fanning himself, propped against the door frame.

"Give me a chair," demanded the general.

"There's a chair."

"God damn you, give me the chair you are sitting on."

Nelson hesitated. "All right; if this chair suits you better than the other, take it."

"You God damned leather-headed son of a bitch, you, sitting down there fanning yourself, God damn you."

"I am fanning myself in my own office and tending to my own business."

"You God damned son of a bitch, you want to have a hole put through you before you can move." At this, one of the mob swept toward Nelson and raised a large pistol.

"Mr. Butler, you know what sort of a man I am," Nelson said, addressing Robert Butler, still in the buggy. "I have always tried to behave when you came in my office."

"Yes," Butler replied, "but, God damn you, this God-damned drilling has got to stop. I want you to go for Rivers."

"I have no right to go for Rivers; and I am not going."

"Well, God damn you, you will be a dead man, and you will wish you had gone." (No one noticed the illogic of this statement.) Nelson was too busy concentrating. He could sense that his life depended on whatever he said next.

"I am but one man," Nelson replied. Something about this broke the tension.

"God damn you," the general muttered again, "sitting down there with your feet cocked up."

"Well, General, I am not dead, but if you are going to kill me, why just kill me, and that is all you can do."

But the general wasn't ready to start killing. He wanted to round up the militia leaders—especially Adams—and executing a constable wasn't going to help.

Rivers came, as promised, at four. By then, as apparently arranged, more whites were drifting into town, by threes and fours, each sitting his horse with his rifle stock in his right hand and the gun barrel draped across his left arm, as if he were carrying a thin corpse. Given the circumstances, it is not surprising that Adams decided not to show. Just before the appointed hour, he had come to Rivers's house to say that as the court could not protect him, he would not make an appearance. Rivers decided to proceed anyway. As he had the regimental colors, he would uphold the law until he couldn't hold it up anymore. Thus, he called the court to order and had Nelson call for Adams. When Adams failed to answer the third call, the court and crowd gradually dissolved. Officially,

Rivers sent Nelson to round up Adams, but he hadn't any real idea that Nelson would succeed. Butler meanwhile drifted down the block to set up a sort of unofficial headquarters at George Damm's grocery, which, also selling liquor, made it a natural hub of activity.[54]

While at Damm's, Butler was approached by various members of Hamburg's town council who had decided to shuttle between Butler's headquarters and the Sibley Building, where the militia had holed up, to see if they could find a solution short of violence. But what was Butler after? What would he accept? Bizarrely, Butler said that he was no longer in Hamburg as an attorney but as *General* Butler. (He did not say general of what, but apparently his Civil War service and authority were, to his mind, ongoing.) If the town wished to avoid catastrophe, he said, Adams and his officers would have to produce themselves, the militia's arms, and a sincere apology. And if they did all this, the council asked, would Butler vouch for their safety? Maybe, Butler said. "It is owing to *how* they apologize to Mr. Butler for how they treated his sons on the 4th."[55]

When the negotiators arrived at the Sibley Building, Attaway called down to them from a second-story window.

"How does it look?" he asked.

"Squally," came the response.[56]

And indeed, things looked "squally." Adams, however, weighed his military options more carefully than he ever had his legal ones. Opening a small trapdoor in the ceiling of the second-floor drilling room, he crawled out onto the Sibley Building's large tin roof, where he could survey his situation unobserved. Looking east, he could see that curiosity and word of mouth were beginning to draw droves of white men in from Augusta. There seemed to be a couple of hundred men in town now. Some were down by the river, directly across from the building, where they occasionally formed in rows, as if about to be inspected, then fell out to lounge in the grass. More were flooding the streets, "strung out . . . like pickets." All were becoming boisterous with liquor and nervous energy, and all were armed, many of them with the new Winchester, the lever-action repeating rifle that would later earn the nickname The Gun That Won the West (but ought really to be remembered as The Gun That Won the South).[57]

Adams could not defeat such a well-armed mob, and he knew it. He had only twenty-five members of his company in the armory, and nineteen of them were boys—under the age of twenty-one and already beginning to panic. Their state-issued arms (Remington single-shot breechloaders) were better than anything Adams had used in the war, but they were no match for the sixteen-shot Winchesters. And then there was the problem of ammo. The South, it must be understood, was a postapocalyptic landscape, and in such places, guns make law. The region's whites, most of them Democrats, constituted a barely demobilized, barely defeated ex-Confederate army with a tradition of exceptional violence. To counter this, the tenuous Republican governments had to arm Black militias while prohibiting ex-Confederates to carry firearms, acts as potentially revolutionary as the idea of breaking up the plantations and giving freedmen forty acres and a mule. Thus, they had moved slowly, rarely distributing weapons and more rarely ammo. Probably there were little more than 120 rounds of ammunition in the entire armory, and the militia had this many only because Adams had gotten approval to stage a picnic and firing demonstration to raise money for uniforms.

If their chance of fighting a way out seemed slim, the chance of negotiating a way out seemed just as bad. Butler wanted three things: the militia's leaders, its guns, and an apology. As the mob's particular target, Adams knew if he went down to Butler's headquarters, he would probably be killed. He was half inclined to go anyway, whether as an act of defiance or as one of sacrifice. Lieutenant Attaway, however, would not go. It wasn't merely that he hadn't Adams's courage. Whether it was merely his nature or the fact that he was a new husband and father, he just had no nihilism in him, no grim gray space in his head where he could hide and pretend that he didn't want to live. Then too there was a problem with the guns. Adams didn't have the authority to surrender the company's arms. The guns, he felt, had been issued by the state and could be returned only to the state. In demanding them, Butler was making a laughable claim to legal authority; he was in Hamburg as a lawyer in a road-obstruction case. Perhaps Adams didn't know a lot about the law. But he knew if he surrendered the guns, he would be surrendering something more than the wood and the metal. So he sent word to Butler; the answer was "no."[58]

Butler took the news badly. The time for parleying was over, he said. "Now, by God I want those guns and I'll be God damned if I ain't going to have them." At approximately six o'clock, as dusk fell on Hamburg, a signal shot was fired from down by the river, and the white men opened up on the Sibley Building. In the drill room, Adams ordered every man to back himself into the spaces between the windows as glass shot from all the panes and the transom lights above the doors. After fifteen minutes, Adams gave the order to return fire, "for it was the only chance of our lives." Making such a shot was difficult, however. Not only were bullets pouring into the very windows his men had to fire out of; the white men doing most of the firing were concealed behind the railroad abutments down at the river crossing. Nevertheless, one of Adams's men was either a very lucky or a very skilled marksman. When a twenty-three-year-old white farmer named Thomas McKie Meriwether stepped out from behind the abutment to take his turn with his Winchester, a bullet from the Sibley Building cut a groove through the top of his head. (Meriwether may have had a rocky afterlife. Earlier in the day, he had threatened not only to kill "every God damned n——r that there was in Hamburgh" but to "try the women and children, and after he had got through with them [to] go up awhile and try Old Jesus Christ.")[59]

The death of young Meriwether amplified the mob's rage. Having shot out all the panes in the Sibley Building, they were beginning to feel a little ineffectual against a brick building. General Butler had a plan for such contingencies. "After dark I could hear them coming across the bridge from Augusta, yelling, whooping, and holl[er]ing," remembered one witness. "I heard them when they brought the cannon across the bridge." Soon the cannon was trained on the front door of the Sibley Building and loaded with grapeshot. The order was given to fire, and twenty-seven egg-sized balls were sent smashing into the armory.[60]

Here Adams proved particularly brilliant. While all the whites were watching the spectacle of a cannonade at the front door, he was moving his people out the back. The only egress from the rear of the Sibley Building was through a set of second-story windows (which is probably why the mob had not thought to station any men there). Adams, a carpenter by trade, tore up some floorboards and quickly created a functional sixteen-foot ladder, which his men lowered into the gloom of the back lot. Attaway, Adams said, should take the bulk of the militia (and all of the townies) down the ladder and wait. Adams, with fifteen men, would maintain a facade by firing sporadically out of the front windows.

Unfortunately, when Adams and his men began descending the ladder themselves, they found that Attaway had panicked, and his men were scattering: Some were rounding the back lot to give themselves up; others were fanning out, trying to find the comfort and cover of shadows. As he looked up, it seemed to Adams that the moon was "shining . . . about as bright as ever you seen it shine . . . brighter than it ever did before." If they were to make it out of the town square, he told his men, they would have to move fast and stick together. By now, the town was in bedlam, as the mob scattered to chase down and shoot at the remnants of Attaway's tattered band. Throwing his men into the commotion, Adams and company fought their way up the street, toward the Butler plantation. As soon as they broke free of the town's limits, they stopped firing altogether and stole silently onto the Butler property, where they hunkered down in the thick bushes surrounding the approach to the house. (It would have been the perfect position from which to ambush the Butlers when they returned, but Adams decided to go back to town to see whom else he could save. Their leader gone, the men dissolved into the countryside.)[61]

Adams had not been back in town long when he realized that any attempt to save others was going to be futile. The mob was dragging his men from underneath houses and buildings; they were breaking down doors and pulling out men who had nothing to do with the militia. Almost caught in a back lot, Adams could only watch as the mob caught up with Hamburg's sheriff, Jim Cook. Surrounded by Tommy and Getzen and three others, Cook made a last plea for his life.

"Mr. Getzen, I know you and will ask you to save my life," Cook said. "I haven't done anything to you. I have only done my duty as town marshal."

"Your knowing me ain't nothing; I don't care anything about your marshalship; we are going to kill you." All five fired.

"O Lord!" Cook cried plaintively. "O Lord!" he said as he crumpled. Even as he lay dying, members of the mob began pawing at his body, taking his boots and watch and whatever else he was carrying.[62]

Adams later admitted that at this point, saving himself had become the priority. His own house, he could see, was already being ransacked, so he decided to try hiding in the back of Schiller's printing office across the street. He had only just made it in the back door when the front door was busted in and the room flooded with whites. "Here's a God damned son of a bitch!" one of the mob shouted. But to Adams's surprise, they weren't talking about him. In tearing the place up, they had discovered under a cabinet a man Adams didn't even know was there, one of his own militiamen, David Freyer. Adams could hear them going to work on Freyer and then on the office even as he crept quietly back out the door. Once in the backyard, Adams sprinted for the fence and had just vaulted it when he heard a loud, "Halt!" His heart in his throat, he realized a moment later that, once again, the mob was talking to someone else. They had caught Moses Parks out in the open as he tried to cross the street. Twenty-five men quickly formed a semicircle around him; at least half of them fired.[63]

Adams next stole into the postmaster's office, vaulted the stairs, and stood in a balcony window, where, from behind the slatted blinds, he could see everything going on below.

"Good boys! God damn it!" Butler shouted as he was presented with one of the new prisoners. "Turn your hounds loose, and bring the last one in." Butler especially wanted Adams, and said so. But by three in the morning, it was clear that there was no one left to find. "Well, we had better go to work and kill all the n——s we have got," said one of the mob. "We won't be able to find that son of a bitch."[64]

"The 'Dead Ring'"

The prisoners sat on the grass surrounded by a densely packed ring of standing white men. Some of the prisoners were leading Republicans or members of Adams's militia; others were simply men against whom local white men had grudges. Attaway was among those in the "dead ring."[65]

"Mays, what do you think of this?" Attaway asked the man sitting next to him. (Jack Mays had been a cook for the Union army; now, by all accounts, he ran a gambling operation in Hamburg.)[66]

"I don't know, Attaway, what to think of it," Mays responded.

"Do you think they will kill any of us?"

"Yes, I do, I think so; just so," said Mays.

"Do you think they will kill me?" Attaway asked finally.

"I do," said Mays. "All you have got to do now is to pray to God to save your soul. Just give up your wife and children and everything else, for they are going to kill you." With that Attaway hung his head and commenced crying.

There was, however, a terrific disagreement among the whites about what to do next. Some thought the prisoners should be simply arrested. Others wanted to open the circle into a firing line and gun them all down.

"All you black sons of bitches get up here; we are going to carry you to Aiken and put you in jail," said one white man.

"No, *we* will start to Aiken," yelled another, "but we will leave *them* on the road!"

"We'll attend to them!" echoed a third.

Finally, Bill Robinson, the son of a judge, spoke up: "Now, gentlemen, the way to do . . . is to go and hold a court-martial, and whatever the court-martial determines you can do, then you can do it." With that, a small detachment moved away from the ring. Probably they consulted with General Butler; certainly they drew up a list.[67]

"Do all you can for me," Attaway begged of Getzen while the court-martial was meeting.

"Yes, God damn you, I will do all I can for you; I will do it in a short while; I will fix you now in a short while." Getzen then went off and came back with Tommy and the men with the list.[68]

Attaway's was the first name called.

"Gentlemen, I am not prepared for death," Attaway said.

"I don't care," said Getzen.

"Will you allow me to prepare to meet my God?"

"I don't care; we are going to kill you." With that, Getzen and Tommy and a few other men carried Attaway across the railroad tracks and down a slope into a little oat field where they shot him.

At the sound of the shots, Dave Phillips turned to the others in the ring. "Why is you all begging so? If they are going to kill us all anyhow, what is the use of begging?"

Dave Phillips's was the next name called. "He got up just like a soldier," a man in the ring remembered. "He looked like he didn't care no more for it than he would about eating, and he walked right along." When they got into the oat field, he was put on his knees and shot down.[69]

"Hamp Stevens!"

Stevens was a large, light-skinned boy, hardly twenty.

"O, gentlemen, I haven't done nothing," he said.

"Come out here," came the response. And Stevens was led away and shot down like the others.[70]

"Alfred Minyard!" Minyard didn't answer. He thought it possible that none of the white men knew who he was. Cursing the delay, someone stepped into the ring and began turning the prisoners' heads to the crowd, asking who knew them. When he finally got to Minyard, Alfred admitted who he was.

"O, let that boy alone," said one of the prisoners, "he is sick."

"O, God damn him; we'll fix him too," came the response, and he was taken off to the oat field.[71]

"Pompey Curry!"[72]

Curry decided to try Minyard's tactic in reverse. At the sound of his name, he jumped up and bolted through an opening in the white men. Several guns went off simultaneously, and Curry went down.

"What better fun do you want than that?" asked one of the gunmen.[73] (But in fact, Curry had not been killed. Shot through the legs, he somehow managed to drag himself out of view and would live to tell everything that had happened in the dead ring.)

Curry's was the last name on the list. "Well, now, what will we do with the rest of them?" asked a member of the crowd.

"By God, let's pile them up like frogs and shoot them off," suggested one.

"O, no," said another. "You have done enough to-night."

The white men did have a problem, however. What were they supposed to do? "Let these damned n——s go?" asked one. "O, no; we ought not to leave none to tell the tale; let's kill them all."

This idea had its proponents. "Let's let them go and shoot after them like rabbits," was the suggestion of some who had liked the sport of shooting at Curry.

Others were ready to call it a night. "Let's swear them before they go not to tell anything," said one, and the rest grumblingly assented. Thus, the remaining prisoners were told to get down on their knees and to swear never to talk or testify about what they had witnessed. And then they were allowed to go. (Most of the prisoners took off and ran, which proved too great a temptation for some members of the crowd. "They shot at us just like they were shooting at birds," remembered one.)[74]

Around four in the morning, the general and the rest of the Butlers retired to their plantation for some watermelon, leaving Hamburg to the mercy of the crowd of drunks who still wanted more. Breaking into houses and rifling the bodies of the men cut down in the massacre, they called out their names and then laughingly responded, "He don't answer." Staring at a corpse, lying on its back in the road, one of the mob noted, "By God, he is looking at the moon and don't wink his eyes." And for reasons that aren't clear, someone went to the unconscious but still living body of Alfred Minyard and "cut off a big piece of meat from off his rump." Perhaps it was the pound of flesh he felt he was owed.[75]

How Rivers escaped the massacre is unknown. Many years later a local newspaper reported that "it was generally believed that Rivers spent the night in the Savannah River to get away." More likely Rivers evacuated *by* river, along with his family. In any case, none of them were at home in the early dawn when a group of rowdies staggered onto his farm on Little Horse Creek, ransacked his house, and tried to set it ablaze. Writing a few days later for *The New York Times*, Higginson was indignant on behalf of a friend. "Allow me to call your attention to a remarkable circumstance in the recent Hamburg massacre," he wrote, "namely that after the captured militiamen had been shot down, the colored magistrate before whom the case had been brought was compelled to flee for his life, and his house was sacked. Yet all accounts agree in saying that his only share in the affair had consisted in an endeavor to keep the peace."[76]

Higginson put his finger on something important. As in the Crozier

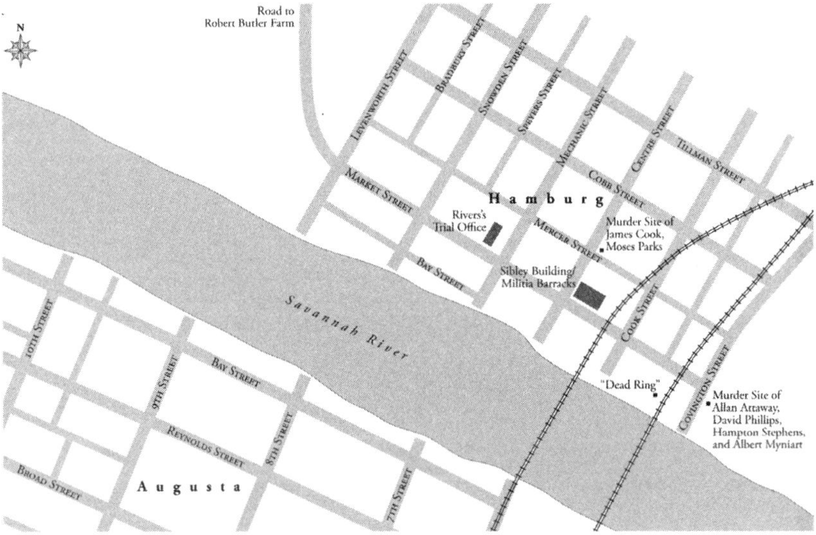

Eighty percent Black and 20 percent white, the "freedom town" of Hamburg, South Carolina, was a political sanctuary for two thousand souls. As intendant/mayor of the town, Rivers was one of the first Black mayors in the United States. Map by Mapping Specialists, Ltd.

affair, so in the Hamburg Massacre, Rivers proved the most strategic, reasonable, and legally faithful of everyone involved.

"The gentleman's time has expired"

Rivers had never imagined anything like the Hamburg Massacre. No one had. Certainly, he knew the murderous intransigence of whites. He had only to close his eyes to conjure the faces of those he'd lost to political violence: Jerome Furman. Alexander Heasly. George Dill. Hamburg was different, however. This wasn't a skulking act of night riding, bushwhacking, or assassination. This was a counterrevolutionary assault on his very seat of power. These were his men dead; his sheriff killed; his town vandalized; his office looted; his home desecrated; his wife's dresses trampled in the dirt.

What could he do with all that anger and impotent rage?

The morning after the massacre, July 9, 1876, Prince Rivers stood over the bodies of his slain townsmen and convened a coroners' inquest. Because that is what you do the morning after a massacre; you forge the first link in the chain of justice. As duly elected trial justice, mayor, and general of the militia, Rivers had a legal obligation to respond, and his response had specific standing before the law. When the inquest was over, Rivers bundled together the pages of testimony and issued arrest warrants for eighty-seven white men, including Matthew Butler, future South Carolina senator, and Ben Tillman, future South Carolina governor. News of the warrants ran in numerous national newspapers, including *The New York Times*.

On July 15, seven days after the massacre, Robert Smalls, now a U.S. congressman from South Carolina, found a way to introduce the subject of Hamburg on the House floor. During the discussion of a joint resolution to reinforce the Texas border against Mexican bandits, Smalls offered an amendment: "That no troops . . . shall be drawn from the State of South Carolina so long as the militia of that State peaceably assembled are assaulted, disarmed, and taken prisoners, and then massacred in cold blood by lawless bands of men." He then had the clerk read into the record an eyewitness account of the Hamburg affair that was particularly damning to Butler and the other whites. When another House member demanded to know the author of the letter, Smalls responded: "I will say to the gentleman that if he is desirous that the name shall be given in order to have another negro killed, he will not get it from me." Smalls's remark was widely applauded on the House floor, but Congressman Samuel S. Cox of New York, a Tammany man and former Copperhead, charged that reading the letter was a political stunt "intended to be shaken in the face of the House for political and bad party purposes."[77]

Cox's calumny aroused the indignation of the only Black congressman who had served the House longer than Smalls, Joseph Rainey, a former barber representing Charleston. "Just think of it!" Rainey demanded:

> What would be thought if here in Washington City, when a military company was parading on the Fourth of July, two men should come up on a buggy and demand of the officers that the company should get out of the way, and if they did not, should at once set to work and murder

> the men of that military company? I ask you, citizens of the United States, would you stand it? I ask you, brave men who fought for your country's liberties long before you took part in the war of the rebellion, would you stand it? I ask you, proud Southern men who boast of your gallantry and your intelligence and your superiority to my race, would you stand it? I ask you, men of the North, who sacrificed your blood and treasure, who sacrificed the lives of your sons and your relatives, would you stand it? Do you, then, expect negroes to stand this? Do you expect my race to submit meekly to continual persecution and massacre by these people in the South? Are you not going to allow us any right of self-defense? In the name of my race and my people, in the name of humanity, in the name of God, I ask whether we are to be American citizens with all the rights and immunities of citizens or whether we are to be vassals and slaves again?[78]

Rainey's words were still ringing in the hall when the House speaker said gently, "The gentleman's time has expired," as he gaveled an adjournment for the weekend.[79]

By the time the House reconvened three days later, Rainey's words seemed like a distant memory. Mississippi Congressman L. Q. C. Lamar, the first former Confederate official allowed back into Congress, rose to proclaim that a discussion of Hamburg had no place on the floor: "I do not propose to discuss or analyze this terrible and disgraceful affair at Hamburg," Lamar said, "although I think that the gentleman [Smalls] has not given a fair and impartial statement of the circumstances in which it originated. But those circumstances are of no moment here upon this question [of frontier reinforcements], nor are the provocations which led to the final fearful tragedy involved in the proposition now before us. Nor are they, in my opinion . . . the legitimate topic of debate or discussion on this floor; they belong to another tribunal."[80]

This ended any discussion of Hamburg in the House of Representatives.

Four days later, South Carolina's Republican governor, Daniel H. Chamberlain, sent President Grant a desperate request for aid. "The recent massacre at Hamburg," Chamberlain said, had caused "widespread terror and apprehension among the colored race and the republicans of this state" and a "feeling of triumph and political elation [among] the democrats." "[W]ill the [federal] Government exert itself vigorously to repress [this] violence? . . . Will the [federal] Government take such precautions as may be suitable . . . to restore confidence to the poor people of both races?" Failure to respond, Chamberlain said, would leave the rule of law in the United States "fatally shaken."[81]

Grant's reply was at once sympathetic and shortsighted. "The scene at Hamburg," he said, was "cruel, blood-thirsty, wanton, unprovoked, and uncalled for." The actions of the whites "would scarcely be accredited to savages, much less to a civilized and Christian people." So, what did Grant intend to do about it? Here he became vague and noncommittal. It was the job of state governors, he said, "to secure a fair trial and punishment of all offenders, without distinction of race or color or previous condition of servitude, and without aid from the Federal Government." Chamberlain was crushed by this. Without the federal army, he would have to activate the militia—meaning organizing more Black men and arming them better—the very provocation that had brought on the Hamburg Massacre in the first place.[82]

In the face of a tepid response from the executive branch, Democratic whites brazenly organized "rifle clubs" and openly plotted to take the whole state back by force. A similar campaign of terror had worked in an off-year election in Mississippi the year before, but, until Hamburg, no one thought it could work in South Carolina. South Carolina was the birthplace of secession; federal troops were still on the ground; 1876 was a presidential election year. Surely a massive campaign of blatant voter intimidation and violence carried out in the open would be met with a swift federal response. Except that it wouldn't. Hamburg had proved that. As the *Aiken Courier-Journal* put it, the "Rubicon [had been] Passed at Hamburg."[83]

Writing many years later about his proud participation in the ensuing terror campaign, Alfred Williams acknowledged that Hamburg had been the gift the white supremacists had never seen coming. "Never were a people more absolutely between the devil and the deep blue sea than

[we] were," Williams confessed. "The weight of sober and prudent argument of journalist[s] and outside pressure were [all] on the side of the mild and persuasive compromise course—until Hamburg. That decided the state's policy and future and brought the uprising and the revolution within ten days."[84]

Only in the United States Senate was a federal effort mounted to deal with Hamburg. Even then, the inquiry was part of a larger investigation into election irregularities and voter intimidation in three states—Florida, Louisiana, and South Carolina—where twenty electoral votes were in dispute. (In the fiercely contested presidential race of 1876, Democrat Samuel J. Tilden won 184 electoral votes to 165 votes for Republican Rutherford B. Hayes. If all disputed electoral votes went to Hayes, he would be declared the winner.)

Election results were in the greatest dispute in South Carolina, where an eye-popping 101 percent of eligible voters cast a ballot. (This was despite the fact that voting was massively down among Republican and Black voters.) In one of the greatest examples of election fraud in United States history, South Carolina's total vote count—182,683—would not be superseded until 1952. Clearly, something was amiss.

In late December 1876, three senators made the trip from Washington, D.C., to Columbia, South Carolina, to interview their first witness, Dock Adams. From the beginning, the senators' partisan preferences were apparent. Angus Cameron, Republican senator from Wisconsin, ably served as chair, but he was forever trying to rein in the verbal fireworks from the other two members of the committee. Isaac Peckham Christiancy, Republican senator from Michigan, had been an antebellum gubernatorial candidate on the Free Soil ticket, and time and again he elicited the most damning testimony from witnesses. Arrayed against him was Augustus Summerfield Merrimon, Democratic senator from North Carolina, whom *The New York Times* called "one of the bitterest partisan Democrats in Congress."[85] Hovering over the entire proceeding was not exactly the question of justice for Hamburg but the fate of a presidential election. Merrimon, particularly, seemed driven to find Democratic cover in the idea that Hamburg was a spontaneous race riot, unconnected to politics, whose fault should be laid at the door of South Carolina's Black (Republican) majority.[86]

In many ways, the resulting three-volume, 2,500-page Senate report was a remarkable achievement. Without it—without the verbatim transcripts from key eyewitnesses—the entire history of the massacre, laid out in detail in the preceding pages, could not have been written. Without it, crimes and crucial details might have been lost. As Lincoln said: "We cannot escape history." Our actions in this life "light us down in honor or dishonor to the latest generation." And there are many men associated with the massacre whose names should be lighted down and whose actions should never escape historical judgment.[87]

Like many Senate reports, however, this one was destined to molder, which is probably why Rivers decided not to show. Charges that he was afraid to set foot in Columbia are ridiculous. Rivers had demonstrated his personal courage too often for this to be plausible. More likely he found the entire exercise pointless. For months the United States government had done nothing in the face of extralegal violence, including the sacking of his own home, and now, instead of sending the army, they were sending a company of paper pushers on a fact-finding mission. Rivers's entire theory of power rested on local control, and he had more pressing problems at home: His citadel was falling.

On January 22, 1877, Rivers received a letter from the office of the newly elected Democratic governor: "Sir: I am instructed by His Excellency the Governor, Wade Hampton, to inform you that he has removed you from the office of Trial Justice, for Aiken County. You will therefore, immediately upon the receipt of this letter, cease to exercise the functions of said office." What does it say that one of the very first official acts of the incoming gubernatorial administration was to strip Rivers of legal authority?[88]

And what does it say that five months later, in one of *its* first official acts, South Carolina's newly elected Democratic legislature revoked Hamburg's town charter? This was obviously another direct blow to Rivers's seat of power. Surviving one massacre, the town was immediately subject to another, one that sought to wipe it from the legal map.

Rivers resisted the revocation of Hamburg's charter with the only means left to him—a petition. "We believe we have a good government in the Town of Hamburg," he and the other petitioners noted, "and we firmly believe that [it] will protect our rights as Citizens and Tax Payers." The document was signed by 131 Black residents of Hamburg, including Rivers and the widows of Allen Attaway and James Cook. The petition was also signed by twenty-four whites, nine of them women, including the very first signatory, a Mrs. B. E. Owing. The inclusion of the whites among the first signatories was obviously intentional. Hamburg was no lawless "Black" town, the petitioners sought to say, but a place even white women were comfortable to call home.[89]

Rivers knew the petition wouldn't work. The second section of the document admits as much: "We have reason to be believe that [a] Certain party or parties have some movement on foot [afoot] to attempt through your Honorable Body to deprive the Citizens and Tax Payers of the Town of Hamburg of their Charter." The petition closes with a humility Rivers must have found galling, hoping "your Honorable Body will give petitioners a Just and favorable consideration."[90]

For the second time in his life, Rivers had a petition denied. He could feel the window closing, time becoming inelastic. Now, he said, it will be a hundred years.

THE COACHMAN

History, like a vast river, propels logs, vegetation, rafts, and debris; it is full of live and dead things, some destined for resurrection.

JACQUES BARZUN

"The purpose of our visit to Hamburg," Ben Tillman later wrote, "was to strike terror, and the next morning when the negroes who had fled [to the swamps] returned to town, the ghastly sight which met them of seven dead negroes lying stark and stiff certainly had its effect. . . . [Their lives] had been offered up as a sacrifice to the fanatical teachings of those who sought to substitute the rule of the African for that of the Caucasian in South Carolina." For months after the massacre, Hamburg remained a favorite haunt of night riders seeking to whoop it up and relive their glory.[1]

With little other choice, Rivers moved with his family to Aiken. He had a smaller community to protect now, especially his young wife and sister-in-law. Their family was not unique. Hundreds of residents moved away from Hamburg, most never to return.

Rubbing salt in the wound, the *Aiken Courier-Journal* welcomed Rivers to the neighborhood with a mocking notice in the paper: "Distinguished Arrivals—Brigadier General Trial Justice Prince R. Rivers and family arrived in Aiken last week and have taken a cottage for the season in lower Aiken."[2]

Rivers gradually sold off his two lots in Hamburg. The first he sold to F. H. Stellings in 1879. The second, at the very heart of the city, he sold in 1886—to Tommy Butler. The sale must have stung, but the property carried heavy memories. Gone were the days when Rivers had stood over his plat map, dreaming of a Black mecca.[3]

Stripped of his civic posts, Rivers worked odd jobs until, like a reluctant horse to harness, he returned to the carriage. "Attired in his livery suit and tall beaver hat," noted a local paper with satisfaction, "he looked like a piece of statuary, so erect in form was he."[4]

The comparison to statuary worked on a number of levels. Rivers bore his disgrace with characteristic dignity. He gave no interviews and made no comment. Instead, he became a museum piece, a walking time capsule, a silent sentinel leaving people to whisper in his wake: "There goes The Black Prince." As one local put it: "This wagon driver's presence summed up nearly 20 years of incredible tumult, years when the world was turned upside down—twice. . . . To see the Major General, the Judge, the Representative, the Sergeant—to see him driving his grocery cart around the dirt streets of Aiken had to jog a person's thinking." Indeed, it did.[5]

At the height of his power, the *Charleston Mercury* had disparaged Rivers's entire political career, calling him a man "here, there, and everywhere except in his proper sphere, with curry comb and horsebrush, on the box of some genteel carriage."[6]

In ways we should appreciate, Rivers had been here, there, and everywhere. He, as much as anyone, helped create the USCT. He, more than anyone, created a sanctuary for his people in the most unforgiving terrain in America. He, better than anyone, proved that Reconstruction could work. Decades before W. E. B. Du Bois and Booker T. Washington, Rivers foresaw the insights of both. Before Du Bois even said it, Rivers believed it would take an especially talented tenth of his race to lead the rest of the formerly enslaved through the gauntlet the white supremacists had prepared for them. Decades before Booker T. Washington established the Tuskegee Institute, Rivers understood that the only color that really mattered in America was green. For Rivers, equality before the ballot box and equality before the jury box were deeply important goals; equality before the cash register was priority one.

I have titled the book *The Original Black Panther* for a reason. Rivers's contemporaries made the animal comparison all the time. "His gait is like a panther's," said his regimental colonel. "He is agile and fleet, like a deer in his speed, and like a panther in his tread," said his regimental surgeon. The comparison to a Black Panther goes deeper, however. Rivers was no Marxist and never engaged in a pitched battle with a cop, but that's not what the Black Panthers were. The Panther program was mostly about self-respect; self-help; policing the police; exercising Second Amendment rights; organizing militarily, politically, socially, and culturally; feeding their kids; and paying their teachers. It is in this sense that Rivers deserves the title, at least as much as any man living in the nineteenth century.[7]

People who fail are rarely the subjects of biographies. They should be. From the humblest of origins, Rivers rose to become "The Power of Aiken County" only to be bound again, like many men, to failing health, dwindling resources, and lost possibilities. The entire arc of Rivers's life—from carriage driver to soldier to legislator to mayor to carriage driver again—encapsulates the window of opportunity that opened and closed on a remarkable generation of African Americans.

After Hamburg, Rivers's titanic will and frame began to falter. "At the time of our marriage," said his wife Louisa, "the general health of my husband was good, but within a year I discovered that he had frequent hemorrhages. Blood would flow from his nose and his mouth but they did not seem to interfere with his daily work."[8]

Rivers died in Aiken, South Carolina, on April 10, 1887, at the age of sixty-four. His official cause of death was Bright's disease—an antiquated term for kidney failure, likely brought on by undiagnosed diabetes, hypertension, or heart disease. A local white paper offered up a typically insulting obituary. "In point of intelligence he was far above the average darkey," the article noted, "and was respected by the white people and looked up to by his colored brethren with much reverence. Always a pronounced Republican, he did what he conceived to be his duty."[9]

Looking for sanctuary, even in death, Rivers had arranged to be buried in the newly created Randolph Cemetery in Columbia, South Carolina. For years, Columbia's Black families had been buried in the potter's field along the river. In 1871 a contingent of the city's Black elite formed a new cemetery association and purchased three acres of land from the white cemetery known as Elmwood. They named the new cemetery after Benjamin F. Randolph, Rivers's fellow delegate to the 1868 constitutional convention, who was assassinated as he stepped down from a train. Randolph Cemetery flourished until 1918 and then gradually fell into disuse as the Great Migration sent many Black families to the north and other interment options opened up in the city. In 1959, an urban renewal project bulldozed the older part of the cemetery where Rivers lay buried before the African American community managed to stop it.[10]

To this day no one knows where the bones of the "Black Prince" lie.

Fade to Black

History and the past are not the same. The past is everything that ever happened. History is whatever we make of the past, a willful act of deciding what to remember and what to forget. In telling one story, we usually forget another.

So, what stories shall we tell here?

First, we could tell the story of a federally sponsored slave insurrection. Rivers's understanding of the Civil War was something very different from ours. For him, the Civil War had been a clash of armies, yes, but it was no white man's fight. Liberation raids of the kind he and his men engaged in have yet to take their place in our conception of what the Civil War was. If Sherman was right—that ultimately the Civil War was won by making war on what makes war itself, the morale of the enemy—then the work of liberating slaves, especially when undertaken by the recently enslaved, needs to be measured in military terms. Every time Rivers and company went out, they put the lie to the very idea that Black people had no future in the United States and dramatically undercut the entire reason the Confederacy was fighting in the first place. Think about it: The only thing the Confederacy ever conceded was the idea that slavery was over. Racism would remain. White supremacy would remain. Jim Crow would descend across the South in a nadir of race relations that wouldn't be lifted for a hundred years. But slavery itself, as it had existed for two centuries, was killed. And who helped kill it? Men like Rivers. This was no small victory. Indeed, it was a monumental victory. And he and his men achieved it just as they had achieved everything else during their long resistance movement—in the interstices between their enslavement and their free will.[11]

The Union army saved the Union. Men like Rivers made the Union "forever worthy of the saving."[12]

Second, we could tell the story of the "Lost City" of Hamburg. Founded in a grudge, the town roared to significance in its first iteration as a cotton and slave transport hub until Augusta beat it out of sight. Debts mounting, the city's founder, Henry Shultz, attempted suicide, putting a gun to his mouth and firing. (Shultz had tilted the gun so far forward that the bullet tore through his soft palate, passing just behind his nose before exiting through his forehead.) Looking exactly like he had blown his own face off, Shultz lived a few years longer. Buried in debt, he is reputed to have been buried for good standing up, facing Augusta, so he could keep a watchful eye on his nemesis.[13]

Refounded in hope by Prince Rivers, Hamburg roared to significance again as a freedom town before again being "lost" in the wake of the Hamburg Massacre. Without its protector, the city went a second time to seed, becoming a marshy demimonde of dead-enders, lawbreakers, and sad memories. The governor's choice to replace Rivers as trial justice was the ultimate extension of the political middle finger: Henry Getzen. With zero law-enforcement experience (except when breaking it), Getzen had murdered two of the town's leading residents before becoming its top law enforcement officer. Getzen immediately went to work, setting up a handsome new trial office, securing a new town charter, and serving as Hamburg's mayor until at least 1897. In his various civic roles, Getzen did exactly what the governor hoped he would do: preside over the "break up of one of the foulest nests of scoundrels that ever-disgraced civilization." Fifteen years after the massacre, Getzen's version of Hamburg was "nothing but . . . a howling wilderness," according to the *Aiken Recorder*. "Hamburg is surely an evidence of what narrowminded illiberal citizens can do," the paper continued. "[The town] now serves but one purpose. It is the battle-ground for game cocks and bull dogs." The

Augusta Chronicle concurred, heralding Hamburg as a local outpost for moonshining, cockfighting, and other "barbaric sports," a place where "dogs, wild cats, and coons [were] made to fight each other." (Ultimately Getzen overachieved in befouling Hamburg, forcing another "veteran" of the massacre, Governor Ben Tillman, to crack down on the illegal moonshining and blood sports in the town.) Getzen died in 1920.[14]

Tommy Butler also spent the rest of his life salting the soil of Hamburg—as the town drunk. He did have one major departure from his barstool—a trip to New York City in 1879. "Some two weeks ago," reported the *Anderson Intelligencer*, "Mr. John Thomas Butler, of Hamburg, S. C. carried a pack of bloodhounds to New York and a negro for them to chase in Central Park, for the purpose of exhibiting the powers of his dogs, which he did very much to the interest of large crowds of spectators on several occasions." The idea of staging a slave-running demonstration in Central Park seems disturbing enough, but apparently Butler then got a temporary gig with a theater troupe and folded his dog exhibition into their production of *Uncle Tom's Cabin*. Butler's plantation theater had a nice run, but local Republicans found the whole thing grotesque and raised a political stink. Certainly, it was a little on the nose for the Democratic Party to be associated with running slave dogs in New York City. The blowback was significant enough that South Carolina papers claimed the whole thing was a false flag operation: "The freak which induced Mr. Butler to go to New York immediately before the elections for the purpose of making this exhibition, indicates to our mind that he has been made the dupe of a political intrigue. . . . He is no doubt satisfied, but the people of the State and of the Democratic party will probably feel like Mr. Butler's proper place is at home."[15]

Tommy returned home to drink away his theater proceeds. The bottle did little to soften him, except around the middle. Even the desolation of his Black neighbors' dreams had done nothing to close the hole in his heart. This is often the case with violence; it leaves everyone associated with it spiritually broken, even the perpetrators.

In 1893, a gunfight broke out in the middle of town between Tommy Butler and the Pettyjohn family, owners of the Arlington Hotel in Augusta. Tommy's grievance with the Pettyjohns was typically piddling.

The cows that supplied the Arlington's milk, butter, and cheese were pastured at his sister's farm, which adjoined Tommy's own. A few of the Pettyjohns' cows had escaped to graze in his oat field, so Tommy impounded them all and refused to release them until restitution was made. Knowing exactly the kind of man they were dealing with, the Pettyjohns—including husband Joseph, his wife, and two sons, Will and Joe—rode out to Butler's farm well armed. Fortuitously, they found the place unoccupied, so they unpenned the cows and led them back to a friendly pasture.

Returning through town, however, they spied Tommy on the porch of the local saloon, shotgun at the ready. Tommy shot first, igniting a general melee. Will Pettyjohn, about twenty years old, took up position behind one of the railroad trestles, near where Thomas McKie Meriwether had died. Tommy managed to shoot him anyway, once in the arm and a second time "in the region of the abdomen," meaning the privates. Joe Pettyjohn, just fifteen, took refuge behind the corner of an adjacent building and escaped unscathed, as did his mother, who stood in the street yelling at her boys to stand their ground. More grievously hurt were the two main antagonists, Joseph Pettyjohn and Tommy. Joseph was so angry he didn't bother to find cover but instead stood in the middle of the road unloading on Tommy, who was partially shielded by the tree at the front of the saloon. After about fifteen rounds, Tommy ran out of ammo and raced back into the bar to reload. Joseph followed right after, but Tommy was quicker and sent a full shotgun blast into Joseph's abdomen just as he entered the building. Tommy then retreated farther into a back room of the bar to load up again. He had just gotten the door shut when Joseph blasted through the door, from a distance of five feet, sending splinters and shot into Tommy's face, neck, and chest. Somehow the saloon's proprietor now managed to convince both men that they should better hobble home to tend to their wounds. The Pettyjohns made it back to their hotel, where they hoped Joseph would recover. He didn't. On his deathbed, he told the press there was simply no living with a "ruffian and brow-beat and bulldozer" like Tommy Butler.[16]

His face "badly peppered" and hand "fearfully mangled," Tommy survived. Sheer cussedness precluded anything else. He even hung around the bar after the melee, knocking back another round and reliving the scene with other local drunks. Some men genuinely enjoy being assholes. Maybe it never occurred to Tommy that he had killed men before on the same spot. Maybe it did occur to him. Maybe that's why he did it.[17]

Nathaniel Hawthorne said it best:

> There is a fatality, a feeling so irresistible and inevitable that it has the force of doom, which almost invariably compels human beings to linger around and haunt, ghost-like, the spot where some great and marked event has given the color to their lifetime; and still the more irresistibly, the darker the tinge that saddens it.[18]

Tommy Butler died five years later, at age forty-three.

Like any sad memory, Hamburg washed away eventually, in this case literally. Henry Shultz had always been proud of "my bridge, my bridge," but nothing made by humans stands forever. In 1888, a flood took out Shultz's bridge and did extensive damage in Augusta. Thereafter the two cities were locked in a new race, less economic than environmental. When Augusta completed its new levee in 1919, its mayor proudly proclaimed: "Our city is now safe from flood waters from the Savannah River." He wasn't entirely right, but the levee itself spelled Hamburg's doom. With nowhere else to go, the floodwaters of August and September 1929 poured over Hamburg, washing everything away. Thirty-seven homes and fourteen barns were obliterated entirely. The rest suffered heavy flooding and damage. Crops were ruined, the water was rendered undrinkable, and 120 citizens caught malaria. The Red Cross appropriated $10,000 in aid, but families could get relief only if they moved. "Under no circumstances will aid be extended to families who remain in Hamburg," the Red Cross reported. "In offering assistance . . . the American Red Cross feels that it will discharge its obligation in Hamburg as a relief agency and at no time in the future will it expect to be called upon to render aid there." Under federal pressure, most of the city's remaining Black population was "forthwith moved to high ground a short distance up the river, and thus was administered the *coup de grace* to the languishing existence of what was for many years the leading interior market of South Carolina." "Hamburg's gone now," one resident said simply.[19]

Today, Hamburg is the golfing community of "River Walk." People golf on Hamburg's graves. The larger environs have been rechristened "North Augusta," even though you're on the South Carolina side of the river. Until recently, the road that ran along the site where Moses Parks, Allen Attaway, David Phillips, Hampton Stevens, and Alfred Minyard were summarily executed carried a formal plaque: the Jefferson Davis Memorial Highway.

To be sure, there are many "lost cities" in America. In a one-hour radius of my house, there are a dozen places where Black folks raised significant centers of cultural, political, and socioeconomic life, only to be displaced. Perhaps the most famous—Oscarville, Georgia—was a successful majority-Black poultry town located just outside Atlanta until the race riots of 1912. Now it's Lake Lanier. If you dive down deep enough you can take a watery tour of the Oscarville graveyard, still intact, because no one bothered to move it. Closer to home is Linnentown, twenty-two acres seized from Black families in Athens, Georgia, in the name of "urban renewal"—meaning student dorms.[20]

Across the United States, from Blackdom, New Mexico, to Freemanville, Florida, there are a thousand "ghost towns" and "drowned towns" resting uneasily beneath our feet (or our kayaks). Hamburg may be the most emblematic of them all. Headed by one of America's first Black mayors and explicitly chartered as an interracial sanctuary, Hamburg was destroyed precisely because it was working. All of the urban renewal and Tennessee Valley Authority projects that ever paved over or flooded a Black town began when the ur-mother of them all—Hamburg, South Carolina—was sacked by white supremacists and the federal government did nothing.[21]

The most important story we could tell is the story of The Black Prince himself. Prince Rivers may be the most consequential American about whom Americans know nothing. Obviously, he never sought to be remembered. He was too busy fighting for his people. Along the way, he created a set of historical impressions, an archive of action, that demands our attention.

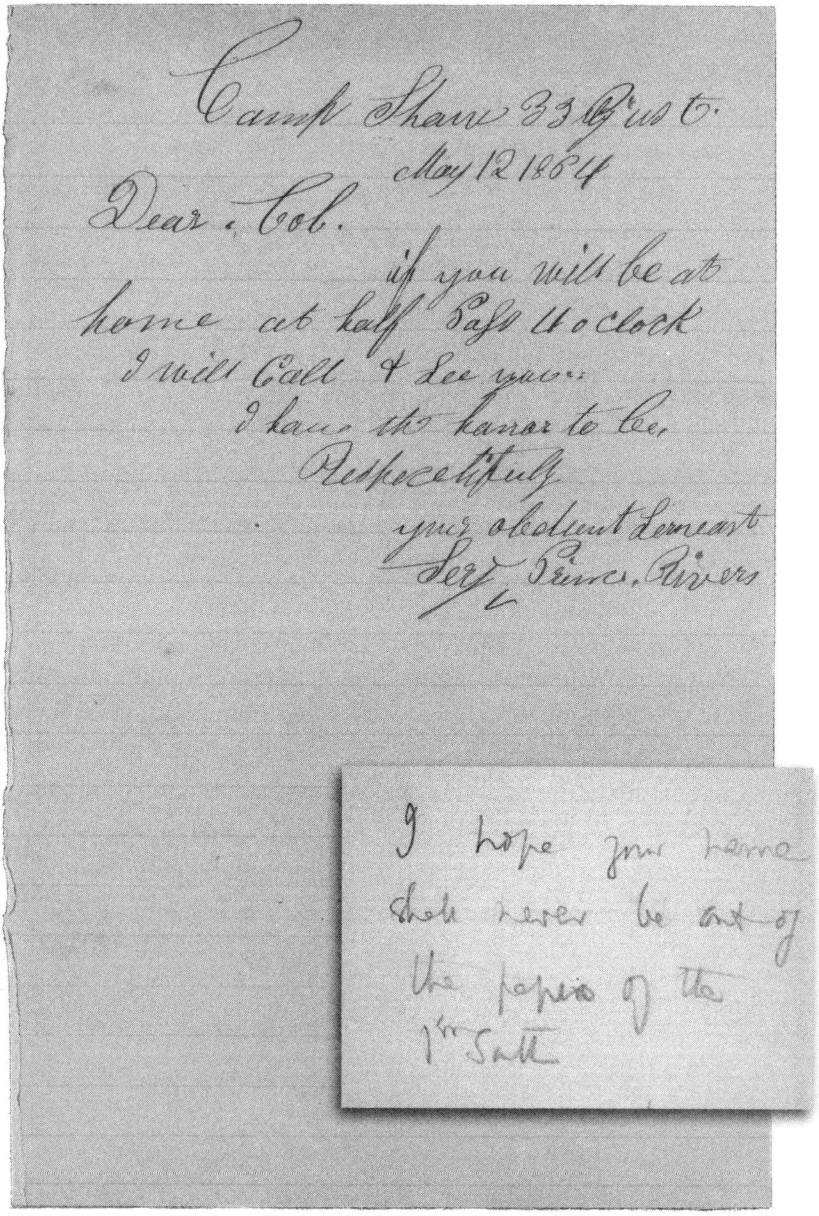
Camp Shaw 33 Regt C.
May 12 1864
Dear Col.
if you will be at home at half past 4 o clock
I will Call & see you.
I have the honor to be,
Respectfully
your obedient servant
Sergt Prince Rivers

I hope your name shall never be out of the papers of the 1st South

As his colonel packed to leave the army, Rivers wrote to say that he would stop in to say goodbye. On the back of the letter Higginson has written: "I hope your name shall never be out of the papers of the 1st South." Rivers to Higginson, May 12, 1864, Higginson, Thomas Wentworth, 1823–1911. Correspondence, 1863–1864, D. Higginson Papers, Houghton Library, Harvard University.

Late in his long life, Thomas Wentworth Higginson, Rivers's old commander, sat at his desk in Cambridge, Massachusetts, sorting his papers for posterity. Among his correspondence, he came across a letter, written in Rivers's own hand. It was the letter Rivers had sent in 1864 arranging for the two men to have a moment to say a proper goodbye. Rereading the letter and stirred by its memory, Higginson turned the paper over and penciled a note on the back: "I hope your name shall never be out of the papers of the 1st South."[22]

We know nothing of Higginson's state of mind when he wrote it. We do know that he penciled nothing like it in the rest of his correspondence. We can also imagine what he meant: Here is a name that might be forgotten, but it never should. Higginson was a student of history; he was also mortal. For all that he'd done to advance the cause of interracial democracy in the United States, he knew some things remain to posterity. This is why a simple note, penciled on the back of a letter among thousands, written to someone long dead, really matters.

We all die twice: first when our heart stops, and then again when no one living bothers to whisper our name. This is the funny thing about time. In the churn of history, some names descend into mud; others buoy back to the surface. If we all die twice, Prince Rivers isn't truly dead. His destiny is not fixed but still unfolding. He put his stamp on his age. He made the USCT a success. He built the greatest experiment in interracial democracy this country has ever known. Rivers never walked but bestrode the land. He will be on a stamp one day. He will be on a bill. He will be on the big screen. Our role is to get out of his way and give him some room. Because here he comes.[23]

Prince Rivers died the first time, of Bright's disease, on April 10, 1887. I have no idea what went through his mind as he passed. I like to think it was a pledge to live twice. I like to think he unhooked his carriage horse for the last time and mounted. I like to think he galloped to everlasting freedom. And I like to think, in the collective breath of horse and man, he began humming one of his regiment's favorite hymns:

> I have known moon-rise . . .
> And I have known star-rise . . .
> And I have walked in the moonlight . . .

And I have walked in the starlight . . .
And I have walked in the graveyard . . .
And I have walked through the graveyard
And now I lie in a grave and stretch out my arms
And I lay this body down
And one day my soul will meet your soul
When you lay your body down.[24]

ACKNOWLEDGMENTS

Every book is its own Sisyphean challenge. In *The Original Black Panther*, I was trying to resurrect a superior human who left inferior records. At times, I wondered whether a full biography of Prince Rivers was even possible. Then I read Tiya Miles's *All That She Carried*, and there were no more excuses.

Acts of resurrection are never the work of the resurrectionist alone. Scholars in their own right, archivists and public historians are the lifeblood of my profession; they know more than most of us academics do, and they share their knowledge with more selfless delight and enthusiasm. In chasing Rivers across the country, I am especially indebted to Robert Adams, director of the Penn Center National Historic Landmark District; Chris Barr and Richard Condon, rangers at Reconstruction Era National Historical Park; Tonya Guy, archivist at the Edgefield County Archives; Wayne O'Bryant, chairman of the Hamburg-Carrsville African-American Heritage District; Lauren Virgo, executive director of the Aiken County Historical Museum; Emily Walhout, reference assistant at the Houghton Library at Harvard University; and Corey Rogers at the Lucy Craft Laney Museum of Black History in Augusta.

Professional friends and colleagues also shared critical research and insights from their toil in neighboring fields. I am particularly indebted to Jared Asser, Melissa DeVelvis, Angela Elder, Wyatt Erchak, Steven Hahn, John Hayes, Kathleen Hilliard, Stephen Kenny, Valinda Littlefield, Kurt Luther, Barbara McCaskill, Lawrence McDonnell, Mary Rolinson, Manisha Sinha, Michael Tadman, and Amy Murrell Taylor. At UGA, close colleagues Nicholas Allen, Cindy Hahamovitch, Stephen Mihm, Scott Nelson, and Scott Nesbit either read drafts or participated in conversations so long they probably felt like they had.

My original idea had been to present Rivers's life as a graphic history, which I still intend to do. My deepest thanks go out to artist Tim Fielder and letterer Leo McGovern for our epic collaboration and all the fun we've had along the way. I also want to thank Andrew Fialka for pushing me (and the profession) to tell our stories in new ways.

At the University of Georgia Press, I have had the steadfast support of Executive Editor Mick Gusinde-Duffy, who championed this project from the beginning. I am indebted also to UGA Press Director Lisa Bayer, who saw the vision of bringing both the bio and the graphic to Georgia Press. Glen Pawelski produced the awesome maps for the volume; Jon Davies and Anne Coulling saved me from many infelicities and errors in copyediting. Profound thanks too to the National Endowment for the Humanities for funding the final sprint to the finish line.

Closest to home, I want to thank my family. At a preternatural age, my siblings and I decided we wanted to be an American version of the Brontës without all the TB. Not (yet) the Brontës and not (yet) stricken with TB, I guess we all have work (yet) to do. My son Will has grown to honorable manhood, and I love him with my whole heart. My daughter Winnie is a ball of pure sunshine. My wife Nell is my all-in-all.

Finally, I want to thank "The Black Prince" himself. In ways I hadn't anticipated, we wrote this book together. Rivers may not have left a strong written record, but he left a strong impression. In reading his "archive of action," I found myself almost conversing with him: "Now, why are you doing that?" and "What's behind your thinking here?" Always his answers revealed political and logistical realities I had never fully considered, and it is fair to say he taught me more about Reconstruction than any scholar ever. As in life, so in this book, Rivers blazed the trail. I close the book because the trail has ended, and it is time for me to mourn the loss of my friend. "Now cracks a noble heart. Good night, sweet Prince / And flights of angels sing thee to thy rest."

NOTES

Preface

1. Historians have long discussed the significance of naming practices among the enslaved. On the one side are those who emphasize the persistence of African naming practices through generations of enslavement. On the other side are those who see a rising tide of enslavers' insistence on naming enslaved children themselves. See especially John C. Inscoe, "Carolina Slave Names: An Index to Acculturation," *Journal of Southern History* 49, no. 4 (November 1983): 527–54.

2. Sojourner Truth, *Narrative of Sojourner Truth, a Bondswoman of Olden Time* (Battle Creek, Mich., 1881), 140; Philip S. Foner, ed., *Frederick Douglass: Selected Speeches and Writings* (Chicago Review Press, 1999), 196.

3. The question of how to build Black biography amid a dearth or biased set of sources is an open one. John Ernest suggests that we need to "reimagine biography altogether"—moving away from individual figures (who are often well documented solely because they worked in unusual proximity to whites) and toward prosopography and community studies that help us to locate Black figures within wider Black networks. (Digital approaches, he suggests, can be especially fruitful in allowing us to aggregate enough fragmentary records that we can begin to see the "complexly contextualized and interconnected lives" of ordinary Black people.) Saidiya Hartman adopts a different approach, one she calls "critical fabulation"—a sort of moral meditation or sponsored melancholia in which we sift through the "detritus of lives," licensed to "imagine what cannot be verified," and write the history of an "unrecoverable past." "How does one tell impossible stories?" Hartman asks. "By playing with and rearranging the basic elements of the story, by re-presenting the sequence of events in divergent stories and from contested points of view." The result, she says, is a "history written with and against the archive," highlighting the ways in which our own age remains tethered to earlier ones.

This book borrows from both approaches. From Ernest I have adopted the spirit of "reimagining biography" and embraced the emphasis on independent Black networks and communities. From Hartman I have borrowed the willingness to push back against the archive in acts of imaginative reconstruction. More generally, I think we should give our subjects a "say" in the forms their own lives take in the retelling. Rivers seems the type of man who would be happy to be judged on the basis of his actions—hence the "archive of action." See John Ernest, "Life Beyond Biography: Black Lives and Biographical Research," *Commonplace* 17, no. 1 (Fall 2016), https://commonplace.online/article/life-beyond-biography/; Saidiya Hartman, "Venus in Two Acts," *Small Axe* 12, no. 2 (June 2008): 1–14; Maria R. Montalvo, *Enslaved Archives: Slavery, Law, and the Production of the Past* (Johns Hopkins University Press, 2024).

4. "Choked voice": Thomas Wentworth Higginson, *Army Life in a Black Regiment* (Penguin Classics, 1994), 41; "This is our time!": *The Independent* (vol. 14, no. 730), November 27, 1862, 1.

The Coachman

1. Will Durant, *The Story of Philosophy: The Lives and Opinions of the Greater Philosophers* (Simon and Schuster, 1926), 87.

2. *Charleston Mercury*, February 1, 1868, 1.

3. "War-Time Letters from Seth Rogers, M.D. Surgeon of the First South Carolina Afterwards the Thirty-Third U.S.C.T. 1862–1863," *Florida History Online* [hereafter Rogers, "War-Time Letters"], accessed November 26, 2024, https://history.domains.unf.edu/floridahistoryonline/projects-proj-b-p-html/cir-index-htm/war-time-letters-from-seth-rogers/.

4. "Young Bloods": Sherman to Henry W. Halleck, September 17, 1863, in *Sherman's Civil War: Selected Correspondence of William T. Sherman, 1860–1865*, ed. Brooks D. Simpson and Jean V. Berlin (University of North Carolina Press, 1999), 545–46; "scarcely sit their horses": H. C. B. Rogers, *The Confederates and Federals at War* (Ian Allan, 1973), 51. Both are quoted in James McPherson, *Ordeal by Fire: The Civil War and Reconstruction* (McGraw Hill, 2010).

5. Frederick Douglass, *Narrative of the Life of Frederick Douglass, An American Slave, As Written by Himself* (London, 1852), 10. The significant exceptions to "Blacks walked, whites rode" were the Black jockeys in the South. For more, see Kathleen Mooney, *Race Horse Men: How Slavery and Freedom Were Made at the Racetrack* (Harvard University Press, 2014).

6. Edw. S. Philbrick to Edw. L. Pierce Esq., March 27, 1862, vol. 19, #106, Port Royal correspondence, 5th Agency, RG 366, as quoted in *The Destruction*

of Slavery, ed. Ira Berlin, Barbara J. Fields, Thavolia Glymph, Joseph P. Reidy, and Leslie S. Rowland, series 1, vol. 1, *Freedom: A Documentary History of Emancipation, 1861–1867* (Cambridge University Press, 1985), 175, https://www.freedmen.umd.edu/.

7. "One long dream": Solomon Northup, *Twelve Years a Slave: Narrative of Solomon Northup, a Citizen of New-York, Kidnapped in Washington City in 1841, and Rescued in 1853* (London, 1853), 260; "feelings were all centered": William Wells Brown, *The Black Man, His Antecedents, His Genius, and His Achievements* (New York, 1863), 76; "thought and dreamed": Lewis Garrard Clarke, *Narrative of the Sufferings of Lewis Clarke, During a Captivity of More than Twenty-Five Years, Among the Algerines of Kentucky, One of the So Called Christian States of America. Dictated by Himself* (Boston, 1845), 31.

8. Guion Griffis Johnson, *A Social History of the Sea Islands* (University of North Carolina Press, 1930), 4.

9. Ibid.

10. See *Beaufort County Atlas*, accessed November 27, 2024, https://www.beaufortcountysc.gov/planning/documents/Sept2021%20Beaufort%20County%20Atlas-2.pdf, p. 30.

11. See especially Daniel C. Littlefield, *Rice and Slaves: Ethnicity and the Slave Trade in Colonial South Carolina* (University of Illinois Press, 1991); Margaret Belser Hollis and Allen H. Stokes, eds., *Twilight on the South Carolina Rice Fields: Letters of the Heyward Family, 1862–1871* (University of South Carolina Press, 2010); Peter H. Wood, *Black Majority: Race, Rice, and Rebellion in South Carolina, 1670–1740* (Norton, 1974).

12. On the natural history of Beaufort, see especially Theodore Rosengarten, *Tombee: Portrait of a Cotton Planter* (University of South Carolina Press, 1994), 37–60; Johnson, *Social History*, 17–30. For a full history of Beaufort before the Civil War, see Lawrence S. Rowland, Alexander Moore, and George C. Rogers Jr., *The History of Beaufort County, South Carolina, Volume 1, 1514–1861* (University of South Carolina Press, 1996).

13. Gilbert P. Voigt, "The 'Periclean Age' of Beaufort," *South Carolina Historical Magazine* 58, no. 4 (October 1957), 218–23; quotation p. 218.

14. William Grayson quoted in Willie Lee Nichols Rose, *Rehearsal for Reconstruction: The Port Royal Experiment* (University of Georgia Press, 1999), 116.

15. William Elliott to Ann Elliott, September 9, 1854, in Beverly Scafidel, "The Letters of William Elliott," PhD diss., University of South Carolina, 1978, 694, 780.

16. William Elliott, *Carolina Sports by Land and Water: Including Incidents*

of Devil-Fishing, Wildcat, Deer, and Bear Hunting, Etc. (University of South Carolina Press, 1994), 101–2.

17. "Plainest people": The full quotation runs: "In proportion to their Fortunes, they are the plainest people I ever meet with, [one woman said of Beaufort's leading men]. [They are] wholly attentive to the Cultivation of Indigo, the profits of which article is most expended in the purchase of Negroes, & nothing is so much coveted as the pleasure of possessing many slaves. These singularities are inherited from their Fore-Fathers—& many follow so closely in the path thru which their Ancestors trod as to deny themselves the Comforts & conveniences of life." See Johnson, *Social History*, 105. "He could not relax": Rosengarten, *Tombee*, 149.

18. "These sands are full of fiddler-crab holes," noted the Freedmen's Bureau teacher Laura Towne, "and are at low tide the resort of negro children with tubs on their heads, crabbing." See Rupert Sargent Holland, ed., *Letters and Diary of Laura M. Towne, Written from the Sea Islands of South Carolina, 1862–1884* (Riverside Press, 1912) [hereafter Towne, *Letters and Diary*], 3. "This land is our family": Queen Quet, "Water Is Life: Climate Change and Cultural Strife," *Gullah/Geechee Nation*, November 19, 2016, https://gullahgeecheenation.com/2016/11/19/water-is-life-climate-change-and-cultural-strife/.

19. "We don't care": The quote continues: "Their morals and manners are in their own keeping." Basil Hall, *Travels in North America in the Years 1827 and 1828* (Edinburgh, 1829), 191. Edda Fields-Black points out in *Combee* that when the raiders disembarked at their first plantation, the enslaved were already in the fields. It was 4 a.m. See Edda L. Fields-Black, *Combee: Harriet Tubman, the Combahee River Raid, and Black Freedom During the Civil War* (Oxford University Press, 2024).

20. Johnson, *Social History*, 127.

21. This saying features prominently in the Ibo Landing historical marker on St. Simons Island, where at least ten Africans drowned rather than be enslaved. See "Ibo Landing: The Legacy of Resisting Enslavement," *Georgia Historical Society*, accessed November 27, 2024, https://www.georgiahistory.com/ghmi_marker_updated/ibo-landing-the-legacy-of-resisting-enslavement/.

22. Rivers's service file includes these details: "DESCRIPTION Age 40 years; height 5 feet 10 inches. Complexion Dark Eyes Light. Hair Curly. Where born Beaufort, S.C. Occupation House-Svt." See Isabel Vandervelde, *Aiken County: The Only South Carolina County Founded During Reconstruction* (Reprint Company, 1999), 149. "Features are not very African": Rogers, "War-Time Letters," February 5, 1863; Rogers's description continues: "Prince Rivers . . . has

a peculiar fineness of texture of skin that gives [him] the most cleanly look . . . and his eye so bright that it must 'shine at night, when de moon am gone away.'" "Raised in the white folks' house": From the deposition of Rivers's daughter, Pattie White, in Vandervelde, *Aiken County*, 152–53.

23. Vandervelde, *Aiken County*, 158–59. Adding to the mystery is Rivers's choice of surname. There were many Rivers families in and around Beaufort, but how he was related to them is unknown. The work on his genealogy is ongoing.

24. Douglass, *Narrative*, 1.

25. "The sweet cake": Frederick Douglass, *My Bondage and My Freedom* (New York, 1855), 53; "after he got his freedom": "Fred Douglass Eulogized," *Washington Post*, February 19, 1896, 2; "birthdays belong": "Old Men Can Be As Bashful As Young Men: An Address Delivered in Washington, D.C., on February 28, 1888," Frederick Douglass Papers Project, Indiana University–Purdue University Indianapolis, https://frederickdouglasspapersproject.com/item/18935.

26. Vandervelde, *Aiken County*, 150.

27. "THE 43rd PRESIDENT; In His Own Words," *New York Times*, December 14, 2000, 23.

28. *Charleston Mercury*, February 1, 1868, 1.

29. As Higginson said of Rivers, "He is a man of distinguished appearance, and in old times was the crack coachman of Beaufort, in which capacity he once drove Beauregard from this plantation to Charleston, I believe." Thomas Wentworth Higginson, *Army Life in a Black Regiment* (Penguin Classics, 1994), 43.

30. Higginson, *Army Life*, 43; Vandervelde, *Aiken County*, 152; Douglass, *Narrative*, 39.

31. Rainer Maria Rilke, *Selected Poems*, trans. Albert Ernest Flemming (Routledge, 1990), 110.

32. Douglass, *Narrative*, 64.

33. *Charleston Mercury*, February 1, 1868, 1.

34. See Marie Jenkins Schwartz, *Birthing a Slave: Motherhood and Medicine in the Antebellum South* (Harvard University Press, 2010); R. J. Knight, "Mothering and Labour in the Slaveholding Households of the Antebellum American South," *Past & Present* 246 (December 2020): 145–66. See also Deirdre Cooper Owens, *Medical Bondage: Race, Gender, and the Origins of American Gynecology* (University of Georgia Press, 2018).

35. "To present a petition": Higginson, *Army Life*, 38. On slavery petitions generally, see the digital project begun by Loren Schweninger, *Race and Slavery*

Petitions, accessed November 27, 2024, https://dlas.uncg.edu/petitions/. On the enslaved as economic actors, especially as consumers, see Kathleen Hilliard, *Masters, Slaves, and Exchange: Power's Purchase in the Old South* (Cambridge University Press, 2014).

36. "The Governor sent him home": Virginia M. Adams, ed., *On the Altar of Freedom: A Black Soldier's Civil War Letters from the Front* (University of Massachusetts Press, 1991), 27; "the power of the master": Mark V. Tushnet, *Slave Law in the American South: State v. Mann in History and Literature* (University Press of Kansas, 2003), 3–4.

37. On the lasting political traditions among the enslaved in rural areas, see Steven Hahn, *A Nation Under Our Feet: Black Political Struggles in the Rural South from Slavery to the Great Migration* (Belknap, 2005). On the Civil War as a labor strike, see especially W. E. B. Du Bois, *Black Reconstruction in America: Toward a History of the Part Which Black Folk Played in the Attempt to Reconstruct Democracy in America, 1860–1880* (1935; repr., Free Press, 1998).

38. Scott Reynolds Nelson, "Livestock, Boundaries, and Public Space in Spartanburg: African American Men, Elite White Women, and the Spectacle of Conjugal Relations," in *Sex, Love, Race: Crossing Boundaries in North American History*, ed. Martha Hodes (NYU Press, 1999), 315. On the enslaved living in self-constituted "neighborhoods," see Anthony E. Kaye, *Joining Places: Slave Neighborhoods in the Old South* (University of North Carolina Press, 2007).

39. Adams, *On the Altar of Freedom*, 27.

40. Ibid.

41. "Left the United States": See Gregory A. Freeman, *Lay This Body Down: The 1921 Murders of Eleven Plantation Slaves* (Chicago Review Press, 1999), 67; "and people talk": Mary Boykin Chesnut, *A Diary from Dixie* (D. Appleton, 1914), 38.

42. P. J. Staudenraus, "Occupied Beaufort, 1863: A War Correspondent's View," *South Carolina Historical Magazine* 64, no. 3 (July 1963) [hereafter Brooks, "Occupied Beaufort"]: 136–44.

43. See Michael Bonner and Peter McCord, *The Union Blockade in the American Civil War: A Reassessment* (University of Tennessee Press, 2021).

44. "Street-like lines": Michael D. Coker, *The Battle of Port Royal* (History Press, 2009), 24. See also Rowland et al., *History of Beaufort*, 443–59; Rosengarten, *Tombee*, 214–24.

45. Coker, *Battle of Port Royal*, 24–28.

46. Brooks, "Occupied Beaufort," 138.

47. Towne, *Letters and Diary*, 27.

48. Brooks, “Occupied Beaufort,” 140.

49. See Cory Callahan, “‘The Day of the Big Gun Shoot’: The Union Occupation of Beaufort and the Rise of the 1st South Carolina Volunteers,” *The Alexandrian* 13, no. 1 (2024). “Much is written about this ‘Port Royal Experiment,’” Callahan rightly notes; “however, little literature exists on one of the greatest achievements during the experiment: the creation of the 1st South Carolina Volunteers.”

50. Brooks, “Occupied Beaufort,” 140.

51. On the varied ways the enslaved found freedom, see the digital project *Visualizing Emancipation*, Digital Scholarship Lab, University of Richmond, accessed November 27, 2024, https://dsl.richmond.edu/emancipation/.

52. Eastman Johnson, *A Ride for Liberty—The Fugitive Slaves (recto)*, Brooklyn Museum, accessed November 27, 2024, https://www.brooklynmuseum.org/opencollection/objects/495.

53. The bounty on Rivers was ten times the typical reward offered for the return of a runaway slave. One study of runaway ads in neighboring North Carolina concludes: “Rewards ranged from two dollars to one hundred, whereas the actual value of a slave in neighboring states averaged around $350.” See Olivia Carlisle, “Trends in the Runaway Slave Advertisements,” Digital Library on American Slavery, accessed December 2, 2024, https://dlas.uncg.edu/notices/trends/. “A placard”: Higginson, *Army Life*, 43. On the feelings of enslavers at the dissolution of their illusions, see Erin Austin Dwyer, *Mastering Emotions: Feelings, Power, and Slavery in the United States* (University of Pennsylvania Press, 2021).

The Soldier

1. See Willie Lee Nichols Rose, *Rehearsal for Reconstruction: The Port Royal Experiment* (University of Georgia Press, 1999); Vernon Burton, *Penn Center: A History Preserved* (University of Georgia Press, 2017); Howard C. Westwood and John Y. Simon, *Black Troops, White Commanders and Freedmen During the Civil War* (Southern Illinois University Press, 1992), 58.

2. “They believed”: Pauli Murray, *Proud Shoes: The Story of an American Family* (Beacon Press, 1999), 169–70; “steady eagerness”: Rupert Sargent Holland, ed., *Letters and Diary of Laura M. Towne, Written from the Sea Islands of South Carolina, 1862–1884* (Riverside Press, 1912) [hereafter Towne, *Letters and Diary*], 281. Higginson was similarly astonished by the freedmen’s thirst for education: “Their love of the spelling-book is perfectly inexhaust-

ible,—they stumbling on by themselves, or the blind leading the blind, with the same pathetic patience which they carry into everything." Thomas Wentworth Higginson, *Army Life in a Black Regiment* (Penguin Classics, 1994), 19. See also Ronald E. Butchart, *Schooling the Freed People: Teaching, Learning and the Struggle for Black Freedom, 1861–1876* (University of North Carolina Press, 2010), 2–6.

3. Whether Hunter's men were absolutely the "first Black troops" of the Civil War is open to interpretation. Technically African Americans could not be employed in federal service before the Second Confiscation and Militia Act of July 17, 1862, which authorized Lincoln to accept Black persons into service for whatever purpose "he may judge best for the public welfare." Preoccupied by the need to find legal cover for emancipation, and worried that arming Black people would alienate the loyal slave states, Lincoln was disinclined to formalize Black service of any kind. Hunter, then, was well in front of the administration when he began freeing and enlisting enslaved people in his district on May 9, 1862. Probably free Blacks in New Orleans were being organized at about the same time, but as Thomas Wentworth Higginson later noted, they were fundamentally different from a regiment of freed slaves. "These pages record some of the adventures of the First South Carolina Volunteers," begins Higginson's *Army Life in a Black Regiment*, "the first slave regiment mustered into the service of the United States during the late civil war. It was, indeed, the first colored regiment of any kind so mustered, except a portion of the troops raised by Major General Butler at New Orleans. These scarcely belonged to the same class, however, being recruited from the free colored population of that city, a comparatively self-reliant and educated race. 'The darkest of them,' said General Butler, 'were about the complexion of the late Mr. [Daniel] Webster.' The First South Carolina, on the other hand, contained scarcely a freeman, had not one mulatto in ten, and a far smaller proportion who could read or write when enlisted. The only contemporary regiment of a similar character was the 'First Kansas Colored,' which began recruiting a little earlier, though it was not mustered in—the usual basis of military seniority—till later." See Higginson, "Appendix B: The First Black Soldiers," *Army Life*, 211–15.

If the First South Carolina were the first Black troops, was Rivers himself the first of the first, meaning the *very first* to join? This question is also the subject of debate. There is no question that he was *among* the first, which would make sense. He was already on the ground at Port Royal when Hunter first began recruiting, and he would be the one Hunter took north as his exemplary Black sergeant. Wyatt Erchak, however, makes a good case that the distinction of being first of the first belongs to William Bronson, who is listed at the top on Hunter's first roster. For more, see Wyatt Erchak, "William Bronson," National Park Service, last updated April 12, 2024, https://www.nps.gov/people/william-bronson.htm.

4. "The Freed Blacks of South Carolina," *The Liberator*, August 8, 1862.

5. See John Bicknell, *The Pathfinder and the President: John C. Frémont, Abraham Lincoln, and the Battle for Emancipation* (Stackpole, 2025).

6. "Sabbath day": *Report of the Proceedings of a Meeting Held at Concert Hall, Philadelphia: On Tuesday Evening, November 3, 1863* (Philadelphia, 1863), 22. On the degree to which the Union army became abolitionized from the ground up, see Chandra Manning, *What This Cruel War Was Over: Soldiers, Slavery, and the Civil War* (Random House, 2007).

7. "I confess": quoted in Stephen W. Sears, *George B. McClellan: The Young Napoleon* (Ticknor & Fields, 1988), 116; "most excellent fellow": quoted in Stanley P. Hirshson, *The White Tecumseh: A Biography of William T. Sherman* (Wiley, 1997), 298; "remember, it requires": "Letters of Dr. Seth Rogers, 1862, 1863," *Proceedings of the Massachusetts Historical Society, Third Series* 43 (October 1909–June 1910) [hereafter "Rogers Letters"], 346. Raised by a Quaker farmer in Vermont, Seth Rogers had been steeped in abolition from an early age. Removed to Worcester, Massachusetts, before the war, he became resident doctor of the Worcester Hydropathic Institution, where he met the Black poet and activist Charlotte Forten and befriended Thomas Wentworth Higginson. When he took over the First South Carolina, Higginson asked Rogers to join him to attend to the medical needs of men. "In our camp," wrote Rogers, "the most curious problems present themselves, as how to keep people from scurvy without vegetables and fresh meat; how to have a good fire in tents without a fireplace, stove or ventilation; how to make bread without yeast and without oven. How to treat the sick without medicines,—how to amputate limbs without knives, all these and many other similarly knotty questions the surgeon of the First Regiment of S.C. Vol's. has to consider,—sometimes when he ought to be sleeping." "War-Time Letters from Seth Rogers, M.D. Surgeon of the First South Carolina Afterwards the Thirty-Third U.S.C.T. 1862–1863," January 18, 1863, *Florida History Online* [hereafter Rogers, "War-Time Letters"], accessed November 26, 2024, https://history.domains.unf.edu/floridahistoryonline/projects-proj-b-p-html/cir-index-htm/war-time-letters-from-seth-rogers/.

8. "Taken by General Hunter": Higginson, *Army Life*, 43; "Serg't Rivers": Rogers, "War-Time Letters," January 3, 1863. A South Carolina newspaper may be referring to the same event when it notes that after Rivers was recruited, "he

subsequently visited New York, where he was a hero. He addressed a meeting in that city, and, be it said to his credit, he gave the most correct and truthful statement about slavery as it existed in the South that his audience ever listened to." See Isabel Vandervelde, *Aiken County: The Only South Carolina County Founded During Reconstruction* (Reprint Company, 1999), 141.

9. Charles Anderson Wickliffe (1788–1869) was a former Kentucky governor and U.S. postmaster general. In 1861 he was elected to Congress from Kentucky's Fifth District, located in the Appalachian, southeast section of the state, a district that was (and continues to be) dominated by conservative poor whites. Wickliffe was apparently not in the chamber when Hunter's formal reply was read to peals of laughter from Republicans. On July 3, 1862, Owen Lovejoy, representative from Illinois, rose to call for an encore performance. "Inasmuch as the gentleman from Kentucky [Mr. Wickliffe] was absent attending a secession meeting when General Hunter's reply to his resolution was received," Lovejoy said, "I wish to ask the consent of the House that that reply may be read again this morning [Laughter]." Wickliffe was not amused: "I do not want it read for my benefit. I intend to answer it at the proper time."

Two days later a resolution was offered formally condemning the tone and spin of Hunter's remarks: "Resolved, That the sentiments contained in the paper read to this body . . . approving the arming of slaves, emanating from Major General D. Hunter, clothed in discourteous language, are an indignity to the American Congress, an insult for the American people and our brave soldiers in arms, for which sentiments, so uttered, he justly merits our condemnation and censure." This led to a heated discussion, particularly between Robert Mallory, representative of Kentucky, and Thaddeus Stevens, representative of Pennsylvania. "I shrink from arming the slave," said Mallory, "using him to shoot down white men, knowing his depraved nature as I do. I would as soon think of enlisting an Indian, and of arming him with the tomahawk and scalping knife, to be let loose upon our rebellious countrymen, as to arm the negro on this contest."

Stevens then replied: "There are many things in the conduct of this war of which I cannot approve. I cannot approve of setting generals who sympathize with slavery at the head of our armies, or setting our generals, under express orders, to pursue and return fugitives from traitors. I cannot consent to that portion of the conduct of the war which sets our armies to watch the property of rebel soldiers in arms against us." Later he said of Black troops: "I am for putting them in the front rank of this battle. I would raise a hundred thousand of them to-morrow. . . . History tells us that they make the best and most docile soldiers in the world. They are not barbarians in nature. They are a people as well calculated to be humanized as any other. From the time of Homer to the present time, the 'blameless sons of Ethiopia' has been a proverb. It is false to say that they are not capable of being made good soldiers and humane soldiers. In St. Domino the slaves, while fighting for liberty, saved their white masters, and sent off many who escaped. Where they could not help it, they killed their masters, as they had a right to do. Sir, I would put these slaves in the front of the battle."

"General Hunter has organized": Cong. Globe, 37th Cong., 2d Sess., Part 3 (June 9, 1862), 2620–21; "I wish to ask" and "I do not want it read": Cong. Globe, 37th Cong., 2d Sess., Part 4 (July 3, 1862), 3102; "Resolved, That": Cong. Globe, 37th Cong., 2d Sess., Part 4 (July 5, 1862), 3109.

10. "Members of Hunter's regiment": John G. Nicolay and John Hay, *Abraham Lincoln: A History* (New York, 1890), 6:444. Higginson's assessment is basically accurate, if made more harsh by his competitiveness and lingering sense that, as incoming colonel, he had inherited some of the ill feelings Hunter had bred. After a bad day with the regiment, for instance, Higginson vented his frustrations about their former commander: "The trouble is in the legacy of bitter distrust bequeathed by the abortive regiment of General Hunter into which they were driven like cattle, kept for several months in camp, and then turned off without a shilling, by order of the War Department. The formation of that regiment was, on the whole, a great injury to this one." The *New York Herald* concurred that not one but many factors doomed the regiment, noting that "General Hunter's experiment . . . was a great[er] parliamentary than military success. There was still too much prejudice in the army itself, and particularly among army officers, against such an innovation. The blacks did not come forward freely to enlist, and when the general undertook to compel them by drafting, it confirmed in their minds the stories which had been told them that it was a renewed slavery; that they were to be sold to Cuba; that they were to be placed in the front rank of battle for slaughter, and many other direful predictions. Under such conditions, though the regiment was formed, it was beset by desertion, by neglect, by contempt, and also by the fatal difficulty that under existing regulations the paymaster could not recognize it. From all these causes it languished, and was, with the exception of one company, formally disbanded about three months afterwards." Seth Rogers disagreed: There was only one problem—the government had recruited a regiment of former slaves, put them to work, and then failed to pay them. "The real drawback to enlistments," he said, "is that the poor fellows who were in the Hunter regiment have never been paid a cent by the Government."

"The trouble is in": Higginson, *Army Life*, 12; "General Hunter's experiment": *New York Herald*, August 16, 1862; "the real drawback": "Rogers Letters," 344. Seth Rogers attested to Prince Rivers's support of aggressive recruiting: "I find my hatred of slop philanthropy deepened by living with these intensely human children. While I reverence them more and more, I am more and more convinced that Robert Sutton and Prince Rivers were in the right when they said at Alberti's Mills: 'That man down know what is good for him. You know that freedom is better dan slavery for him and you ought to force him to away wid us.' The most intelligent men in our regiment urge the policy of conscription on the same ground, and that it will give them a 'chance to get sense.'" "Rogers Letters," 394.

11. See Higginson, "Appendix B," *Army Life*.

12. *New York Herald*, August 16, 1862.

13. "He prided himself": Brenda Wineapple, *White Heat: The Friendship of Emily Dickinson and Thomas Wentworth Higginson* (Knopf, 2009), 93; "had an invitation": Higginson, *Army Life*, 2.

14. "The only Phi Beta Kappa": Quoted in Edward J. Renehan, *The Secret Six: The True Tale of the Men Who Conspired with John Brown* (University of South Carolina Press, 1997), 84–85. On Anthony Burns, see Virginia Hamilton, *Anthony Burns: The Defeat and Triumph of a Fugitive Slave* (Laurel Leaf, 1993); Gordon S. Barker, *The Imperfect Revolution: Anthony Burns and the Landscape of Race in Antebellum America* (Kent State University Press, 2010).

15. Renehan, *Secret Six*, 64–65.

16. Edward A. Miller Jr., *Lincoln's Abolitionist General: The Biography of David Hunter* (University of South Carolina Press, 1997).

17. "Streaks of lavender": Carl Sandburg, *Abraham Lincoln: The Prairie Years* (Harcourt, Brace, 1926), 266; "the birds are as real": Mary Thacher Higginson, ed., *Letters and Journals of Thomas Wentworth Higginson, 1846–1906* (Houghton Mifflin, 1921), 349;

18. Higginson, *Army Life*, 2.

19. Higginson, *Army Life*, 5. It is one thing to believe in Black liberation; it is another to suddenly be one of the only white faces in a sea of Black ones. In taking over as colonel, Higginson embarked on a journey toward another level of racial consciousness. There is no question that he was committed to ending slavery, but he had not yet been emancipated of all prejudice. He tended, for instance, to see Black people as inherently spiritual, childishly innocent, and Edenic—a nineteenth-century version of what filmmaker Spike Lee has called "the magical negro." "They are simple, docile, and affectionate almost to the

point of absurdity," Higginson noted in his camp diary, "[y]et I should not fear any wanton outrage from them. After all their wrongs, they are not really revengeful; and I would far rather enter a captured city with them than with white troops." This proved prescient, but his reasoning was problematic: He attributed Black restraint to an inherent religiosity and gentleness rather than to a calculated conscience and emotional control. Seth Rogers, who may have had romantic feelings for Black poet Charlotte Forten, came closer to a true understanding: "Every day deepens my conviction that if we are true to them they will be true to us. The Col. arrives at the same conclusion. When I think of their long suffering at the hands of the whites, and then of their readiness to forgive, I feel reverence for the race that I did not know before coming among them."

"They are simple": Higginson, *Army Life*, 8; "Every day deepens": "Rogers Letters," 345.

20. Higginson, *Army Life*, 5–7.

21. "A single mutiny": Higginson, *Army Life*, 5; "discipline must come first": Higginson, *Army Life*, 7. In her journal, Charlotte Forten offers a description of Higginson's camp: "They have a beautiful situation, on the grounds once occupied by a very old fort, 'De La Ribanchine,' built in 1629 or 30. Some of the walls are still standing." See *The Journals of Charlotte Forten Grimké* (Oxford University Press, 1988), 429.

22. Higginson, *Army Life*, 202.

23. Ibid., 43–44.

24. Ibid.

25. Marlene L. Daut, *The First and Last King of Haiti: The Rise and Fall of Henry Christophe* (Knopf, 2025), xiii.

26. Wineapple, *White Heat*, 93–94.

27. The question of John Brown's sanity is a debated one. I would myself ascribe the word "madness" to Brown, and I do not support the controversial conclusions of James Malin's *John Brown and the Legend of '56* (Haskell House, 1982). Here I use the term because I am inhabiting Higginson's mind, and he ascribed the term to Brown.

28. Higginson, *Army Life*, 7.

29. Ibid., 4.

30. As mentioned, the conception of the Civil War as coincident with, even semisynonymous with, a massive labor strike among the enslaved population goes back to W. E. B. Du Bois, *Black Reconstruction in America* (1935). On the political and military context for Lincoln's Preliminary Emancipation Proclamation, see especially Allen C. Guelzo, *Lincoln's Emancipation Proclama-*

tion: The End of Slavery in America (Simon & Schuster, 2006); Glenn David Brasher, *The Peninsula Campaign & the Necessity of Emancipation: African Americans & the Fight for Freedom* (University of North Carolina Press, 2012).

31. Among those who attended the Emancipation Day celebration was Black activist, educator, and poet Charlotte Forten. Born into the robust free Black community of Philadelphia, Forten had been the first Black schoolteacher to join the Port Royal Experiment. A year earlier, she had met Seth Rogers when she traveled to Worcester to visit his water cure facility, and they forged a personal connection. When Rogers arrived at Camp Saxton in December 1862 ahead of the Emancipation Day celebration, the two rekindled their acquaintance and perhaps more. In her diary, Forten speaks often and fondly of Rogers and the time they spent together "taking walks and riding horseback, having dinner, traveling together to nearby plantations, playing chess, reading to one another, and just talking about themselves[,] their work, and literature." It is unclear, however, whether the two were having an affair. The two corresponded, and Rogers sent her gifts, but he also requested that she think of him "as a brother." In 1878 she married Francis James Grimké, pastor of the Fifteenth Street Presbyterian Church in Washington, D.C., and mixed-race nephew of famed abolitionists Sarah and Angelina Grimké. See Brenda Stevenson, "Charlotte Forten (1837–1914)," in *Portraits of American Women: From Settlement to the Present, ed.* G. J. Barker-Benfield and Catherine Clinton (Oxford University Press, 1998), 291–92. "The old year": *The Independent,* November 27, 1862, 1.

32. Christopher Looby, ed., *The Complete Civil War Journal and Selected Letters of Thomas Wentworth Higginson* (University of Chicago Press, 1999) [hereafter Looby, *Journal & Letters*], 88.

33. Grace Bigelow House, "How Freedom Came to Big Pa," *Southern Workman* 45, no. 4 (April 1916): 217–26, Penn School Papers, Southern Historical Collection, University of North Carolina, https://finding-aids.lib.unc.edu/03615/.

34. Ibid.

35. Ibid.

36. "Nothing could have been more unexpected": Rogers Letters, January 1, 1863; "Col. Higginson had [just] received the flag": "Late News," *Circular,* January 22, 1863. Seth Rogers may have explained best what it was like to be in the white audience during the Emancipation Day celebration near Camp Saxton. "After the presentation speech had been made," he wrote home, "and just as Col. Higginson advanced to take the flag and respond, a negro woman standing near began to sing 'America,' and soon many voices of freedmen and

women joined in the beautiful hymn, and sang it so touchingly that every one was thrilled beyond measure. Nothing could have been more unexpected or inspiring. . . . To know what I mean you must stand in the midst of the disenthralled and feel the inspiration of their birth into freedom. For once I heartily cheered for stars and stripes. There is nothing in history more touching and beautiful than the spontaneous outburst of these freed men and women just at the moment when our gallant colonel was receiving the flag of the regiment. None of us had ever heard them sing America, and the most infinite depth and tenderness of 'My country 'tis of thee Sweet land of Liberty,' was inspiring to the last degree. I doubt if our Col. ever spoke so well and he justly attributed inspiration to the unexpected singing of the hymn." Charlotte Forten was similarly overcome by the day's events: "I cannot give a regular chronicle of the day. It is impossible. I was in such a state of excitement. It all seemed and seems still like a brilliant dream." "After the presentation": "Rogers Letters," January 2, 1863; "I cannot give": Ray Allen Billington, "A Social Experiment: The Port Royal Journal of Charlotte L. Forten," *Journal of Negro History* 35, no. 3 (July 1950): 254–55.

There has been speculation, then and now, about the spontaneity of this performance of "My Country, 'Tis of Thee." Certainly, the white teachers at the Penn Center had been teaching their students the song, but the Black attendees chose to sing it, following Polite's lead. No other interpretation makes sense. Obviously, Penn Center personnel would never have deliberately organized a feature for the program that surprised and even discombobulated the attending whites. According to one witness, moreover, it was specifically the sight of Sutton and Rivers taking the flags that elicited the performance: "Mr. French presented to Colonel Higginson for his black regiment two new flags given by Dr. Cheever's church in New York. They were received by Higginson's color-bearers, Corporal Robert Sutton and Sergeant Prince Rivers, both of St. Helena. At this point, the people could not longer contain their joy. Someone in the crowd suddenly began singing 'My Country 'Tis of Thee,' and the entire assemblage burst into song. It was one favorite the blacks had learned well from their white friends and it gave them a perfect outlet for their pent-up emotions." "New Years Day at Port Royal," *New York Tribune*, January 22, 1863, 2.

37. *Free South*, January 10, 1862.

38. Ibid.

39. The Saint Mary's River runs along the eastern border between Georgia and Florida, meandering from its source in the Okefenokee Swamp to its mouth on the Atlantic Ocean at Fernandina Beach, Florida. The town of

Woodstock was a small village forty miles upriver and the source of many of the original bricks for Fort Clinch. "Rebellious to the last degree": "Rogers Letters," 352; "question to solve": "Rogers Letters," 356.

40. Rogers, "War-Time Letters," January 30, 1863.

41. Higginson, *Army Life*, 65–66.

42. William Wells Brown, *Narrative of William W. Brown, An American Slave. Written by Himself* (Charles Gilpin, 1949), 56, 126. On the domestic slave trade, see Steven Deyle, *Carry Me Back: The Domestic Slave Trade in American Life* (Oxford University Press, 2005). On the magistrates and freeholders court system, see Philip N. Racine, "The Spartanburg District Magistrates and Freeholders Court, 1824–1865," *South Carolina Historical Magazine* 87, no. 4 (October 1986), 197–212. On Lewis Robards, see Stephen Berry, *House of Abraham: Lincoln & The Todds, A Family Divided by War* (Houghton Mifflin, 2008).

43. Higginson, *Army Life*, 70.

44. Ibid.

45. Ibid., 76–77.

46. Ibid., 78.

47. Rogers, "War-Time Letters," March 12, 1863.

48. Higginson, *Army Life*, 82.

49. Ibid., 93.

50. Like the Union commanders who occupied Jacksonville before and after him, Higginson had made his headquarters at the Sanderson house. An attorney before the war, John P. Sanderson had built an ostentatious, three-story brick mansion on the corner of Ocean and Forsyth Streets with a double veranda and mounting cupola, a sort of down payment on what the city would become. During the first occupation of Jacksonville, Sanderson had stridden his rose gardens for a last time and then fled the city, telling his servants to seek out the Union commander and show him every courtesy. The house would serve as headquarters for every Union commander in every occupation thereafter. Like many of the South's great houses, the Sanderson mansion was slave made. "Our headquarters are grand," Seth Rogers noted during the First South Carolina's occupations of the city. "The new brick house we occupy was owned by Col. Sanderson, one of the ablest lawyers in the state and one of the most traitorous. . . . I just asked Serg't Hodges if he knew Sanderson. 'Oh yes, I was one of the carpenters who worked many a hard day on that fine house.'" "Our headquarters are grand": "Rogers Letters," 372.

51. Higginson, *Army Life*, 94–95.

52. Higginson described the regiment's encounter with the Blakely in

great detail: "Straining our eyes to look along the reach of level railway which stretched away through the pine barren, we began to see certain ominous puffs of smoke, which might indeed proceed from some fire in the woods, but were at once set down by the men as coming from the mysterious locomotive battery which the Rebels were said to have constructed. Gradually the smoke grew denser, and appeared to be moving up along the track, keeping pace with our motion, and about two miles distant. I watched it steadily through a field-glass from our own slowly moving battery: it seemed to move when we moved and to halt when we halted. Sometimes in the dim smoke I caught a glimpse of something blacker, raised high in the air like the threatening head of some great gliding serpent. Suddenly there came a sharp puff of lighter smoke that seemed like a forked tongue, and then a hollow report, and we could see a great black projectile hurled into the air."

Higginson, *Army Life*, 124–25. "These magnificent specimens": C. R. Horres Jr., "Charleston's Civil War 'Monster Guns,' the Blakely Rifles," *South Carolina Historical Magazine* 97, no. 2 (April 1996), 115–38; "mysterious locomotive battery" and "ten thousand rifles": Higginson, *Army Life*, 124–25. For a description of the wounds among the white regiment, see Stephen Ash, *Firebrand of Liberty: The Story of Two Black Regiments That Changed the Course of the Civil War* (Norton, 2008), 150.

53. "General Hunter is expected": Higginson, *Army Life*, 172; "this is one of the saddest days": "Rogers Letters," 383.

54. *Weekly National Intelligencer*, April 23, 1863, 2.

55. Fortunately for the regiment, the fact that the First South Carolina played no part in the burning of Jacksonville circulated quickly in the public print. The *Boston Journal*, for instance, noted: "The colored regiment had nothing at all to do with it; they behaved with propriety throughout." In a later article the editor lamented: "We know not whether we are most rejoiced or saddened to observe, by the general concurrence of accounts, that the negro soldiers had nothing to do with the barbarous act." These sentiments were echoed by the *New York Tribune*: "The negro troops took no part whatever in the perpetration of this Vandalism." *Boston Journal* and *New York Tribune* articles quoted in Higginson, *Army Life*, 97; "groped his way": Wineapple, *White Heat*, 133–34; "with heavy hearts": Higginson, *Army Life*, 175.

56. Abraham Lincoln to David Hunter, April 1, 1863, Abraham Lincoln Papers, Library of Congress, https://www.loc.gov/item/mal2276700/; "the latter theory": Higginson, *Army Life*, 97.

57. See Anna Berkes, "Wolf by the Ear (Quotation)," Monticello, May 31,

2007, https://www.monticello.org/research-education/thomas-jefferson-encyclopedia/wolf-ear-quotation/.

58. As historian George Fredrickson has persuasively written, the Black image in the white mind was a bifurcated one, a simultaneous projection of white hopes and white fears. In the white mind, Black men were both Sambo (childlike and gentle) and Nat Turner (terrifying and vengeful). The former justified paternalism. The latter justified punishment. Neither embraced the full scope of Black humanity, and both were particularly designed to contain the power of Black masculinity. Consider: The U.S. Army names military hardware after Native Americans (Apache helicopters and Tomahawk missiles) and army bases after Confederate generals (Fort Benning or Fort Bragg). Why? Because those versions of masculinity are culturally vanquished and appropriated. Black masculinity remains unvanquished, lying in wait, barely contained. "I tremble for my country," Jefferson had said, "where I reflect that God is just, that His justice cannot sleep forever."

"When armed," Cong. Globe, 37th Cong., 2d Session, Part 4 (July 5, 1862), 3127; George M. Fredrickson, *The Black Image in the White Mind: The Debate on Afro-American Character and Destiny, 1817–1914* (Wesleyan University Press, 1987); "I tremble": Thomas Jefferson, *Notes on the State of Virginia* (Penguin, 1999), 169.

59. "There is no doubt": Looby, *Journal & Letters*, 145. On Lincoln's decision to enlist Black soldiers, see especially the appendix, "Historians and the Lincoln Administration's Decision for Full-Scale Black Recruitment," in Stephen Ash, *Firebrand of Liberty*, 210–13. "So far, their expedition": *Washington Evening Star*, March 24, 1863, quoted in Ash, *Firebrand of Liberty*, 200.

60. "Rogers Letters," February 1, 1863. On the pressure Higginson felt in the delicacy of the historical moment, see Higginson, *Army Life*, 46–47: "Our success or failure may make or mar the prospects of colored troops. [And yet] military success . . . may depend on a moment's turn of events, and . . . may be determined by some trivial thing, neither to be anticipated nor controlled. All that one can expect is, to do one's best, and to take with equanimity the fortune of war."

61. Higginson, *Army Life*, 202.

62. "This is our time!": *The Independent*, November 27, 1862, 1; "it is extraordinary": *New York Times*, February 25, 1864, 4.

63. "The destiny": Frederick Douglass, "The Future of the Colored Race in America" (1886), in *The Portable Frederick Douglass, ed. John Stauffer and Henry Louis Gates Jr.* (Penguin, 2016), 513; "it is almost impossible": Higginson, *Army Life*, 161.

64. "With the rest": Clinton Cox, *Undying Glory: The Story of the Massachusetts 54th Regiment* (Scholastic, 1991), 98. See also Martin Henry Blatt, Thomas J. Brown, and Donald Yacovone, eds., *Hope & Glory: Essays on the Legacy of the Fifty-Fourth Massachusetts Regiment* (University of Massachusetts Press, 2001); Robert Gould Shaw and Russell Duncan, *Blue-Eyed Child of Fortune: The Civil War Letters of Colonel Robert Gould Shaw* (University of Georgia Press, 1999).

65. The fundamental nature of the Civil War has been debated so endlessly that the war is in danger of an identity crisis. Was the Civil War a grand sequence of battles—as most historians and the lay public understood it from roughly 1865 to 1965? Or was it a "people's war"? A "household war"? A "war of occupation"? A "war of liberation"? Yes. All of the above.

66. Higginson, *Army Life*, 127.

67. Ibid., 130.

68. Ibid., 131.

69. Returned to camp, Higginson was examined by a doctor who believed a shell had passed six inches from his side. Higginson made light of it in a letter home to his wife: "Well dearest I am having a nice lazy time for a week, in a contentment that makes a so called wound appear a great humbug. I feel just as if I had had some mishap at the Gymnasium, lamed my hip a little & weakened me enough for decent excuse for going home." Looby, *Journal & Letters*, 296; "some prize fighter": Higginson, *Army Life*, 136.

70. Higginson, *Army Life*, 134.

71. Ibid., 138.

72. Ibid., 204.

73. Ibid.

74. Ibid., 136. These words belong to Higginson, but he was expressing the feelings of many of his men.

75. The three treasury agents were James Melyn Latta, Hiram Reed, and Lyman Stickney. According to the Library of Congress, "Historians have speculated that their motivations were primarily commercial in nature, and indeed, an estimated quarter of all columns in the *Free South* were filled with notices of federal tax sales. James Gordon Thompson meanwhile contributed fiery editorials that would have hardly endeared the *Free South* to any native Southerners." "A rebel has but two rights": *Free South*, May 16, 1863. See "About the Free South," Library of Congress, accessed November 29, 2024, https://www.loc.gov/item/sn84026962/.

76. Looby, *Journal & Letters*, 348.

77. Ibid., 351.

78. Ibid., 360. On Olustee, see Robert P. Broadwater, *The Battle of Olustee, 1864: The Final Union Attempt to Seize Florida* (McFarland, 2006).

79. Looby, *Journal & Letters*, 358.

80. "The Colonel commanding": General Orders No. 27, May 11, 1864, in "Higginson, Thomas Wentworth, 1823–1911, Correspondence," Harvard University [hereafter Higginson Papers, Harvard], https://hollisarchives.lib.harvard.edu/repositories/24/archival_objects/339798; "as to the war": Higginson to Mary, May 11, 1864, Higginson Papers, Harvard.

81. Tubman to Higginson, September 10, 1864, Higginson Papers, Harvard.

82. "Dear Col.": Rivers to Higginson, May 12, 1864, Higginson Papers, Harvard; "one invalided": Looby, *Journal & Letters*, 360.

83. Special Orders No. 368. October 27, 1864. "The following named officers having tendered their resignations are hereby honorably discharged the service of the United States on account of physical disability. . . . Colonel T. W. Higginson 33d U.S.C. Troops." For other cases where the loss of a colonel had a significant impact on the morale and bearing of a regiment, see Lesley J. Gordon, *Dread Danger: Cowardice and Combat in the American Civil War* (Cambridge University Press, 2024). Gordon argues that the loss of popular colonels Elmer Ellsworth and William Rogers had devastating psychological effects on the Eleventh New York and Second Texas respectively.

84. Trowbridge was also good-looking, which never hurts. See Susie King Taylor, *Reminiscences of My Life in Camp with the 33rd United States Colored Troops, Late 1st South Carolina* (Boston, 1902), 46. Both Trowbridge and Seth Rogers deserve full biographies.

85. Loudon S. Langley to Thomas Wentworth Higginson, August 14, 1864, Higginson Papers, Harvard.

86. Ibid.

87. Ibid.

88. Higginson, *Army Life*, 191.

89. Loudon S. Langley to Thomas Wentworth Higginson, August 14, 1864, Higginson Papers, Harvard.

90. Ibid.

91. "We have the honor": Loudon S. Langley to Thomas Wentworth Higginson, September 2, 1864, Higginson Papers, Harvard; "having commanded": Looby, *Journal & Letters*, 148.

92. "It was one of those instances": Higginson, *Army Life*, 355. The other blow to morale was the simple fact that men like Rivers couldn't rise in the

ranks. "I should have tried to obtain commissions for him and several others before I left the regiment," Higginson noted, "had their literary education been sufficient; and such an attempt was finally made by Lieutenant-Colonel Trowbridge, my successor in immediate command, but it proved unsuccessful. It always seemed to me an insult to those brave men to have novices put over their heads, on the ground of color alone; and the men felt it the more keenly as they remained longer in service." See Higginson, *Army Life*, 349.

93. Don E. Fehrenbacher and Virginia Fehrenbacher, *The Recollected Words of Abraham Lincoln* (Stanford University Press, 1999), 441.

94. William Tecumseh Sherman, *Memoirs of General William T. Sherman by Himself* (New York, 1875), 2:109.

95. Sherman to Grant, October 9, 1864, in Brooks D. Simpson and Jean V. Berlin, *Sherman's Civil War: Selected Correspondence of William T. Sherman, 1860–1865* (University of North Carolina Press, 1999), 731.

96. Sherman to Halleck, September 4, 1864, in *The War of the Rebellion: A Compilation of the Official Records of the Union and Confederate Armies*, ser. 1, v. 38, pt. 5 (Government Printing Office, 1891), 793. Sherman later protested that his letter was never meant for circulation, but he never disavowed its contents. See Michael Fellman, *Citizen Sherman: A Life of William Tecumseh Sherman* (Random House, 1995), 161.

97. Higginson, *Army Life*, 263.

98. Charlotte Forten to Higginson, December 24, 1864, Higginson Papers, Harvard.

99. Joseph T. Glatthaar, *The March to the Sea and Beyond: Sherman's Troops in the Savannah and Carolinas Campaigns* (Louisiana State University Press, 1995).

100. Ira Berlin, Steven F. Miller, Joseph P. Reidy, and Leslie S. Rowland, eds., *The Wartime Genesis of Free Labor: The Upper South Freedom*, series 1, vol. 2, *A Documentary History of Emancipation, 1861–1867* (Cambridge University Press, 1993), 777–78. See also Lawrence T. McDonnell, "Killing Calvin Crozier: Honor, Myth, and Military Occupation After Appomattox," in *Reconstruction Beyond 150: Reassessing the New Birth of Freedom*, ed. Vernon Burton and J. Brent Morris (University of Virginia Press, 2023).

101. "Six Months in the Freedmen's Bureau with a Colored Regiment, Address by Lieut. Col. Chas. Tyler Trowbridge, Thirty-Third Regiment U. S. C. T., October 11, 1904," in *Glimpses of the Nation's Struggle*, sixth series, vol. 31(1), "Papers Read Before the Minnesota Commandery of the Military Order of the Loyal Legion of the United States, January 1903–1908" [hereafter Trowbridge,

"Six Months"], accessed January 4, 2025, http://www.sandersweb.net/ed/TrowbridgePaper.htm.

102. Trowbridge, "Six Months." Trowbridge's recollections are invaluable as they betray a tendency toward reconciliationism and make free use of the N-word, further signs that he hadn't Higginson's "colored man heart."

103. McDonnell, "Killing Calvin Crozier," 274.

104. Trowbridge, "Six Months."

105. Ibid.

106. Ibid. See also Rod Andrew Jr., "In Search of Manse Jolly: Mythology and Facts in the Hunt for a Post–Civil War Guerrilla," in *The Civil War Guerrilla: Unfolding the Black Flag in History, Memory, and Myth*, ed. Joseph M. Beilein Jr. and Matthew C. Hulbert (University Press of Kentucky, 2015).

107. Trowbridge, "Six Months."

108. Hight's accomplices were acquitted. Hight was found guilty but his death sentence was commuted to fifteen years' imprisonment in Auburn, New York. See "Acquittal," *Edgefield Advertiser*, November 15, 1865, 2.

109. Trowbridge, "Six Months."

110. McDonnell was the first to suggest that Rivers and company had purposely blocked the track. See McDonnell, "Killing Calvin Crozier."

111. McDonnell, "Killing Calvin Crozier," 276.

112. Ibid., 277.

113. Ibid., 280.

114. Ibid.

115. Ibid.

116. Ibid., 281.

117. R. G. Crozier to Andrew Johnson, November 4, 1865, Letters Received, Record Group 94: Records of the Adjutant General's Office, National Archives, Washington, D.C.

118. During the war, Perry had served as district attorney and district judge under South Carolina's Confederate government before being appointed provisional governor in June 1865, just two months after Lincoln's assassination. In this role, he had been the whip hand imposing Johnson's preferred version of Reconstruction, resisting both the Thirteenth and Fourteenth Amendments and overseeing the implementation of the new Black Codes, which sought to return the freedmen to a state of serfdom. "You are all now": N. W. Stephenson, "Southern Nationalism in South Carolina in 1851," *American Historical Review* 36, no. 2 (January 1931): 334; "the African": "Letter from Hon. B. F. Perry of South Carolina," *Charleston Daily Courier*, October 1, 1866, 4.

119. Charles T. Trowbridge, 33rd USCT (Case MM3193), November 8, 1865, in Court Martial Case Files, Record Group 153: Records of the Office of the Judge Advocate General, National Archives.

120. Ibid.

121. Ibid.

122. Ibid.

123. Higginson, *Army Life*, 356.

124. After the ceremony the flag would be folded up, sent to the National Archive, and apparently lost.

125. Higginson, Appendix E: "Farewell Address of Lt. Col. Trowbridge," *Army Life.*

126. Samuel G. Morse to Higginson, October 1865, in Higginson Papers, Harvard.

The Legislator

1. Rupert Sargent Holland, ed., *Letters and Diary of Laura M. Towne, Written from the Sea Islands of South Carolina, 1862–1884* (Riverside Press, 1912) [hereafter Towne, *Letters and Diary*], 167.

2. Ibid.

3. "No friend": John Lobb, ed., *The Life and Times of Frederick Douglass from 1817–1882, Written by Himself* (London, 1882), 319; "I know that damned Douglass": Lawanda Cox and John H. Cox, "Johnson and the Negro," in *Andrew Johnson: A Profile,* ed. Eric L. McKitrick (Hill & Wang, 1969), 152–53.

4. Andrew Johnson, from an interview with General John A. Logan on May 31, 1865. See "Andrew Johnson and Reconstruction," National Park Service, accessed December 16, 2024, https://nps.gov/anjo/andrew-johnson-and-reconstruction.htm.

5. While some few whites saw forty acres and a mule as the least the enslaved were owed, others supported Sherman's parcel as something closer to Black reservation. See Claude F. Oubre, *Forty Acres and a Mule: The Freedmen's Bureau and Black Land Ownership* (Louisiana State University Press, 1978).

6. The full text of Rivers's letter reads: "Morris Island, South Carolina. November 26, 1865. General, I have the honor to ask for a[n] understanding. I was told that the Government has given Land to Soldiers. If this land were given will [it] be just for the time being or will [it] be hereafter held by the Soldiers? I would like very much to know if any Part of the Mainland. If so I would like to get a piece on Mr. H. M. Stuart plantation, Oak Point, near

Coosaw River." See Dorothy Sterling, ed., *The Trouble They Seen: The Story of Reconstruction in the Words of African Americans* (Doubleday, 1976), 37.

7. The play in question, *Our American Cousin*, is perhaps more frivolous than terrible. The three-act farce, written by English playwright Tom Taylor, features an American goober coming to England to claim an estate he thinks he is heir to. Booth timed the assassination to a moment when he knew the audience would be laughing.

8. Towne, *Letters and Diary*, 167. On the legal history of Reconstruction's tax titles, see Cynthia Nicoletti, "Robert Smalls's Tax Title and the Endurance of Land Redistribution in Port Royal, South Carolina," in *The War That Made America: Essays Inspired by the Scholarship of Gary W. Gallagher*, ed. Caroline E. Janey, Peter S. Carmichael, and Aaron Sheehan-Dean (University of North Carolina Press, 2024), 141–62.

9. *New South*, June 16, 1866, 2; Towne, *Letters and Diary*, 167.

10. On Black marriages in the period generally, see Tera M. Hunter, *Bound in Wedlock: Slave and Free Black Marriage in the Nineteenth Century* (Belknap Press, 2019); Darlene Goring, "The History of Slave Marriage in the United States," *John Marshall Law Review* (2006): 300–347.

11. In her history of Aiken County, Isabel Vandervelde notes: "Much data is provided from the voluminous pages of [Rivers's pension] file." Unfortunately, that file cannot now be found. Vandervelde offers a full transcriptions testimony given by Louisa Rivers (his second wife) and Pattie White (his daughter) and notes that "three other depositions say that probably Elsie was living with Simmons by the time Prince returned home from the army." See Isabel Vandervelde, *Aiken County: The Only South Carolina County Founded During Reconstruction* (Reprint Company, 1999), 153, 443–44.

12. Rivers's primary duties as color sergeant and provost sergeant were to oversee basic discipline and cleanliness in camp, but he was also tasked with overseeing the regimental jail and running down deserters. He handled these tasks with his usual aplomb, making him few friends among the enlisted men.

13. See Cate Lineberry, *Be Free or Die: The Amazing Story of Robert Smalls' Escape from Slavery to Union Hero* (Picador, 2018).

14. Ibid.

15. Thomas Wentworth Higginson, *Army Life in a Black Regiment* (Penguin Classics, 1994), 48; Edith M. Dabbs, *Sea Island Diary: A History of St. Helena Island* (Reprint Company, 1983), 174.

16. "The Freed Blacks of South Carolina," *The Liberator*, August 8, 1862.

17. Jack Kenny Williams, *Vogues in Villainy: Crime and Retribution in*

Ante-bellum South Carolina (University of South Carolina Press, 1959), 33. See also Elliott J. Gorn, "'Gouge and Bite, Pull Hair and Scratch': The Social Significance of Fighting in the Southern Backcountry," *American Historical Review* 90 (February–December 1985): 18–43.

18. The list of biographies that have grappled with Sickles's political buoyancy includes Garry Boulard, *Daniel Sickles: A Life* (iUniverse, 2019); W. A. Swanberg, *Sickles the Incredible: A Biography* (Butternut and Blue, 1991); Thomas Keneally, *American Scoundrel: The Life of the Notorious Civil War General Dan Sickles* (Doubleday, 2002); and James A. Hessler, *Sickles at Gettysburg: The Controversial Civil War General Who Committed Murder, Abandoned Little Round Top, and Declared Himself the Hero of Gettysburg* (Savas Beatie, 2010). "One of the bigger bubbles": George Templeton Strong, *Diary: The Turbulent Fifties* (Macmillan, 1952), 77.

19. "Letters Received Concerning Recommendations of Persons for Appointment as Registrars of Voters in North and South Carolina, 1867," National Archives, RG 393, part 1, entry 4363, box 2. The author is indebted to Kathleen Hilliard for pointing out this source.

20. Ibid.

21. "Delegates to the Convention.—The following are the delegates elected to the Reconstruction Convention of the State. Of one hundred and twenty whose names are given, fifty-four are white and sixty-three are negroes: . . . Edgefield—George D. Meddes, John Wooley, F. Arnaim (W.), R. C. Elliott, P. R. Rivers, J. Bonum D. Harris (C.)." *Charleston Mercury*, November 30, 1867, 1.

22. "Nothing quite like this": "Great Moments in Black History No. VI: The People's Convention," Lerone Bennet Jr., *Ebony*, February 1976, 64; "the commendation of every lover," *Proceedings of the Constitutional Convention of South Carolina* (Charleston, 1868) [hereafter *Proceedings*], 16; "God help the people": *Proceedings*, 639; "Sketches of the Delegates," *Charleston Mercury*, February 1, 1868, 1.

23. *Proceedings*, 925.

24. Du Bois dubbed the entire Black-led Reconstruction government of South Carolina the "South Carolina Commune." See W. E. B. Du Bois, *Black Reconstruction in America* (1935; repr., Free Press, 1998). "In the teaching of U.S. history," notes American historian Noel Ignatiev, "Reconstruction occupies a position analogous to the Revolution in France or the Khyber Pass in military affairs: whoever controls it controls the terrain below." See Noel Ignatiev, "'The American Blindspot': Reconstruction According to Eric Foner and W.E.B. Du Bois," *Labour / Le Travail* (Spring 1993): 243.

25. See Allen C. Guelzo, *Lincoln's Emancipation Proclamation: The End of Slavery in America* (Simon & Schuster, 2006), 25.

26. *Charleston Mercury*, February 24, 1868, 1.

27. Ibid., 7.

28. Ibid.

29. Ibid., 6.

30. Ibid., 5.

31. *Daily Phoenix* (Columbia, S.C.), January 29, 1869, 4.

32. "Shown his wisdom": *Charleston Mercury*, February 1, 1868, 1; "P.R. Rivers": *Edgefield Advertiser*, February 26, 1868, 3.

33. *Proceedings*, 639.

34. Ibid., 637.

35. Ibid., 869.

36. Ibid.

37. On June 4, 1868, just after dark, a mob surrounded Dill's house. At the sound of whispers, his bodyguard, an older African American named Nestor Ellison, rose from his chair and opened the door to investigate. He was shot in the head. Simultaneously, Dill was fired on through a window, the bullet crashing into "the cervical portion of the spine." The mob then opened fire on the house generally, hitting Dill's wife, Rebecca, in the leg. Her guest, Nancy Burnett, ran out of the house to beg not for her own life but for the lives of the three children who were still inside. From the darkness an exultant voice answered, "By God, I've got all I want," and the mob withdrew. See "The State vs. the Dead Body of S. G. W. Dill, Nestor Ellison," CSI:Dixie, accessed January 15, 2020, https://csidixie.org/inquests/2847.

38. "An Act to Raise Supplies for the Year One Thousand Eight Hundred and Twenty-two; and For other Purposes Therein Mentioned," *The Statutes at Large of South Carolina: Containing the Acts from 1814, Exclusive, to 1838, Inclusive* (Columbia, S.C., 1839), 171.

39. *Charleston City Gazette*, May 20, 1822.

40. See Eugene Alvarez, *Travel on Southern Antebellum Railroads, 1828–1860* (University of Alabama Press, 2007), 8; "a few years since": *Edgefield Advertiser*, December 27, 1838.

41. "Slave Trading in Georgia," *Anti-Slavery Bugle*, October 27, 1848.

42. Richard David Ralston, *A Second Middle Passage: African Student Sojourns in the United States During the Colonial Period and Their Influence Upon the Character of African Leadership* (University of California Press, 1972). Study of the internal slave trade exploded with the publication of Frederic

Bancroft, *Slave Trading in the Old South* (1935; repr. University of South Carolina Press, 1996), which devastated the idea that the slave traders were a marginalized class. See especially Michael Tadman, *Speculators and Slaves: Masters, Traders, and Slaves in the Old South* (University of Wisconsin Press, 1989); Steven Deyle, *Carry Me Back: The Domestic Slave Trade in the American Life* (Oxford University Press, 2005); Walter Johnson, *Soul by Soul: Life Inside the Antebellum Slave Market* (Harvard University Press, 1999); Diana Ramey Berry, *The Value of the Enslaved, from Womb to Grave, in the Building of a Nation* (Beacon Press, 2017); and Tiya Miles, *All That She Carried: The Journey of Ashley's Sack, A Black Family Keepsake* (Random House, 2022).

43. William Goodell, *The American Slave Code in Theory and Practice: Its Distinctive Features Shown by Its Statutes, Judicial Decisions, and Illustrative Facts* (New York, 1853), 54–55; Tadman, *Speculators and Slaves*, 262–63.

44. Quoted in Michael Tadman, "The Reputation of the Slave Trader in Southern History and the Social Memory of the South," *American Nineteenth Century History* 8, no. 3 (2007): 247–71.

45. *Anti-Slavery Bugle*, October 27, 1848, 3.

46. "Monied aristocrats": *The State* (Columbia, S.C.), October 14, 1951, 65. See also Thomas L. Stokes, *The Savannah* (University of Georgia Press, 1982).

47. John L. Knight to James Evans, April 27, 1851, South Caroliniana Library, University of South Carolina.

48. See Karen L. Cox, *No Common Ground: Confederate Monuments and the Ongoing Fight for Racial Justice* (University of North Carolina Press, 2021); Thomas J. Brown, *Civil War Monuments and the Militarization of America* (University of North Carolina Press, 2019); Adam H. Domby, *The False Cause: Fraud, Fabrication, and White Supremacy in Confederate Memory* (University of Virginia Press, 2022).

49. "Northern Teacher to the Freedmen's Bureau Commissioner," Halls Hill, Virginia, August 4, 1865, Freedmen and Southern Society Project, University of Maryland, accessed July 9, 2025, https://www.freedmen.umd.edu/J%20Johnson.htm.

50. Rivers purchased two key properties in town, Lots 1 and 2, on the corner of Market and Mechanic Streets, on March 9, 1872. The first he purchased from Amanda Hill, the second from E. P. Alexander. See "Aiken County Deed Cross Index," quoted in Vandervelde, *Aiken County*, 162.

51. "A Bill to Incorporate the Rivers Guards," originally introduced on December 19, 1871, then referred to the Committee on Military Affairs on January 8, 1872, in *Journal of the House of Representatives of the State of South Carolina,*

Regular Session 1871–1872 [hereafter *Journal of the House*] (Columbia, 1872), 171, 192; "A Bill to Incorporate the Knights of the Circle Tie," January 17, 1872, in *Journal of the House*, 265; "A Bill to Incorporate the Hamburg Warehouse Company," October 24, 1873, in *Journal of the House of Representatives of the State of South Carolina, Special Session, Commencing Tuesday, October 21, 1873* (Columbia, 1873), 50; "An Act to Charter the Town of Hamburg," February 28, 1871, in *Journal of the House*, 104; "An Act to Construct and Keep in Repair a Certain public Road," February 14, 1871, in *Journal of the House*, 89. Tellingly, Rivers also sponsored "A Bill Prohibiting the Organization of Armed Bodies Other than the Regular Constituted Militia of the State," in *Journal of the House*, 33.

52. Because our attention focuses on the national-level figures in the struggle for civil rights—from Harriet Tubman and Frederick Douglass to Martin Luther King and Malcolm X—we tend to forget the organizers who remained on the ground. The creation of Aiken County is a testament to Rivers's ingenuity and commitment to erecting a stronghold for his people.

53. Aiken County Charter, 1868, South Carolina Department of Archives and History.

54. John Oldfield, "The African American Bar in South Carolina, 1877–1915," in *At Freedom's Door: African American Founding Fathers and Lawyers in Reconstruction South Carolina*, ed. James Lowell Underwood and W. Lewis Burke Jr. (University of South Carolina Press, 2000); Isabel Vandervelde, *Biography of Samuel Jones Lee* (Art Studio Press, 1997).

55. Eric Foner, *Freedom's Lawmakers: A Directory of Black Officeholders During Reconstruction* (Louisiana State University Press, 1996), 99.

56. See Vandervelde, *Aiken County*, 171–78.

57. Too often politics in the period is understood as a struggle *between* Black and white populations, when it was also a struggle *within* Black and white populations.

58. *Radical Members of the First Legislature After the War, South Carolina*, Library of Congress Prints and Photographs Division, Washington, D.C., accessed December 18, 2024, https://www.loc.gov/resource/ppmsca.30572/.

59. The Gibbeses' Saluda River Factory ruins are now listed in the National Register of Historic Places. See "National Register Properties in South Carolina: Saluda Factory History District, Lexington County," South Carolina Department of Archives and History, http://www.nationalregister.sc.gov/lexington/S10817732003/index.htm. The author is indebted to Kurt Luther for helping with the provenance of this image.

60. See Ronald S. Coddington, "Cardomania!: How the Carte de Visite

Became the Facebook of the 1860s," *Military Images* 24, no. 3 (Summer 2016): 12–17.

61. "He and I were antipodes": *Proceedings in the General Assembly and Supreme Court of South Carolina, on the Death of Hon. Lemuel Boozer, Judge of the Fifth Judicial Circuit* (Columbia, 1870), quoted in Hyman Rubin III, *South Carolina Scalawags* (University of South Carolina Press, 2021), 14–15. See also Ulysses Robert Brooks, *South Carolina Bench and Bar*, vol. 1 (State Company, 1908), 175; James Alex Bagget, *The Scalawags: Southern Dissenters in the Civil War and Reconstruction* (Louisiana State University Press, 2004), 44.

62. "Most perfect scalawag": Robert H. Woody, "Franklin J. Moses Jr., Scalawag Governor of South Carolina, 1872–1874," *North Carolina Historical Review* 10, no. 2 (April 1933): 111. See also Benjamin Ginsberg, *Moses of South Carolina: A Jewish Scalawag During Radical Reconstruction* (Johns Hopkins University Press, 2010).

63. "Radical Members of the South Carolina Legislature," Graphic Arts Collection, Princeton University Library.

The Mayor

1. Rivers served in each assembly of the state legislature from November 24, 1868, to November 24, 1873. In the forty-eighth and forty-ninth general assemblies he represented Edgefield County; in the fiftieth general assembly he represented Aiken County. See "The South Carolina General Assembly—Historical Information," *Carolana*, accessed June 10, 2025, https://www.carolana.com/SC/Legislators/sc_legislature_historical.html.

2. Isabel Vandervelde, *Aiken County: The Only South Carolina County Founded During Reconstruction* (Reprint Company, 1999), 151.

3. Ibid.

4. Rev. E. J. Adams, "These Are Revolutionary Times," *Charleston Courier*, March 22, 1867.

5. See Rebecca Price Janney, *Then Comes Marriage: A Cultural History of the American Family* (Moody Publishers, 2010), 66. As one enslaved man noted about his own marriage: "We slaves knowed that them words wasn't bindin'. Don't mean nothin' lessen you say, 'what has jined, cain't no man pull asunder.' But dey never would say dat. Jus' say, 'Now you married.'"

6. In the 1880 U.S. Census, Jack Rivers is listed as a carpenter, age thirty-three, with a wife, Caroline, keeping house, age thirty-two, and four children: Prince, age twelve; Edward, age nine; Madison, age seven; and Ann, age five.

7. "Province of Africa": "A Black Solon on the War Path," *Charleston Daily News*, February 16, 1870, 1; "Africanized town": "Sports in Hamburg," *Charleston Daily Courier*, February 23, 1870, 4; "perfect Sodom": *Raleigh News and Observer*, December 1, 1877, 2; "once the great cotton mart": *Georgia Weekly Telegraph and Georgia Journal & Messenger*, March 21, 1871, 8; "poor old . . . Hamburg": *Edgefield Advertiser*, March 9, 1871.

8. Quoted in the *Charleston Daily Courier*, March 31, 1871, 1.

9. *The Southern Baptist*, Atlanta, April 14, 1881, 5.

10. William L. Barney, *The Passage of the Republic: An Interdisciplinary History of Nineteenth Century America* (Heath, 1987).

11. Vandervelde, *Aiken County*, 141.

12. Hamburg Township, 1870 U.S. Census.

13. Frederick Douglass, "What to the Slave Is the Fourth of July," in *Frederick Douglass: Selected Speeches and Writings*, ed. Philip S. Foner (Lawrence Hill, 1999), 194.

14. "The Fourth of July [has] ceased": *Richmond Enquirer and Examiner*, July 6, 1868; "sack-cloth of humiliation": *Edgefield Advertiser*, July 3, 1867. For more on the Fourth of July during Reconstruction, see Mitchell Snay, *Fenians, Freedmen, and Southern Whites: Race and Nationality in the Era of Reconstruction* (Louisiana State University Press, 2010), 146–48. According to Louis Schiller, the festivities in Hamburg began in earnest about three o'clock with the reading of the Declaration of Independence; the militia began marching sometime after 4:30 p.m. See testimony of Louis Schiller, "South Carolina in 1876: Hearings Before the United States Senate Committee on Privileges and Elections," 44th Cong., 2d Sess. (Dec. 30, 1876; Jan. 1–6, 8–12, 18, 1877) [hereafter Senate Investigation], 145.

15. Republican governors in Southern states had no illusion about how difficult it was going to be to reconcile former slaves and former enslavers. One of the more creative solutions was compulsory state militia service, where Black and white soldiers would serve together. (Certainly, Truman's integration of the army would have a salutary effect eighty years later.) In some places, this worked. In Aiken township, for instance, a count of the eighteen- to thirty-year-olds in militia service in 1870 reveals ninety-six Blacks and ninety-five whites, roughly proportional to the town's population. Hamburg's militia was also integrated and representative, which is to say 80 percent Black and 20 percent white. According to law, whites who refused militia service (usually because they didn't want to serve in integrated units) would be forced into the National Guard. This did not happen. The result was a gradual segregation of the militia

units or abandonment of them altogether as whites flooded into alternative "rifle clubs."

In testimony before the U.S. Senate, M. C. Butler tried to make the case that the Hamburg militia was illegitimate, but there is no evidence for this. While it is true that Hamburg's militia had been relatively inactive for a period, its reorganization under Adams had been perfectly lawful, as were its state-issued arms. Hamburg's militia rolls listed eighty-five men; probably about half of them were drilling that night. Multiple witnesses attest to the fact that Adams was an excellent drillmaster, who had done much to recover the luster of the organization. In the subsequent Senate investigation, M. C. Butler's implication of the militia's illegality was specifically undermined by Louis Schiller, who served as the militia's keeper of the rolls:

"Q[uestion]. Have you sufficient knowledge of the statute law of the State to state whether it [the Hamburg militia] was organized under law? A[nswer]. I have, sir; it was organized in accordance with the laws of the State of South Carolina. . . . I am positive, I being one of General Rivers's staff-officers, being in the militia myself, I know this to be a fact; that, under his orders, they organized and had an election; and after election, during a private drill that they had of the company, General Rivers, myself, and a gentleman of the name of Simms, were judges of the drill for the company. Under General Rivers's orders they met and elected this man Adams as captain. The rolls were made out, for I made out their rolls myself. . . .

"Q. How happened it that the negroes formed and the whites did not? A. The whites refused to join the militia of the State; they refused to be in the same regiment with the negroes. Q. And the law provided that they must be if they organized? A. Yes, sir; that they must go into the national guard. They refused to do that. . . .

"Q. How did they escape when the statute required them to do it? A. For the reason that a great many escape in this State; that there was nothing to enforce it, we hadn't power enough to enforce the law. Q. Did you not have the whole machinery of the State government, the republicans? A. Yes, sir; they had. Q. Governor, judges, legislature, and all? A. Very true; but the legislature may pass a law, the judges may pass a sentence, or may decide a question, but who is to enforce it? A negro militia? If the governor had ordered out the negro militia to enforce the law, it would have created a civil war right there. There was not force enough to do it."

Louis Schiller further testified that it was the successful reorganization of the militia, not its illegality, that enraged local whites: "Q. So far as you know, were the colored people of that town and county disposed to be quiet and peaceable? A. Why, they were, sir. There was no difficulty at all; none at all. They never interfered with any white men unlawfully; they never had done anything; I never knew them to do anything of the kind. The only objections were, that they were drilling, and they have told me—this R. J. Butler told me himself—that it was wrong for them to be drilling; that they should not have no militia company. . . . I say, 'Why, over in Augusta, right across the river, they drill every night—the white militia companies.' He says, 'Well, it is wrong for the n——s to drill.'"

On July 12, shortly after the Hamburg Massacre, the Democratic *Augusta Chronicle and Sentinel* all but admitted that the legality of Hamburg's militia was not in dispute: "The colored militia may as well accept the situation and return their guns and ammunition to the State. We say this in all kindness and with a sincere desire to avert bloodshed. It may be said that the militia have been organized and armed according to law. Granted. But there is a higher law than that—the Law of Self-Preservation. This is the law which demands they shall disarm and disband."

"Have you sufficient knowledge": testimony of Louis Schiller, Senate Investigation, 157–59; "so far as you know": testimony of Louis Schiller, Senate Investigation, 156; "the colored militia": *Augusta Chronicle and Sentinel*, July 12, 1876; see also Vandervelde, *Aiken County*, 435; "most equal to any company": testimony of Louis Schiller, Senate Investigation, 156.

16. Thomas Butler was the twenty-one-year-old unmarried son of Robert J. Butler, the "old negro-hunter" who lived up the hill on the farm northwest of town. When asked during the later Senate investigation what his profession was, Tommy said: "Well, I have not been doing much business. I have not been long from school. I am just stopping around home, living with my father." Apparently in "stopping around home" Tommy had frequent run-ins with the residents of Hamburg. In later testimony, Tommy would swear that he never cursed the militia and was "very mild and peaceful." If so, responded John Williams, "it is the first time that he ever was." John Henry Getzen was Tommy's twenty-six-year-old brother-in-law, having married Tommy's sister, Frances Julia Butler, in 1866. Getzen's father had died in Alabama at age thirty, after which Getzen and his mother lived with her brother, the Edgefield Baptist minister J. P. Mealing. "My nephew I raised as my own child," Mealing said of Getzen. After marrying into the Butler clan, Getzen had set up as a farmer, near or on the Butler property. Both young men traveled often to Augusta, a trip that took them directly through Hamburg.

"Well, I have not": testimony of J. T. Butler, Senate Investigation, 308; "it is the first time": testimony of John Williams, Senate Investigation, 708; "my nephew I raised": testimony of J. P. Mealing, Senate Investigation, 1063. In support of the notion that sons had inherited "some of [the Civil War's] bitterness and none of its resignation," see testimony of Jerry Thornton Moore, Senate Investigation, 7: Atkinson [a white witness]: "We will have it [meaning, 'home rule'] if we have to wade in blood knee deep." [Moore]: "Mr. Atkinson, look here. You tried that once, and what's the use to start that thing again?" Atkinson: "But, I tell you, our sons won't stand it. We can't keep them down."

17. Michael S. Smith, *The Lost Freedmen's Town of Hamburg, South Carolina* (History Press, 2021), 32.

18. *Georgia Weekly Telegraph and Georgia Journal & Messenger*, August 31, 1875, 2.

19. On the power of language and on Reconstruction as a linguistic/conceptual fight as well as an actual one, see Manisha Sinha, *The Rise and Fall of the Second American Republic: Reconstruction, 1860–1920* (Liveright, 2025).

20. On the rise of the peonage system, see Douglas Blackmon, *Slavery by Another Name: The Re-Enslavement of Black Americans from the Civil War to World War II* (Anchor, 2009); Earl Swift, *Hell Put to Shame: The 1921 Murder Farm Massacre and the Horror of America's Second Slavery* (Mariner, 2024).

21. Alan Friedlander and Richard Allan Gerber, *Welcoming Ruin: The Civil Rights Act of 1875* (Haymarket Books, 2020).

22. On the ensuing noninsurrection (and resulting panic), see William Rawlings, "The Freedmen's Land Insurrection of 1875," *Georgia Backroads*, Autumn 2014, 39–48; Ridgeway Boyd Murphree, "Rebel Sovereigns: The Civil War Leadership of Governors John Milton of Florida and Joseph E. Brown of Georgia, 1861–1865" (PhD diss., Florida State University, 2006).

23. "Secret Clubs and Armed Drills," *Georgia Weekly Telegraph and Georgia Journal & Messenger*, October 6, 1874, 4.

24. *Sandersonville Herald*, October 3, 1873, 3.

25. *Georgia Weekly Telegraph, Journal, and Messenger*, August 24, 1875, 4.

26. "The Negro Conspiracy," *Augusta Daily Constitutionalist*, August 19, 1875; "The Insurrection: The Trouble in Middle Georgia," *Augusta Daily Chronicle and Sentinel*, August 20, 1875.

27. Rawlings, "Freedmen's Land Insurrection," 44.

28. Hill Jordan, James I. Robertson Jr., and J. H. Segars, eds., *The Bell Irvin Wiley Reader* (Louisiana State University Press, 2001), 108.

29. Thomas G. Dyer, *Secret Yankees: The Union Circle in Confederate Atlanta* (Johns Hopkins University Press, 2001).

30. Rawlings, "Freedmen's Land Insurrection," 47.

31. "The Black Cloud," *New York Daily Herald*, August 20, 1875, 7.

32. *Georgia Weekly Telegraph and Georgia Journal & Messenger*, August 24, 1875, 4.

33. *Georgia Weekly Telegraph and Georgia Journal & Messenger*, August 31, 1875, 2.

34. "Once-ler" is a reference to Dr. Seuss's classic children's book, *The Lorax*. For the property values of Robert Butler Sr., see 1850 U.S. Census.

35. Philip Henry Gosse, *Letters from Alabama, Chiefly Relating to Natural History: An Annotated Edition* (University of Alabama Press, 1993), 252–53.

36. Since he had earned "quite a reputation" for his dogs, people had come from fifty miles away to have Butler run down criminals or lost children. Mostly, though, he ran down slaves. During the later Senate investigation into the Hamburg Massacre, Republican senators were clearly curious, if not a little appalled, to meet an actual "negro-hunter," and they kept dragging Butler back to the real purpose for his dogs: "Q. You kept a pack of dogs and hunted runaway negroes before the emancipation? A. Yes, sir; I used to run everybody, black or white, that stole or murdered in the county. I done it for ten years. Q. You had a pack of dogs? A. Yes, sir, I had but the negroes killed them. I have not got a dog now. Q. That was your business? A. No, sir; my business was farming, but when a man was murdered in the neighborhood they came to me, and when they did so I would set my dogs after him. Q. When a negro ran away, if they came for you did you not go out with your dogs and run them down? A. Yes, sir; and I have caught children that run away from their home. I have trailed them up and caught them. I have had dogs that I have been sent for as far as fifty miles, and hunted both black and white. Q. You had quite a reputation in that business? A. I had, sir."

In his testimony, Louis Schiller made it clear to the committee that Butler was more "negro-hunter" than farmer: "I recognized that man, Robert J. Butler. Q. How old a man is he? A. He must be about sixty-seven years old, with large gray whiskers. I know him to be a very determined man; that he wouldn't lose any opportunity to kill me if he could. He is an old negro-hunter. He has made his living, all he had made, by hunting negroes before the war. He kept a large number of hounds. Q. He was a professional negro-hunter? A. Yes, sir."

"Quite a reputation," "kept a pack of dogs": testimony of R. J. Butler, Senate

Investigation, 346–47; "old negro-hunter": testimony of Louis Schiller, Senate Investigation, 152.

37. *Edgefield Advertiser*, October 30, 1873; "such a home": Orville Vernon Burton, *In My Father's House Are Many Mansions: Family and Community in Edgefield, South Carolina* (University of North Carolina Press, 1987), 39.

38. *Charleston Mercury*, October 11, 1864, 2.

39. "Fatal Rencontre," *Edgefield Advertiser*, September 21, 1864, 2.

40. "Dash and daring": *Charleston Mercury*, April 2, 1864; "Twiggs was a gentleman": *Edgefield Advertiser*, September 21, 1864; "he has fallen": *Charleston Mercury*, October 11, 1864, 2; "unpleasant occurrences": "Fatal Encounter in Hamburg," *Charleston Daily Courier*, September 19, 1864, 1.

41. See Cormac Broeg, "Killing Butler's Bloodhounds: An Act of Political Violence by Iowa Soldiers in Reconstruction South Carolina," *The Annals of Iowa* 78 (Spring 2019): 131.

42. Ibid., 131–32.

43. The slaughter of dogs by soldiers and freedmen was a common occurrence in the period. For generations, dogs had been integral to the enforcement of the South's carceral landscape (just as they would become integral to the system of Jim Crow, debt peonage, and chain gangs). As Higginson put it, "Dogs are the detective officers of Slavery's police." Thomas Wentworth Higginson, *Army Life in a Black Regiment* (Penguin Classics, 1994), 35. As the Confederacy lost its grip on power, however, the dogs paid a frightful price. As *The Iowa City Weekly Republican* reported during Sherman's March to the Sea, "wherever our army has passed everything in the shape of a dog has been killed" to protect "negroes and our escaped prisoners." Broeg, "Killing Butler's Bloodhounds," 131.

44. "Another war brewing": *Augusta Chronicle & Sentinel*, as reprinted in *The Charleston Daily Courier*, March 13, 1871, 1.

45. According to Butler's and Getzen's later testimony, they had been innocently making their way home from Augusta when the militia purposely impeded their progress, refusing to let them pass while abusing them verbally and threatening them physically. Every other eyewitness, Black and white, claimed Butler and Getzen purposely steered their wagon into the militia and demanded the right-of-way. Any theory of the case must weigh all of the testimony. Dock Adams claimed to have seen Butler and Getzen "on one side of the street, sitting in a buggy, looking at us drill up and down the street, I reckon, for about half an hour. After a while they went back down the street from where we were drilling, and went around on the street called Main Street. Afterward they came back on the street." He further claimed that Getzen and Butler had actu-

ally been present when, at the beginning of the drill, he had ensured that none of his militiamen had any ammunition. (For obvious reasons, militia maneuvers are executed with unloaded weapons.) Adams mentioned this fact to Getzen at a later hearing and, at least according to Adams, Getzen didn't deny it, saying only that some of the militiamen might have had a secret cache of bullets, thereby justifying his contention that his life had been credibly threatened by armed men. These are very specific details for Adams to have invented; if true, they suggest (1) that Butler and Getzen had had ample time to find an alternate route home, and (2) that they appear to have been purposely seeking a confrontation. This theory of the case is also supported by the testimony of Louis Schiller: "They [Butler and Getzen] stopped and watched them drill for nearly half an hour. Afterward they drove back again in front of a bar-room, and staid there, and had a conversation with some one for some time. And after they again drove back around to where the company was. . . . They drove right up to the center of the company." This theory is further supported by the testimony of John Williams: "Q. Getzen and Butler had turned out of that [the usual wagon track] in order to meet the company? A. Yes, sir. Q. You are certain about that? A. I am certain about that."

"On one side of the street": testimony of D. L. Adams, Senate Investigation, 35; "stopped and watched": testimony of Louis Schiller, Senate Investigation, 146; "Getzen and Butler had turned": testimony of John Williams, Senate Investigation, 707.

46. The exchange between Adams and Getzen is taken verbatim from the testimony of D. L. Adams, Senate Investigation, 35–36. Similar exchanges arranged as dialogue below are likewise verbatim testimony. See testimony of Robert J. Butler, Senate Investigation, 1056–57.

47. A major point of contention in the subsequent Senate investigation revolved around whether Butler and Getzen could or could not have driven around the militia. As a matter of law, no road rage in the world can justify a subsequent public massacre, but for argument's sake, let's have the argument. Market Street, the main road running along the Hamburg side of the Savannah River, was 158 feet wide. Much was made of the fact that, at the Mechanic Street intersection, the road had a supposedly nonnavigable ditch on the left and a well in the middle, creating some sort of "pinch point" that the militia effectively, and perhaps purposely, blocked. This argument was repeatedly demolished by eyewitness testimony, however. Take, for instance, the remarks of Henry Sparnick, a white lawyer from Aiken: "Q. Could there have been any difficulty in the buggy going up the street and turning to the right of that pump

or well and passing right on? A. None. Q. Was that ditch or gutter any obstruction or trouble in passing at all? A. I should think not, sir, in the least. My impression is that two buggies could have passed there perhaps. Q. And that ditch would have been no obstruction? A. None, in my judgment, whatever.... Q. It was stated that there was a ditch running from that well down to this cross street that would prevent a carriage going up this way from crossing. A. If there is such a ditch my memory is very badly at fault.... I examined the ground carefully, and I saw nothing on the ground that would obstruct the passage of a buggy at that well on either side." Testimony of Henry Sparnick, Senate Investigation, 497.

Or take the testimony of John Williams: "Q. How wide was the street at that point? A. About 150 feet. Q. How much width of the street did the company occupy? A. I suppose they occupied but very little over one-third of it. Q. Was there any difficulty in a horse and buggy driving right by the company on either side. A. No, sir; none. They could have driven either side if they had went there. Q. There was a good road on each side? A. Yes, sir." Testimony of John Williams, Senate Investigation, 701.

Or take the testimony of Louis Schiller: "Q. State whether there was sufficient space on each side of the company for them to have ridden by. A. Yes, sir; there was enough space for three or four trains of cars to pass on each side. Q. State whether the street was level or whether there were any obstructions in the way. A. No, sir; it was very level. Q. Could they have turned out without any difficulty? A. O, yes, sir; there is not doubt about that; the street is one hundred and fifty feet wide." Testimony of Louis Schiller, Senate Investigation, 146.

The best theory of the case, then, is that Butler and Getzen purposely drove into the militia. Adams and Getzen agreed about very little else, but they both testified that when the wagon pulled up, the militia was executing a maneuver called "interval march, open order," in which the men are arrayed in a broad line, ten feet separating each man. If Butler and Getzen were looking for a confrontation, they had certainly found one in the moment when the militia executed the only maneuver that maximized the possibility of collision.

An alternative theory of the case is that Adams waited until just the right moment and then executed the only movement that would splay his men across the road and impede the Butler boys' progress. Among the many other problems with this theory, it absolutely fails to square with the emotions attested to by all parties in their reaction to the collision. No witness, white or Black, claimed the militia reacted with secret delight at the execution of so clever a trick; no witness—not even Butler and Getzen themselves—claimed Butler and

Getzen reacted with surprise at being suddenly accosted. Instead, all parties agreed that the militia reacted with startled indignance, precisely because they were the ones who were taken aback after being driven into.

Getzen's insistence on traveling "the rut I always travel" is freighted with metaphorical overtones. Butler and Getzen would not adjust course, literally or figuratively, for their Black neighbors, even and perhaps especially on the Fourth of July. Too young to have fought in the Civil War, they saw themselves as soldiers in a different racial conflict in which they were determined to excel. As they saw it, Market Street was "their" road. In his Senate testimony, Tommy's father referred so many times to Market Street as "my road" that Republican Senator Isaac Peckham Christiancy finally interjected: "Q. Is not that street to which you have referred a public street, in which everybody has an equal right to travel? A. Of course; it is a public street in Hamburgh. Q. When you speak of it as your street, it is no more yours than anybody's else? A. No, sir. . . . Q. You call it your street. You mean, simply, that it is one that you have occasion to use mostly? A. I have to use it all the time; it is our common road. Q. But still it is a common road to every one else who chooses to use it? A. Of course it is a common road." Senate Investigation, 143.

48. "Respect [Rivers] no how": Senate Investigation, 36.

49. Testimony of J. P. Mealing, Senate Investigation, 1064–65.

50. James Morris Morgan, *Recollections of a Rebel Reefer* (Houghton Mifflin, 1917), 362. The full quotation reads: "General Butler was an extraordinarily handsome man—tall and graceful, and possessed of the manners of a Chesterfield. His courtesy and winning smile made friends of all who came in contact with him. At one of the battles in Virginia a shell had struck his horse in the breast and exploded inside of the animal, shattering the general's leg so badly that it had to be amputated below the knee; but so well did he manage his artificial limb that for several years after the war was over he used to dance at balls, and it was difficult to convince strangers that he was a one-legged man. In the hour of danger he was one of the coolest men I ever saw, and he feared neither man nor devil."

51. Matthew Butler would later claim that he had come to Hamburg merely to serve as counsel to the other Butlers in their continued prosecutions of Adams. There are clear signs, however, that violence was anticipated (indeed orchestrated) from the beginning. In his testimony before the Senate investigation, Dock Adams remembered noting that in addition to the sixteen-shot, repeating Winchesters all the men were carrying, Robert Butler "had about seven or eight pistols in the buggy; large Navy pistols." This was corroborated

by Frank Robinson: "The first buggy I seen come in, it contained General M.C. Butler and some other man, I don't know who he was. It was in front; and next I seen Robert Butler in his buggy and another man in there, with guns and pistols there in the buggy." Testimony of D. L. Adams, Senate Investigation, 37; testimony of Frank Robinson, Senate Investigation, 611.

In his Senate testimony, Henry Getzen flatly denied that there were additional arms in the vehicles: "Q. Did you have arms? A. I had a carbine, and Tommy Butler had a carbine. Q. Did the old man have any arms? A. I suppose they all had pistols; I didn't see none. Q. How many arms did they have in the buggy? A. Tommy had his rifle in the buggy, and I had my rifle on my horse; those were all the guns I saw." M. C. Butler also claimed to have been unarmed: "I had no pistol, and nothing more dangerous than a copy of the Revised Statutes of South Carolina." Similarly Tommy Butler couldn't remember seeing a single other gun in Hamburg, except the one he carried because he feared for his life: "Q. You are the only person who had a gun on that occasion? A. I had my gun. My life had been threatened, and I had carried my gun for my own protection. Q. I asked you if you were the only person there that had a gun? A. I didn't see any one else there with a gun. Q. You had the only gun that was there? A. The only gun; yes, sir. Q. You swear positively to that? A. That I was the only person I seen with a gun." Testimony of Henry Getzen, Senate Investigation, 329; testimony of M. C. Butler, Senate Investigation, 100; testimony of J. T. Butler, Senate Investigation, 313.

The weight of evidence suggests the Butlers were well armed, however, and they had also apparently sent word to area white rifle clubs to descend on Hamburg. Louis Schiller would later testify that Harrison Butler, the other of Robert's sons, had threatened earlier in the day "that he had 1,500 men ready to come to Hamburgh, and they would make us suffer for it; that this company had to quit drilling; that the white people wouldn't stand it. . . . A rumor came to me that the rifle-clubs were coming into town, and that there was going to be a riot. They came there to see that Adams and Attaway [were] dealt with." Testimony of Louis Schiller, Senate Investigation, 147.

This construction of events is corroborated by Henry Sparnick, who heard the rumor from Robert Butler himself, when he bumped into Butler in Augusta that morning. Having acted as unofficial counsel for Adams in the matter of the original summons, Sparnick volunteered to Butler that there was simply nothing to his legal case and that "to push it further would be merely to excite feeling between the two peoples at a time when I thought it was necessary to have as much peace as possible, at the beginning of the [political] campaign

. . . and I asked him to abandon the prosecution. He said he would do no such thing; that the negroes at Hamburgh had been very offensive . . . that some of his friends and neighbors from the country had been informed that the trial was to take place that evening, and that they would be there present. He said there would be twenty-five or thirty or something of that kind. I said to him, 'Mr. Butler, perhaps there will be two or three hundred.' He said, 'well, yes, damn it, two or three thousand.' He seemed to be very much inflamed about it, and from his general talk and demeanor I apprehended trouble." Testimony of Henry Sparnick, Senate Investigation, 491.

In this theory of the case, then, Robert J. Butler, the "old negro-hunter," was the ultimate architect of the Hamburg Massacre. This is further supported by a comment attributed to J. P. Mealing, Robert Butler's in-law, who strongly implied that the massacre had been prearranged by the Butlers. Moving through Hamburg with a friend the day before the trial, he pointed at the Sibley Building and said: "That is where that damned militia company drills. . . . To-morrow they are going to have a trial, and we intend to kill the captain of that company before he gets away from that court." D. L. Adams, Senate Investigation, 52. What cannot be perfectly determined by the record is whether Robert invited M. C. Butler to Hamburg as his lawyer or as "General Butler," a man who could oversee a military operation.

52. The conversation between Nelson and Butler is drawn verbatim from the testimony of William Nelson, age thirty-three, a constable for the town of Hamburg who assisted Rivers in the running of the trial office. See testimony of William Nelson, Senate Investigation, 603.

53. "Highly sulphurated vocabulary": Morgan, *Recollections of a Rebel Reefer*, 372. The full quote reads: "The general was the possessor of a most highly sulphurated vocabulary when his passions were aroused, and he was using it with unstinted prodigality."

54. Like many nineteenth-century "groceries," Damm's store was effectively a saloon. According to Adams, virtually all of the whites were "getting drunk very fast, or drinking liquor and appearing like they were drunk, and saying they were going to kill ever God damned n——r in Hamburgh that day, and especially Dock Adams; that was myself." In his testimony, M. C. Butler did not deny that the men were drunk but presented it as an excuse. When asked by Senate investigators, "Did you have any control of that mob at all?" he answered, "Not the least. No human power could have controlled them after the first shot was fired. It was an unbridled mob. The men that brought that artillery over there I did not know. . . . I remarked to this man Conway that it was curious that I did

not recognize these people, and he said to me, 'These are factory people, and the Irish have come over here for the purpose of plunder, and these men are drunk.'" Testimony of D. L. Adams, Senate Investigation, 37; testimony of M. C. Butler, Senate Investigation, 100.

55. There is ample evidence that the militia did not occupy the Sibley Building to make a stand but were driven to it by a lack of options. Witness John Freyer, for instance, had tried to go home as the toughs rolled into town "but the people told me if I was to go there I would be killed going there. They told me I better not go, and concluded I would not go, and I went into the drill room . . . for protection. It was a good brick house." Similarly, Needham O'Bryant told himself "the best thing for you to do is to go in that room and bar yourself up. It's the only safe place there is in town. Bar up every window and door, and let nothing nor anybody in the world get in, and by this means they will have nothing to fight, if they want to fight, but themselves." Testimony of John Freyer, Senate Investigation, 525; testimony of Needham O'Bryant, Senate Investigation, 161.

In the subsequent Senate investigation, North Carolina Senator Augustus Summerfield Merrimon seemed intent on questioning their decision, implying that the militia had aggressively occupied a well-armed "fortress." But each witness had the same answer, pointing out that the Sibley Building was not the strongest offensive position but the only defensive position. In interrogating Frank Robinson, for instance, Merrimon first asked: "Q. How did you happen to go into that drill-room that night? A. I happened to go in there because I thought that was safest place for me to go. Q. That was the most dangerous place for you to go to. A. I didn't think so when I could not get home." Merrimon had a similar exchange with Spencer Harris: "Q. Tell us what you went to the drill-room that night for. A. I went in there for safety; to keep from getting hurt. Q. Why, that was the most dangerous place you could go to, in the drill-room. A. If it was, I didn't think so, because most all the men went up there, and I thought it was a heap the best to be where the most men was." Merrimon's questioning of William Nelson followed the same pattern: "Q. What did you run to the drill-room for? A. I ran to the drill-room for protection, sir. Q. How did you expect protection there; why, was not that the very point of danger? A. Why, because most of the men were there, and I went there for protection, thinking that if we went into the drill-room that those men would not fire on us or try to injure us in any way, sir. Q. Instead of going to a place of safety you really went to the very place of danger? A. A good many times men think they is going to a place of safety and goes right into danger."

Testimony of Frank Robinson, Senate Investigation, 610; testimony of Spencer Harris, Senate Investigation, 711; testimony of William Nelson, Senate Investigation, 605.

56. "By that time I walks right back to the armory; Attaway opens the windows and asks me how it looks; I said, 'It looks squally.'" Testimony of Needham O'Bryant, Senate Investigation, 162.

57. "Strung out": Testimony of Needham O'Bryant, Senate Investigation, 162.

58. Rivers did not testify at the Senate investigation, and, as a result, his precise movements during the Hamburg Massacre are unknown. His detractors, mostly white supremacists, occasionally imply that he somehow could have or should have done more to avoid the catastrophe that befell his town. This is, frankly, an absurd instance of victim blaming. All witnesses agree he did all he could to avoid disaster, and that he survived should not somehow be held against him. Adams escaped with his life also, and regardless, there is nothing cowardly about choosing not to get massacred. In every Civil War engagement for which we have qualitative evidence of his conduct, Rivers was invariably cited for bravery. In the years after the Civil War, unreconstructed whites paid him the perverse compliment of being afraid of him, precisely because they knew what he was capable of. In the entirety of his military career, Rivers had never been tactically stupid. Instead, like a wily veteran, he probably saw the Hamburg situation precisely for what it was: militarily hopeless. Adams, he probably believed, had misplayed the whole affair; he should have kept his cool and allowed himself to be dressed down at the first hearing. Failing this, he and Attaway should have appeared as scheduled at the second trial. Their every move had played into the whites' hands, providing them a pretext and an opportunity to escalate the situation. Even so, Rivers worked harder than anyone to avert disaster. Late in the afternoon, he met with the militia's officers, accompanied by Samuel Spencer, Aiken County commissioner, and Sparnick: "We canvassed the matter, and we urged them to do it; that is, Spencer, Rivers, and myself united in urging these men to go down there and see General Butler. They were willing to do it, with the exception of Attaway. Attaway objected, because he said he was afraid of his life." Testimony of Henry Sparnick, Senate Investigation, 493.

Sparnick suggested that perhaps Rivers should go alone, through the town, through an army of racist drunks, to talk to Butler. "He agreed with me in that view," Sparnick later testified, "and went, so far as I know, alone. . . . In the meanwhile the colored people were becoming very much excited, and were gathering in the streets. I went among them and told them all to go in their houses, and not to stand on the streets . . . to leave this whole matter to be adjusted by Rivers and General Butler, if it could be adjusted." According to Needham O'Bryant, when Butler saw Rivers he said, "By God you had better go and do something; there is going to be hell to pay here." Testimony of Henry Sparnick, Senate Investigation, 2:490–98; testimony of Needham O'Bryant, Senate Investigation, 162.

Rivers made a final suggestion: He would ensure that the militia's arms would be boxed up and sent back to the governor. If it was the guns he was really after, Butler could have them. Butler refused; he wanted the arms but also the militia captains, and what's more, he wanted an apology. And, Rivers asked, would that suffice? It would depend, Butler replied, on "how they apologize to Mr. Butler for how they treated his sons on the 4th." Negotiations, in effect then, were over. Soon after this exchange, the white mob "fell into line there [at the river bluff]," Sam Spencer remembered. Rivers and the other white negotiators asked Butler a last time "if there was anything that we could do. We saw what was going on. We saw that the matter had been brought down to such a point that it was impossible for anything to be done, and we knew that we were helpless. Nothing was more unexpected to us, however; we hadn't a single thought—well, nothing was further from my mind than [the resulting slaughter]." Spencer here makes an important point: Only after the massacre did Hamburg's residents, including Rivers, realize that the whites meant to inaugurate a policy of total war. See testimony of Samuel B. Spencer, Senate Investigation, 710.

59. "I want those guns": testimony of Samuel B. Spencer, Senate Investigation, 709; "for it was the only chance": testimony of D. L. Adams, Senate Investigation, 40; "every God damned": testimony of D. L. Adams, Senate Investigation, 55. Butler's baseless demand for guns legally issued to the Hamburg militia by the state was part of a broader move by unreconstructed whites to disarm Black citizens. See David H. Schenk, "Freedmen with Firearms: White Terrorism and Black Disarmament During Reconstruction," *Gettysburg College Journal of the Civil War Era* 4 (2014): 9–44.

60. Another point of contention in the subsequent Senate investigation was the question of who fired first, the Blacks or the whites. Again, this has little bearing on the legality of a subsequent massacre, but let's weigh all the evidence. Predictably, the whites being investigated for murder claimed the first shots came from the Sibley Building. This is hard to credit. Every eyewitness inside the drill room testified that the mix of thirty-five to forty militiamen and civilians were all hunkered down, a theory that is consistent with the notion they had occupied the

building as a purely defensive position in the first place. Typical questions and responses during the investigation include the testimony of S. Picksley ("Q. The volley came from whom? A. White people") and from Frank Robinson ("Q. You don't know who fired the first gun? A. No, sir, but I am pretty confident it was fired from the river bank"). Testimony of S. Picksley, Senate Investigation, 80; testimony of Frank Robinson, Senate Investigation, 610.

There is evidence too that M. C. Butler specifically gave the signal to fire. According to John Freyer, "Late in the evening the answer came, 'The general says we must give up our arms.' Q. General Butler? A. Yes, sir; said he would give us fifteen minutes. . . . Well, fifteen minutes rolled around [Butler] came from down the street, horseback, and he stopped within about fifteen yards of the corner of the drill room, Sibly's building, and he turned his face toward these other five mens, and he gave them a signal. Q. What sort of a signal? A. He sort of motioned his hand; and they all rode right off, and went on down toward the Augusta bridge, and shortly after that I seed a great crowd of them on the street. Q. White men? A. Yes, sir; coming on the river bank with their guns . . . and the street was just filled full as it could hold of them; and some of them commenced firing. . . . Q. Had any shots been fired from the drill-room? A. No, sir; we all were that scared we couldn't shoot from the drill-room; they shot so rapid till we all just betwixt the widows and got behind there, and they fired so regular they shot all the window-glass out and nobody could get to the windows. Q. Tommy Butler testified here that the first shot was fired from the drill-room. What I want to get at is who fired the first shot. A. Well, sir, I know the first shot were fired from the abutment of the bridge; I is sure of that, for every man in there was too scared to get up to the windows; and the orders was from the captain for every man to hold his place, and get from in front of those windows; if they didn't they would be shot." Testimony of John Freyer, Senate Investigation, 524–25.

In 1916, a marker was erected in Meriwether's honor as the lone casualty of the "Hamburg Riot." The marker claims: "In life he exemplified the highest ideal of Anglo-Saxon Civilization. By his death he assured to the children of his beloved land the supremacy of that ideal." The unveiling ceremony was followed by a screening of *Birth of a Nation*.

61. "Shining . . . about as bright": testimony of D. L. Adams, Senate Investigation, 67. On Adams's escape plan, see testimony of John Freyer, Senate Investigation, 525.

62. On the death of Cook, see, especially, testimony of Samuel B. Spencer, Senate Investigation, 711.

63. "Here's a God damned": testimony of D. L. Adams, Senate Investigation, 67.

64. Ibid., 43.

65. For the most part, the whites did not summarily kill but instead rounded up all the Black males they could capture and carried them down to what they came to call the Dead Ring. According to John Freyer, most of the Black individuals in the ring were just boys. "There was just as many white people around there as could get around there," he testified, "fifty or sixty, guarding. . . . They were there as thick as hail around us." See testimony of John Freyer, Senate Investigation, 526.

66. The conversation between Attaway and Mays comes from the testimony of Harry Mays, Senate Investigation, 33. Attaway had a similar conversation with Andrew J. Griffin: "This man Attaway asked me if I thought there was any danger, and I said that I believe that those men intended to do some damage. . . . He says, 'Griffin, I wish you would go and see, and try and see what you can do, and see if there is any way for us to get out of here.'" See testimony of Andrew J. Griffin, Senate Investigation, 608.

67. Testimony of Harry Mays, Senate Investigation, 33–34.

68. In his subsequent Senate testimony, Getzen specifically denied saying, "I will fix you now in a short while": "Q. Did you see him [Attaway] after he was arrested? A. No, sir; I did not see him after he was arrested. Q. I ask you if, after he was arrested, he did not call to you and says this, 'Mr. Getzen, do what you can for me;' and that you answered him, 'God damn you, I will do what I can for you directly; I know you'? A. No, sir; I didn't say anything like that at all; I never saw him at all, and never had no conversation with him."

"Do all you can": testimony of John Freyer, Senate Investigation, 527; "did you see him": testimony of Henry Getzen, Senate Investigation, 334–35.

69. Testimony of Harry Mays, Senate Investigation, 34.

70. Unlike the first two men executed, Hampton Stevens did not serve in the Hamburg militia, so he probably thought he was going to be safe. It is unclear why the mob singled him out for execution. See testimony of Harry Mays, Senate Investigation, 34.

71. Testimony of John Freyer, Senate Investigation, 527.

72. The final name called from Butler's list was Pompey Curry. Curry is listed as a twenty-two-year-old farmer on the Hamburg Roll of Citizens and, like three of the men summarily executed, he was a member of the militia. He was also vaguely accused of robbing wagons in testimony given by Archy B. Griffin: "Q. You heard of wagons being also robbed about there? A. Yes, sir; not

in Hamburgh; up the road. Q. Some distance from Hamburg? A. Yes, sir; but the white people all know, and this n——r will tell himself, that he will do that—Pompey Curry."

Hamburg Roll of Citizens, in Vandervelde, *Aiken County*, 367; testimony of Archy B. Griffin, Senate Investigation, 699; on the shooting of Pompey Curry, see testimony of John Freyer, Senate Investigation, 527.

73. "What better fun": testimony of John Freyer, Senate Investigation, 527.

74. Stephen Budiansky, *The Bloody Shirt: Terror After Appomattox* (Viking, 2008), 221–54.

75. "Cut off a big piece": testimony of Harry Mays, Senate Investigation, 34. The sixth Black man killed in the massacre was Moses Parks, who, according to the testimony of William Nelson, was murdered by Robert Butler: "Q. You saw Robert Butler there? A. To the best of my knowledge; he says, 'Here he goes;' and I known him very well, and I know his voice. I have had a great deal of dealing with R. J. Butler, and, as he jumped over, Davis Lepfield says, 'Who is that?' and Butler says, 'There goes one of the God-damned sons of bitches,' and fired—bam, bam—that was two fires; and he says, 'God damn him, I got him.' Q. What colored man was it that got shot there? A. Moses Parks." Robert Butler denied killing Moses Parks, claiming that he had retired early: "I was very unwell myself, and I went into a man's store with him and his family, and remained there until the difficulty ceased, about twelve o'clock." He was probably referring to George Damm, on whom he relied for an alibi. Damm claimed, "I closed my house up and never went out" after the firing started. Testimony of William Nelson, Senate Investigation, 605; testimony of Robert J. Butler, Senate Investigation, 1054–55; testimony of George Damm, Senate Investigation, 553–55.

After the release of the prisoners, the whites turned to taunting the corpses of their victims before engaging in a general looting of the town. According to Samuel Spencer: "Q. State generally what their exclamations or statements were. A. They would say, 'By God, they thought they had Hamburg all right now; thought that they had killed a sufficient number to prevent n——r rule any longer in Aiken County; that that they had put a quietus on the n——r rule in Aiken County for all time to come. . . . [Then they] went on hollering and calling the names of the men that they had killed; and one would say, 'He don't answer,' and another would say, 'By God, he is looking at the moon and don't wink his eyes;' and they went on in that way, making sport of the men that they had already killed. Well, about the time they were going out, after they got through killin, they commenced robbing. You could hear them burst open the doors, and you hear the doors all over town. It looked like they had parted themselves up in squads for the purpose of robbing, and you could hear them going to a man's store and burst it open and go in, all the way down the street." Louis Schiller survived by hiding three days in the swamp: "What they couldn't break they carried off. I didn't have a thing left; had to borrow a spoon to eat with." Testimony of Samuel B. Spencer, Senate Investigation, 712; testimony of Louis Schiller, Senate Investigation, 153.

76. "Generally believed": "A Point on the Hamburg Riots," *Augusta Chronicle*, July 22, 1885; "allow me": "The Hamburg (S.C.) Massacre," *New York Times*, July 19, 1876, 4.

77. The Copperheads were "Peace Democrats" who had opposed the Civil War and favored a quick settlement with the Confederacy. "A Centennial Fourth of July Democratic Celebration. The Massacre of Six Colored Citizens of the United States at Hamburgh, S. C., on July 4, 1876. Debate in the U.S. House of Representatives, July 15th and 18th, 1876" (Washington, D.C., 1876) [hereafter Hamburg House Debate], https://babel.hathitrust.org/cgi/pt?id=hvd.32044037451077&seq=7.

78. Ibid.

79. Ibid. Rainey's sentiments were broadly shared, especially in the Charleston Black community. On July 17, 1876, for instance, Black residents of Charleston held a mass meeting to organize a response to atrocities committed in Hamburg: "ATTENTION! Colored Citizens Attention! There will be a mass meeting of the Colored Citizens on Monday night, July 17th, in front of Market Hall, to express our indignation, and to adopt resolutions setting forth the enormity of General M.C. Butler's outrage in Hamburg So. Ca. The following gentlemen will address the Meeting: Rev. R. H. Cain, Genl. R. B. Elliott, Rev. E. Adams, Hon. W. J. Wipple." See "Proclamations, Politics, and Commerce: Broadsides from the Colonial Era to the Present at the South Caroliniana Library," digital collection, South Caroliniana Library, University of South Carolina, accessed December 27, 2024, https://digital.tcl.sc.edu/digital/collection/bro/id/437/rec/12.

80. Hamburg House Debate.

81. Daniel H. Chamberlain to Ulysses S. Grant, July 26, 1876, in *The Papers of Ulysses S. Grant: January 1–October 31, 1876* (Southern Illinois University Press, 2005) [hereafter Grant Papers], 199.

82. Ulysses S. Grant to Daniel H. Chamberlain, July 26, 1876, in Ronald C. White, *American Ulysses: A Life of Ulysses S. Grant* (Random House, 2016), 576. In testimony before the Senate investigation, Louis Schiller went right to

the heart of this catch-22: "Q. Did you not have the whole machinery of the State government, the republicans? A. Yes, sir; they had. Q. Governor, judges, legislature, and all? A. Very true; but the legislature may pass a law, the judges may pass a sentence, or may decide a question, but who is to enforce it. A negro militia? If the governor had ordered out the negro militia to enforce the law, it would have created a civil war right there. There was not force enough to do it." Testimony of Louis Schiller, Senate Investigation, 159. In his reply to Chamberlain, Grant expressed a similar fatalism. To not act risked perfect civic failure; to act risked renewed civil war; he promised Chamberlain he would "give every aid for which I can find law or constitutional power," but he gave no sense of when that aid would materialize or what form it might take. This was undoubtedly exacerbated by the fact that Grant was, by the summer of 1876, effectively a lame duck, having determined, at the end of eight years of scandal, not to seek a third term. The whole of his attitude is best captured by a sense that he had thrown up his hands: "How long these things are to continue," he said, "or what is to be the final remedy, the Great Ruler of the universe only knows." Grant Papers, 199.

83. Quoted in Budiansky, *Bloody Shirt*, 244.

84. Alfred B. Williams, *Hampton and His Red Shirts: South Carolina's Deliverance in 1876* (Porirua Publishing, 2024), 28.

85. *New York Times*, October 14, 1878.

86. Anyone reading the resulting three thousand pages of testimony can see precisely the game that Merrimon determined to play: "Q (Merrimon). Was it commonly said in Augusta and round about in South Carolina, outside of Hamburgh, that Hamburgh was a terribly bad place? A (witness). I can't say that." "Q (Merrimon). Do they not say in Augusta that Hamburgh is a mighty bad place? A (witness). Of course they say so. Q. They say it is a perfect Sodom? A. No, sir." "Q (Merrimon). Was it not alleged, and generally alleged, that Hamburgh was a regular Sodom, and that negroes in the town could go out and steal hogs and cattle and whatever they could get, and take them in there? . . . A (witness). No, sir; they made an allegation afterward that it was harbor for thieves." Testimony of Samuel B. Spencer, Senate Investigation, 713; testimony of Archy Griffin, Senate Investigation, 700; testimony of Louis Schiller, Senate Investigation, 156.

Merrimon returned so often to this line of questioning that the Republican senators began to push back. In one cross-examination, for instance, Senator Christiancy had the following exchange with a witness: "Q. I will continue your attention to the time previous to these riots only. Was there any more crime committed at Hamburgh than in any other village around, so far as you know anything about it? A. I don't think there was, sir. Q. Did you ever know a place that did not have some crimes committed there at times? A. None, sir; I have never known any." Christiancy pursued a similar line of questioning with another witness: "Q. So far as you know, were the colored people of that town and county disposed to be quiet and peaceable? A. Why, they were, sir. There was no difficulty at all; none at all. They never interfered with any white men unlawfully; they never had done anything; I never knew them to do anything of the kind." Testimony of Samuel B. Spencer, Senate Investigation, 714; testimony of Louis Schiller, Senate Investigation, 156.

Ruled out of order for returning again to his pet theme, a frustrated Merrimon revealed his true motivation: "It is alleged before this committee that the Hamburgh riot grew out of political considerations, and that with a view to rebut, it is competent and necessary, *if it can be shown* [emphasis added], to show that there was a state of lawless misrule there; that a set of desperate negroes occupied the town, and that they paraded its streets with guns, which they allege were militia guns, and that the condition of things there had become intolerable." Senate Investigation, 922. Here, in miniature, was the theory that would dominate Reconstruction historiography for almost a hundred years: Reconstruction failed because Black people could not govern themselves, and the governments they created were corrupt and "intolerable." There is no historical evidence that Hamburg was particularly unlawful except for the imputations of its unlawfulness by those who (a) were bigoted and apt to conflate Blackness and criminality generally, and (b) were politically motivated to create historical "cover" for the very real crimes committed by whites. Merrimon and the apologists for Hamburg always backed up and up and up, searching for some origin point where it might all be the fault of the Black people themselves: Maybe if they hadn't shot first (they didn't). . . . Maybe if they hadn't holed up in the armory (they had no other choice). . . . Maybe if they hadn't created an impassable road (they didn't). . . . Maybe if they hadn't lived in a perfect Sodom (they didn't). . . . When you don't want to believe something, your mind searches for any justification, any palliation, rather than submit.

87. Abraham Lincoln, "Second Annual Message to Congress" (1862), *The American Presidency Project*, accessed October 27, 2025, https://www.presidency.ucsb.edu/documents/second-annual-message-9.

88. Quoted in Budiansky, *Bloody Shirt*, 249.

89. "An Act to Repeal an Act Entitled, 'An Act to Charter the Town of Hamburg Approved February 28, 1871,'" no. 289, June 9, 1877, Acts of the General

Assembly, South Carolina Department of Archives and History; "Citizens of Hamburg, Petition Protesting the Repeal of the Town's Charter," undated, South Carolina Department of Archives and History. Other white women who signed the petition included Mrs. P. Schiller, Martha B. Kenningham, and Kenningham's two daughters, May and C. One hundred fifty signatures may not seem like a lot compared to the size of the town, but we must bear in mind that signing your name to such a document in the immediate aftermath of the massacre took significant courage.

90. "An Act to Repeal an Act Entitled, 'An Act to Charter the Town of Hamburg'"; "Citizens of Hamburg, Petition Protesting the Repeal of the Town's Charter."

The Coachman

1. Peter Irons, *White Men's Law: The Roots of System Racism* (Oxford University Press), 101.

2. *Aiken Courier-Journal*, August 17, 1876.

3. Isabel Vandervelde has speculated that Rivers had to sell his lots to pay his medical bills: "Rivers owned at least two pieces of real property, Lots 1 and 2 in the town of Hamburg, but both were sold before his death, one in 1879, the other in 1886. He did not own a house in the town of Aiken. He was very ill for a period of at least a year, according to both his physician and his wife, and both pieces of land were sold prior to his death, probably to help pay medical expenses. There is no record of any estate probate or will for Prince Rivers in the Probate Office in Aiken County." See Isabel Vandervelde, *Aiken County: The Only South Carolina County Founded During Reconstruction* (Reprint Company, 1999), 155.

4. *Aiken Review*, April 13, 1887.

5. "This wagon driver's presence": *Aiken Standard*, April 30, 1985. In the 1870 census, Prince R. Rivers, age forty-five, is listed as living in Hamburg as a trial justice with $500 in personal assets and $250 in real estate assets. In the 1880 census, Prince R. Rivers, age fifty-six, is listed as a painter living in Aiken (dwelling 197) with Louisa R. Rivers, seamstress, age thirty-two, and his sister-in-law, Sarah Edwards, "at school," age twelve. Rivers's 1887 obituary notes that "for a number of years he has been a trusted employee of Mr. B. P. Chatfield, at the Highland Park Hotel . . . and as a driver for Mr. Wm. C. Langley." See *Aiken Review*, April 13, 1887.

6. *Charleston Mercury*, February 24, 1868, 6.

7. "His gait": Thomas Wentworth Higginson, *Army Life in a Black Regiment* (Penguin Classics, 1994), 78; "he is agile": "Letters of Dr. Seth Rogers, 1862, 1863," *Proceedings of the Massachusetts Historical Society, Third Series* 43 (October 1909–June 1910), February 5, 1863.

8. Vandervelde, *Aiken County*, 443–44.

9. The latest medical science suggests one possible diagnosis in Rivers's death: salt-sensitive hypertension (SSHT). If Rivers's ancestors hailed from a West African region relatively unaccustomed to salt, his years of army service (and his resulting steady diet of salt pork and bacon), coupled with a typical Southern diet, might have aggravated an underlying genetic sensitivity. See Constance B. Hilliard, "A Key to Black Americans' Health May Lie in a Misunderstanding of the Slave Trade," *STAT*, December 17, 2024, https://www.statnews.com/2024/12/17/black-americans-sodium-kidney-disease-genetics-slave-trade-amkd/. "In Point of Intelligence": *Aiken Review*, April 13, 1887.

10. Rivers's "obit," published in the *Aiken Review*, notes: "Since August last he has been confined to his bed, a great sufferer. He was a member and officer of the colored Methodist church, and was also at the head of the lodge of Odd Fellows. His funeral took place at the Cumberland A.M.E. Church, Rev. W. R. Beamer officiating, and in obedience to his request his remains were taken to Columbia by a delegation of Odd Fellows, and buried in the Randolph cemetery of that city." See *Aiken Review*, April 13, 1887. In 2005, the city of Columbia formed the Downtown Columbia Cemetery Task Force, focused primarily on restoring Randolph Cemetery. See "Randolph Cemetery Survey," 2007, Richland Library, accessed January 2, 2025, https://localhistory.richlandlibrary.com/digital/collection/p16817coll12/id/1627/; Michael Trinkley and Debi Hacker, "A Small Sample of Burials at Randolph Cemetery" (Chicora Foundation, 2007), https://www.chicora.org/pdfs/RC461.pdf; "Randolph Cemetery, Richland County," *South Carolina Department of Archives and History*, accessed January 2, 2025, http://www.nationalregister.sc.gov/richland/S10817740105/index.htm.

11. On the First South Carolina as a government-inspired slave insurrection, see Stephen Ash, *Firebrand of Liberty: The Story of Two Black Regiments That Changed the Course of the Civil War* (Norton, 2008), 197: "The Florida expedition of 1863 thus stands as unique in the annals of the Civil War and perhaps in the annals of all military history. Conceived and commanded by radical abolitionists in uniform, in a shining moment of optimism inspired by the Emancipation Proclamation, it was intended first and foremost to ignite the destruction of slavery within the world's most powerful slaveholding society and

to establish and defend a homeland for the freed people." On the importance of liberation raids, see also Edda L. Fields-Black, *Combee: Harriet Tubman, the Combahee River Raid, and Black Freedom During the Civil War* (Oxford University Press, 2024).

12. Abraham Lincoln, "Speech at Peoria," October 16, 1854, in Lewis E. Lehrman, *Lincoln at Peoria: The Turning Point* (Stackpole Books, 2008).

13. Details of Schultz's suicide attempt can be found in Michael S. Smith, *The Lost Freedmen's Town of Hamburg, South Carolina* (History Press, 2021), 34.

14. "Foulest nests": "Some of the Work of the Legislature," *Weekly Union Times*, June 15, 1877; "howling wilderness": "A Story About Hamburg S.C.," *Aiken Recorder*, June 19, 1891; "barbaric sports": *Augusta Chronicle*, March 5, 1891.

15. "What Bloodhounds Can Do," *Anderson Intelligencer*, October 23, 1879; Smith, *Lost Freedmen's Town*, 34. Tommy's father, Robert, "the old negro hunter," died nine years later. See "Mr. Robert Butler Dead," *Augusta Chronicle*, August 10, 1888.

16. "In the region": "Bloody Battle Waged," *Edgefield Advertiser*, June 1, 1893; *Savannah Morning News*, May 26, 1893, 2: "Augusta contributed two well-known citizens to a lively shooting scrimmage in Hamburg, S.C., this afternoon, and Tom Butler, the leader in the Hamburg riot of 1876, held up the Carolina side of the controversy. . . . Joseph Pettyjohn, proprietor of the Arlington hotel, in Augusta, has a farm across the river in Carolina, adjoining the property of the Butlers. He has a drove of cows, and supplies the butter and milk for the hotel and garden truck for the table. There have been a number of petty disagreements between the Pettyjohns and Butlers, and there has grown to be a great deal of bad blood between them. To-day matters culminated when Pettyjohn's cows got into Butler's oat field, and had thirty-odd cows impounded." See also *Laurens Advertiser*, May 30, 1893: "Mr. Pettyjohn had twenty-eight head of cows in the pasture of Mrs. Henry H. Getzen, a sister of Mr. Butler. This morning the cows got out of the pasture and were grazing on Mr. Butler's oat crop, and he penned the cows up and gave orders not to release them until damages to his oats were paid. . . . Mr. Pettyjohn says . . . Butler is mad with them because they will not discharge a farm hand who Butler claims he hired for the year. Butler used small buckshot and the Pettyjohns' guns were loaded with turkey shot."

17. "Bloody Battle Waged," *Edgefield Advertiser*, June 1, 1893.

18. *The Complete Works of Nathaniel Hawthorne*, vol. 5 (Boston, 1896), 103.

19. Barbara Seaborn, *Monumental Legacy: The Rise and Fall of Hamburg,*

South Carolina (iUniverse, 2021), 171; "Red Cross Work in Hamburg Ends," *Aiken Journal and Review*, February 5, 1930; "Hamburg Must Go, States Red Cross," *Aiken Standards*, November 22, 1929; "Hamburg Problem Solution Planned," *Aiken Journal and Review*, December 11, 1929.

20. On the epic and continual displacement of African Americans throughout history, see Barbara J. Fields, "Dysplacement and Southern History," *Journal of Southern History* 82, no. 1 (February 2016): 7–26.

21. See Anna Webb, "The Atlas of Drowned Towns," *Humanities: The Magazine of the National Endowment of the Humanities*, Fall 2024, https://www.neh.gov/article/atlas-drowned-towns.

22. Rivers to Higginson, May 12, 1864, "Higginson, Thomas Wentworth, 1823–1911. Correspondence," Harvard University, https://hollisarchives.lib.harvard.edu/repositories/24/archival_objects/339798.

23. Undoubtedly Rivers's own descendants continue to whisper his name, and this book is written in the hope that additional attention will help us flesh out his family tree. In an unpublished manuscript, the late historian Isabel Vandervelde assembled the most complete genealogy we have of Rivers, which includes numerous surviving children and grandchildren by multiple partners and wives. See Isabel Vandervelde, "The Family of Prince R. Rivers," Aiken County Historical Museum. As has been mentioned, Rivers and his first wife, Elsie, had two children survive to adulthood, Jack and Pattie. Jack (born around 1846) fathered at least five children before, according to Pattie, "he was killed by accident before Pa died." (The circumstances of this accident are unknown.) Pattie (born around 1848) married Isaac White and had at least one daughter, Florence (White) Grayson, with whom she was living in 1920. (When Pattie died in 1929, Florence served as witness to her mother's death certificate, suggesting the two were close.) While Rivers had no children with his second wife, Louisa, Vandervelde suggests he had as many as sixteen children with four domestic partners, all of whom were mistresses before the war and two of whom he moved to Hamburg and then to Aiken. This pattern is suggestive of several possibilities, including that he was, in his early days, a serial womanizer, or that he was pressured to reproduce by his enslaver (and then protected the women for years afterward), or anything in between. Unless and until more information comes to light, historians should proceed cautiously.

24. Higginson's curiosity about his men occasionally resembled that of an anthropologist who had fallen in love with his subject of study. Nowhere was this quality of mind more apparent than in his meticulous quest to document his men's favorite spirituals. "I Know Moon-Rise" surprised him the most.

“With all my experience of their ideal ways of speech,” he said, “I was startled when first I came on such a flower of poetry in that dark soil . . . ‘I’ll lie in de grave and stretch out my arms.’ Never, it seems to me, since man first lived and suffered, was his infinite longing for peace uttered more plaintively than in that line.” Higginson, *Army Life*, 160.

INDEX